# with **Chapter-wise Previous 10 Year**
## (2013 - 2022) Questions

**DISHA**™
Publication Inc

# DISHA Publication Inc.

45, 2nd Floor, Maharishi Dayanand Marg,
Corner Market, Malviya Nagar, new Delhi -110017
Tel: 49842349/ 49842350



**Typeset By**

DISHA DTP Team

**Buying books from DISHA**

# Just Got A Lot More Rewarding!!!

We at DISHA Publication, value your feedback immensely and to show our apperciation of our reviewers, we have launched a review contest.

To participate in this reward scheme, just follow these quick and simple steps:

- Write a review of the product you purchase on Amazon/Flipkart.
- Take a screenshot/photo of your review.
- Mail it to *disha-rewards@aiets.co.in*, along with all your details.

Each month, selected reviewers will win exciting gifts from DISHA Publication. Note that the rewards for each month will be declared in the first week of next month on our website.

**https://bit.ly/review-reward-disha.**

**Write To Us At**

feedback_disha@aiets.co.in

# Preface

We are pleased to launch the thoroughly revised 4th edition of **Olympiad Champs Science Class 2** which is the first of its kind book on Olympiad in many ways.

The Unique Selling Proposition of this new edition is the inclusion of past year questions till 2022 of different Olympiad exams held in schools.

The book is aimed at achieving not only success but deep rooted learning in children. It is prepared on content based on National Curriculum Framework prescribed by NCERT. All the text books, syllabi and teaching practices within the education programme in India must follow NCF. Hence, Olympiad Champs become an ideal book not only for the Olympiad Exams but also for strengthening the concepts for Class 2.

There is an exhaustive range of thought provoking questions in MCQ format to test the student's knowledge thoroughly. The questions are designed so as to test the knowledge, comprehension, evaluation, analytical and application skills. Solutions and explanations are provided for all questions. The questions are divided into two levels-Level 1 and Level 2. The first level, Level 1, is the beginner's level which comprises of questions like fillers, analogy and odd one out. When the children covers Level 1, it means his basic knowledge about the subject is clear and now he is ready for Level 2. The second level is the advanced level. Level 2 comprises of techniques like matching, chronological sequencing, picture, passage and feature based, statement correct/ incorrect, integer based, puzzle, grid based, crossword, venn diagram, table/ chart based and much more.

The first concern which each parent faces is how to make their children read a book especially when it is based on academics. Keeping this in mind interesting facts, real life examples, historical preview, short cuts to problem solving, charts, diagrams, illustrations and poems are added.

With the vision to remove all the misconception a child may have pertaining to the subject, to relate his knowledge to the real world and to develop a deeper understanding of the subject, this book will cater all the requirements of the students who are going to appear in Olympiads.

While preparing this book, some errors might have crept in. We request our readers to identify those errors and send it across on **feedback_disha@aiets.co.in**.

We wish you all the best for your Olympiads and happy reading…….

**Team Disha**

**For feedback : feedback_disha@aiets.co.in.**

# CONTENTS

# CHAPTER FOREWORD

We see so many things around us. Some are living and some are non-living things. Non-living things are different from the living things as they cannot grow, move, felt, eat, and reproduce. But living things can move, grow, feel, eat and reproduce.

**Directions:** Circle the things that are non-living but are obtained from living things.

(i)

(ii)

(iii)

(iv)

(v)

(vi)

(vii)

(viii)

(ix)

After reading this chapter, you will know more about living and non-living things. You will also learn to differentiate between them.

# Chapter 1

# Living and Non-Living Things



❖ **Misconcept:** Things that cannot move on their own are non-living things.

❖ **Concept:** Living things like plants have all the characteristics of life but are fixed at one place and cannot move. However, some plants show movement like sunflower. Some plants like, sunflower have slow movement.

## LEARNING OBJECTIVES

**This lesson will help you to:**

❖ know about living and non-living things.

❖ differentiate between living and non living things.

❖ learn about characteristics of living and non-living things.

## INTRODUCTION

We see so many things around us. Some are living and some are non-living. Non-living things are different from the living things as they cannot grow. Similarly, there are other characteristics also which differentiate living things from non-living things. Let us study the characteristics of both living and non-living things in detail.

- The things which have life in them and can grow are living things. For example: plants, fishes, animals birds and human beings.

- The things which do not have life in them and cannot grow are non-living things. For example: book, table, fan, aeroplane, car and bus.

- Some non-living things like water, wood and rock that are found in nature. These are called **natural** things.

- Non-living things like paper, pen, train, house and clothes are not found in nature. These are made by man. Hence, these are called **man-made** things.

## CHARACTERISTICS OF LIVING THINGS

### 1. Living things can move:

Living things can move from one place to another. For example: fishes swim, birds fly, animals move from one place to another.

Some plants also show movement. For example: Sunflower moves in the direction of sun.

**2.   All living things grow on their own:**

Seeds grow to become trees. Living things can grow on their own.

**3.   All living things need food, air and water:**

To grow and live, living things need food, water and air. Without them living things cannot live.

**4.   All living things can feel:**

We feel pain when we get hurt by someone. We feel hot when we touch a hot object. These things show that we can feel the changes happening in our surroundings.

**5.   All living things can reproduce:**

Human beings give birth to babies. Animals either lay eggs or give birth to young ones. Birds lay eggs and plants produce seeds which give rise to a new plant.

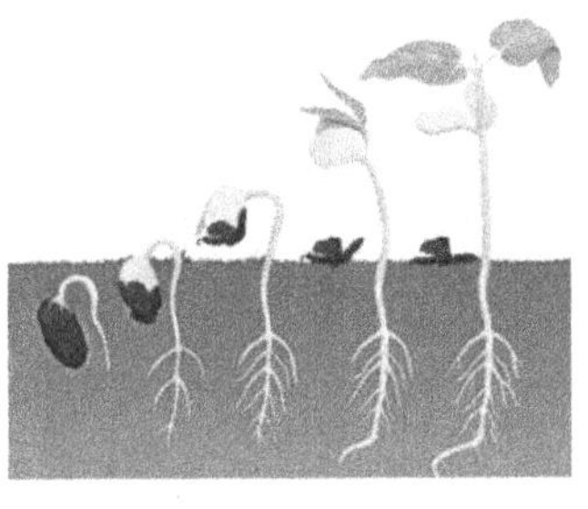

## CHARACTERISTICS OF NON-LIVING THINGS

1.   Non-living things cannot move on their own.
2.   Non-living things do not grow.
3.   Non-living things do not eat food, do not grow old and do not die.
4.   Non-living things do not feel.
5.   Non-living things do not reproduce.

# Multiple Choice Questions

## LEVEL 1

1. **Which of the following is a living thing?**

   (a) A pen      (b) An ant      (c) An aeroplane   (d) A kite

2. **Which of the following is a non-living thing?**

   (a) A rose plant    (b) A mouse      (c) A car      (d) A penguin

3. **Which one of the following is true about the non living things?**     [2012, Tricky]

   (a) Non-living things have ability to think   (b) Non-living things eat food

   (c) Non-living things need water to survive (d) Non-living things do not need air

4. **Which of these is a non-living thing?**

   (a) A tree      (b) A table      (c) A snake      (d) A monkey

5. **Which of the following is/are characteristic features of all living things?**   [Tricky]

   (a) Living things need food       (b) Living things breathe

   (c) Living things reproduce      (d) All of the above

6. **Which of the following things cannot move by itself?**

   (a) Bus      (b) Bird      (c) Fish      (d) Boy

7. **Car is considered as non-living thing because _________.**       [Tricky]

   (a) it moves       (b) it doesn't move

   (c) it responds      (d) it doesn't grow or reproduce

8. **Which of the objects given below is / are living things?**       [2013]

   (a) Horse, car    (b) Horse, chair    (c) Horse, aeroplane    (d) Horse

9. **Living things need _________ to grow.**

   (a) food      (b) water      (c) kite      (d) both (a) and (b)

10. **Living things die if they do not get _________.**       [Tricky]

    (a) air       (b) food

    (c) water      (d) All of the above

11. **Which of the things below can grow?**

    (a)        (b)

    (c)        (d)

12. A plant is different from a rock because a plant __________.     [Tricky]

    (a)   can grow          (b)   can reproduce     (c)   can breathe     (d)   All of these

13. Which of the following is a living thing?     [2015]

    (a)          (b)

    (c)          (d)

14. Why do plants come in the category of living things?     [Tricky]

    (a)   They can grow          (b)   They can sing

    (c)   They can talk          (d)   None of the above

**Direction (Qs. 15 to 19): Select the odd one out**     [Critical Thinking]

15. (a)   paper          (b)   pen          (c)   water          (d)   train
16. (a)   plant          (b)   animal          (c)   rock          (d)   bird
17. (a)   water          (b)   wood          (c)   rock          (d)   truck
18. (a)   fish          (b)   aeroplane          (c)   bus          (d)   train
19. (a)   spoon          (b)   cow          (c)   cat          (d)   plant

20. Identify the picture that can move from one place to another on its own.   [2016]

    (a)          (b)

    (c)          (d)

21. A ______________ eats to survive.

    (a)   knife          (b)   lion          (c)   basket          (d)   vase

22. Which of the following is true?     [Tricky]

    (a)   A tiger does not eat          (b)   An elephant does not eat

    (c)   A chair eats          (d)   A tiger eats

**23.** Which of the following is not true about the animal given in the picture below?

[Critical Thinking]

(a) It can fly     (b) It can reproduce     (c) It can eat     (d) It can move

**24.** A male and a female dog takes part in reproduction to give birth to a ______________

(a) baby cat     (b) baby dog     (c) baby cow     (d) baby lion

**25.** Read the following statements :     [Critical Thinking]

**Statement 1** : Movement is the main characteristic feature of a living thing.

**Statement 2** : Growth is the main characteristic feature of a living thing.

Which one of the following is correct about the above statements?

(a) Statement 1 is true and 2 is false     (b) Statement 1 is false and 2 is true

(c) Both statements are false     (d) Both, statements are true

**26.** For which of the following images, breathing is must to survive?     [2017]

(a) 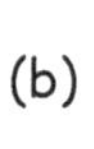

(b) 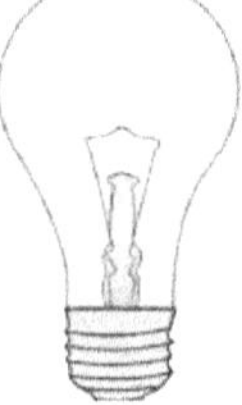

(c)  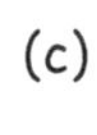 

(d) 

**27.** Which one of the following will grow?

(a) Key     (b) Lock     (c) Bottle     (d) Boy

**28.** Which one of the following is a true statement?

(a) Peacock is a non-living thing     (b) Rabbit is a non-living thing

(c) Elephant is a living thing     (d) Cat is non-living thing

**29.** Study the characteristics of H, I, J and K in the given table.  [2015]

| | Moves from place to place | Needs water | Reproduces | Has legs |
|---|---|---|---|---|
| H | | ✓ | ✓ | |
| I | ✓ | ✓ | ✓ | ✓ |
| J | ✓ | ✓ | ✓ | |
| K | ✓ | | | |

**Which one is most likely to be a non-living thing?**

(a)  H  (b)  I  (c)  J  (d)  K

**30.** Tanvi kept two rabbits under different conditions as shown below.  [2018]

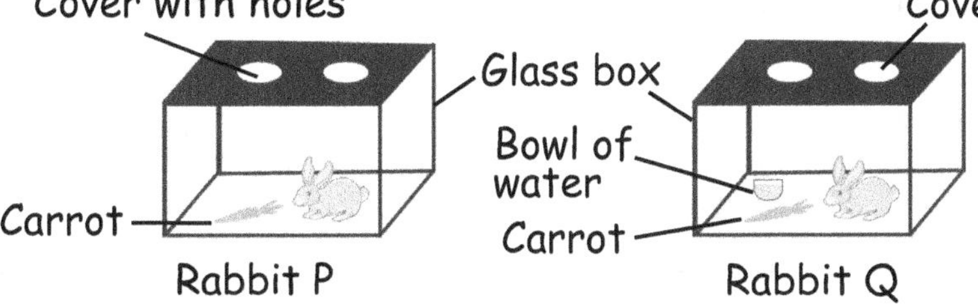


**Which rabbit will die earlier and why?**

(a)  Rabbit Q because it does not have sufficient air to breathe.

(b)  Rabbit P because it has no water to drink.

(c)  Rabbit Q because it has very little water to drink.

(d)  Cannot be predicted

**31.** Which of the following shows living things together?  [2018]

(a)   (b)   (c)   (d)  Both A and B

**32.** A dog gets the energy it needs to run from –  [2018]

(a)  Water  (b)  The Sun  (c)  The air  (d)  Food

**33.** Which of these is a nonliving thing that mice need to live ?  [2018]

(a)  Water  (b)  Rocks  (c)  Grass  (d)  Seeds

**34.** Which of the following represents growth in living things?  [2019]

(a)  A gel bead increasing in size when put in water

(b)  A balloon increasing in size when inflated

(c)  Money plant spreading on wall

(d)  None of these

**35.** Which of the following is a living thing?  [2020]

(a) 

(b) 

(c) 

(d) 

**36.** Select the odd one out on the basis of living and non-living thing.  [2021]

(a) 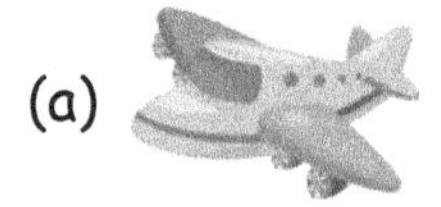   (b)    (c) 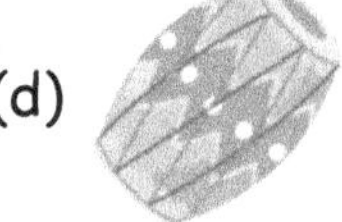   (d) 

**37.** Touch-me-not plant droops its leaves when touched. It shows that living things  [2022]

(a) Can breathe
(b) Can give birth to young ones
(c) Can grow
(d) Can move on their own

**38.** Which of the following is a natural non-living thing?  [2022]

(a) 

(b) 

(c) 

(d) 

**39.** Choose the non-living things from the following:  [2022]

1. 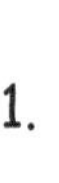   2.    3.    4. 

5. 

(a) 1 and 2 only  (b) 2 and 4 only
(c) 1, 3 and 5 only  (d) 1, 2, 3 and 4 only

## LEVEL 2

1. Which of the following is/are natural things? **[2013, Tricky]**

(a) 
Rock

(b) 
Water

(c) 
Wood

(d) All of the above

2. Study the given classification table. **[2015]**

Select the INCORRECT option regarding it.

(a) A dead fish should be placed in group 1.

(b) A pearl oyster should be placed in group 2.

(c) A toy car should be placed in group 1.

(d) A newspaper should be placed in group 2.

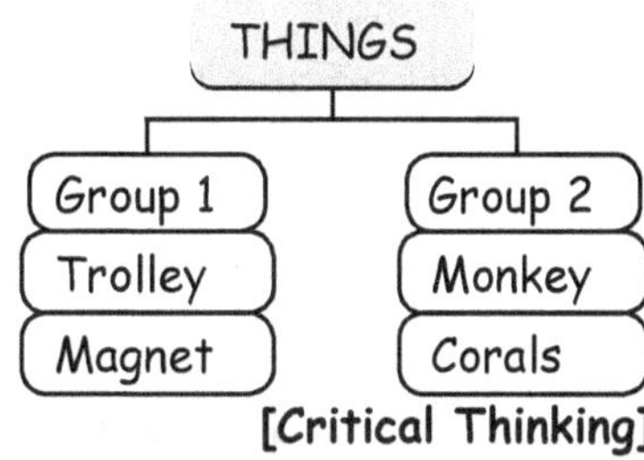


3. Which of the following has been wrongly classified? **[Critical Thinking]**

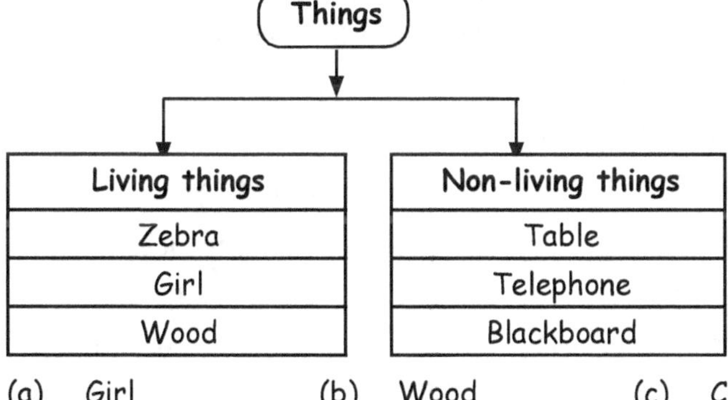


(a) Girl  (b) Wood  (c) Coin  (d) Blackboard

4. Look at the box below and answer the following question.

Car, stone, fish, plants, door, cow, spoon, clothes, pencil.

How many living things are there? **[Tricky]**

(a) 3  (b) 2  (c) 4  (d) 6

**Direction (Qs. 5 to 9):** Fill in the blanks in the passage given below:     (Critical Thinking)

The things which have life in them are called _____ (5) _____ things. For example: birds have life and they can _____ (6) _____. Living things can _____ (7) _____ as birds lay eggs. Non-living things cannot reproduce and they cannot _____ (8) _____ on their own. Some of the non-living things like water, wood and rock are _____ (9) _____ things.

5.   (a) non-living    (b) living    (c) man-made    (d) none of these
6.   (a) dance    (b) water    (c) grow    (d) All of these
7.   (a) reproduce    (b) run    (c) eat    (d) talk
8.   (a) drink    (b) move    (c) air    (d) water
9.   (a) natural    (b) man-made    (c) living    (d) both (a) and (b)

10. **Which of these is NOT correct?**     [2014]
    (a) Non-living things do not grow    (b) Non-living things feel
    (c) Non-living things do not breathe    (d) Non-living things do not reproduce

11. **Which one of these refer only to living things?**     [Tricky]
    (a) Clouds, fire, rivers    (b) Birds, trees, butterflies
    (c) Rivers, birds, trees    (d) All of these

12. **The sunflower turns towards the sun in the morning. This shows that a sunflower can:**     [Tricky]
    (a) grow    (b) reproduce
    (c) move    (d) take in air and water

13. **Which of the thing below cannot live without food?**

    (a)     (b)     (c)     (d)

14. **What would happen if a living thing did not get food?**     [Tricky]
    (a) It will be stronger    (b) It will die
    (c) It will remain healthy    (d) It will reproduce

15. **Read the sentences given below and choose the correct option.**   [Critical Thinking]
    **T stands for true and F stands for false.**

    A. A plant can grow     B. Birds cannot fly
    C. A table can reproduce     D. A fish can reproduce
    (a) TTTF    (b) TFFT    (c) FTFT    (d) TFTF

16. **Match the column (I) with the column (II)**     [Critical Thinking]

|     | Column (I) |     | Column (II) |
| --- | --- | --- | --- |
| A. | Birds reproduce by | 1. | Food, air and water to live |
| B. | Table cannot grow because | 2. | Laying eggs |
| C. | Plants need | 3. | It is a non-living thing |
| D. | House, cloth, pen | 4. | Man-made things |

|     | A | B | C | D |
|-----|---|---|---|---|
| (a) | 1 | 2 | 3 | 4 |
| (b) | 4 | 3 | 2 | 1 |
| (c) | 2 | 3 | 1 | 4 |
| (d) | 3 | 2 | 1 | 4 |

17. Which of the following is a living thing?  [2014]

(a) Cloud  (b) Bird  (c) Rock  (d) Star

18. Water, rock and wood are the examples of __________

(a) living things  (b) natural things

(c) man-made things  (d) Both (a) and (c)

19. Which of the following is a man-made thing?

(a) Train  (b) Clothes  (c) House  (d) All of these

20. 

The diagram above shows a living thing. Which of the following characteristic it shows?  [Tricky]

(a) Move  (b) Grow  (c) Breathe  (d) All of these

21. A grasshopper with some leaves is placed in a glass jar, The jar is tightly closed with a lid.  [2015, Tricky]



The grasshopper will die because there is no __________ in the glass jar.

(a) food  (b) air  (c) light  (d) water

22. Ramu kept some fishes in the fish bowl and filled it with water. Then, he covered it from the top and forgot to add food into the fish bowl. After few days, he noticed that, few of the fishes stopped moving. He started crying. As a friend, how will you stop Ramu from crying?

(a) You will not say anything to Ramu.

(b) Advise him to put some food in the fish bowl.

(c) Remove the cover from the fish bowl.

(d) Both (b) and (c)

23. Which of the following is/are natural, non-living thing?

(a) Mountain  (b) Toy  (c) Rock  (d) Both (a) and (c)

24. Out of all these, which one belongs to the same category as plants?

    (a)  Toy              (b)  Teddy bear      (c)  Boy              (d)  River

25. Which of the following belongs to the category of belong/s man-made, non-living thing?

    (a)  Chair            (b)  Table           (c)  Train            (d)  All of these

26. Rani planted a plant in a flower pot and kept it in a closed, dark room. She gave water to the plants daily. After 3-4 days, she noticed that plants were not growing and all the leaves got dried. She got upset and started crying. How will you help her?  **[Critical Thinking]**

    (a)  Give some chocolates to her.

    (b)  Tell her to give some food to the plants.

    (c)  Tell her to keep the flower pots in the open garden.

    (d)  Tell her to give more water to the plants.

**Direction (Qs. 27 to 30): Look at the following picture carefully and answer the following questions**  **[Tricky]**

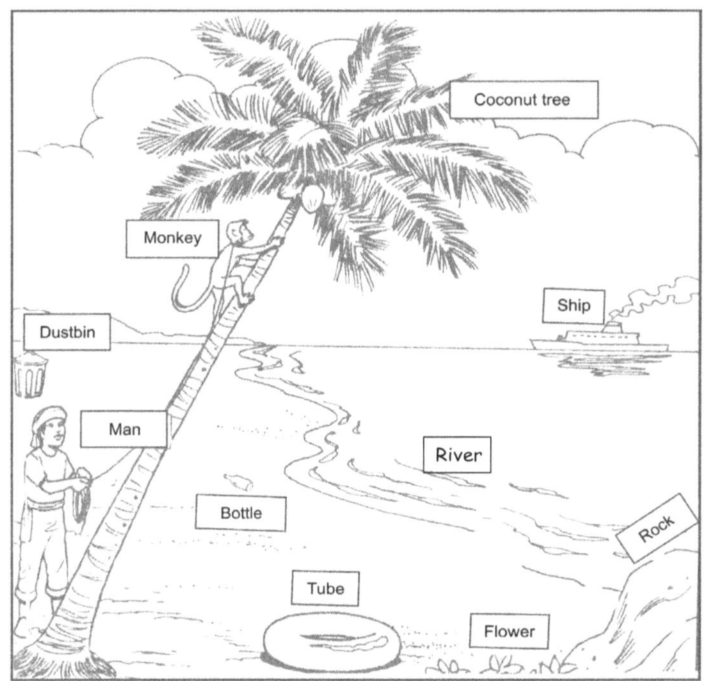


27. Which of the following is a man-made, nonliving thing?

    (a)  Tree            (b)  Ship            (c)  Rock            (d)  Monkey

28. Which of the following is a non-living thing?

    (a)  Man             (b)  Monkey          (c)  Tree            (d)  River

29. Count the number of natural, non-living things in the diagram shown above?

    (a)  2               (b)  1               (c)  3               (d)  2

**30.** Identify the living thing that can make its own food. [2016, Tricky]

(a) Monkey (b) Tree (c) Snake (d) Bird

**31.** Which of the following statement is NOT correct? [Critical Thinking]

(a) All non-living things are man-made

(b) All living things grow

(c) Some non-living things are found in nature

(d) Living things need air, food and water to stay alive

**32.** Which of the following does NOT belong to the group formed by the others?

[Critical Thinking]

(a)     (b)

(c)     (d)

**33.** Read the sentences below and choose the correct option.

(A) Non-living things can move an their own. (B) You are a living being

(C) Humans can not grow (D) Plants need water and air to grow

(a) FFTT (b) TFTT (c) FTFT (d) FTFF

**34.** Select the statement that is INCORRECT about man-made things. [2021]

(a) They cannot give birth to young ones. (b) They can make noise

(c) They can feel the pain. (d) They cannot breathe.

**35.** Which of the following statements is correct about the picture shown below?

[2022]

(a) It needs food to survive. (b) It is a nonliving thing.

(c) It needs oxygen to breathe. (d) None of these

## RESPONSE GRID

### LEVEL 1

1. a b c d    2. a b c d    3. a b c d    4. a b c d    5. a b c d
6. a b c d    7. a b c d    8. a b c d    9. a b c d    10. a b c d
11. a b c d    12. a b c d    13. a b c d    14. a b c d    15. a b c d
16. a b c d    17. a b c d    18. a b c d    19. a b c d    20. a b c d
21. a b c d    22. a b c d    23. a b c d    24. a b c d    25. a b c d
26. a b c d    27. a b c d    28. a b c d    29. a b c d    30. a b c d
31. a b c d    32. a b c d    33. a b c d    34. a b c d    35. a b c d
36. a b c d    37. a b c d    38. a b c d    39. a b c d

### LEVEL 2

1. a b c d    2. a b c d    3. a b c d    4. a b c d    5. a b c d
6. a b c d    7. a b c d    8. a b c d    9. a b c d    10. a b c d
11. a b c d    12. a b c d    13. a b c d    14. a b c d    15. a b c d
16. a b c d    17. a b c d    18. a b c d    19. a b c d    20. a b c d
21. a b c d    22. a b c d    23. a b c d    24. a b c d    25. a b c d
26. a b c d    27. a b c d    28. a b c d    29. a b c d    30. a b c d
31. a b c d    32. a b c d    33. a b c d    34. a b c d    35. a b c d

# Answers with Explanations

## LEVEL 1

1. **(b)** Ant is a living thing. Pen, aeroplane and kite are non-living things.

2. **(c)** Car is a non-living thing. Rose, mouse and penguin are living things.

3. **(d)** Non-living things do not need air.

4. **(b)** A table is a non-living thing, but tree, snake and monkey are living things.

5. **(d)** Living things have all the three features. They need food, can breathe and can reproduce also.

6. **(a)** Bus cannot move by itself.

7. **(d)** Car is considered as non-living thing because it does not more.

8. **(d)** Horse is a living thing.

9. **(d)** Living things need both food and water to grow.

10. **(d)** Living things will die if they do not get air, water and food.

11. **(d)** Frog can grow because it is a living thing.

12. **(d)** A plant is different from a rock because a plant can grow, reproduce and breathe.

13. **(c)** A bird is a living thing which can give birth to babies.

14. **(a)** Plants can grow, thus they come in the living things category.

15. **(c)** Water is a natural thing. Pen, paper and train are man-made, nonliving things.

**16.** **(c)** Rock is a non-living thing. Plant, animal and birds are living things.

**17.** **(d)** Truck is a man-made, non-living thing. Water, wood and rock are natural, non-living things.

**18.** **(a)** Fish is a living thing. Bus, train and aeroplane are non-living things.

**19.** **(a)** Spoon is a non-living thing. Cow, cat, and plant are living things.

**20.** **(c)** Cow can move from one place to another.

**21.** **(b)** A lion eats to survive. A lion is a living thing and needs food to survive.

**22.** **(d)** A tiger eats because it is a living thing and it needs food to survive.

**23.** **(a)** A tiger cannot fly.

**24.** **(b)** Dogs give birth to young ones.

**25.** **(b)** Growth is the main characteristic feature of living thing.

**26.** **(c)** Bear is a living thing. It breathes to live.

**27.** **(d)** A boy is a living being. He will grow.

**28.** **(c)** Elephant is a living thing. Peacock, rabbit and cat are also living things.

**29.** **(d)** Non-living things do not reproduce, do not need water to live and may and may not have legs. They can move from one place to another with the help of a battery or a human. For example: toy, car, bus and so on.

**30.** **(b)** Rabbit P will die earlier because it has no water to drink.

**31.** **(c)** In option (a), the plant and the butterfly are living things and in option (b), the tree and the bird are the living things. In option (c), the fish is a living thing, but the pot is a non-living thing.

**32.** **(d)** A dog is a living thing and gets energy from food.

**33.** **(a)** Water is a non-living thing. A mice needs water to live. All living things need water to live.

**34.** **(c)** A money plant is a living thing. The money plant spreading on wall shows growth.

**35.** **(b)** Trees are living things.

**36.** **(c)** Snake is a living thing while all other are non-living things.

**37.** **(d)** Living things can move on their own.

**38.** **(b)** Rock is natural non-living thing.

**39.** **(c)**

## LEVEL 2

**1.** **(d)** Rock, water and wood, all these are natural things.

**2.** **(d)** According to the given classification table, things are divided into two groups. Group 1 contains non-living things and group 2 contains living things. Newspaper is a non-living thing hence, it should be placed in group 1.

**3.** **(b)** Wood is not a living thing. It is a non-living thing.

**4.** **(a)** In the given box, there are 3 living things (cow, fish and plants).

**5.** **(b)** living things

**6.** **(c)** grow

**7.** **(a)** reproduce

**8.** **(b)** move

**9.** **(a)** natural

**10.** **(b)** Non-living thing do not feel.

**11.** **(b)** Birds, trees and butterflies, all these are living things.

**12.** **(c)** Sunflower shows movement.

**13.** **(b)** A plant is a living thing which needs food and water to live and grow.

14. **(b)** If a living thing did not get food, then it will die.

15. **(b)** A bird can fly and a table cannot reproduce.

16. **(c)** Birds reproduce by laying eggs. Table is a man-made thing. Plants need food, air and water. House, cloth and pen are man-made things.

17. **(b)** Bird is a living thing. It needs food, air and water to live.

18. **(b)** Water, rocks and wood are the examples of natural things.

19. **(d)** All of these (train, clothes and house) are man-made things.

20. **(d)** Chicks are living things which can move, grow and breathe.

21. **(b)** The grasshopper will die because there is no air in the glass jar.

22. **(d)** Advise him to put some food in the fish bowl as without food they will die.

23. **(d)** Mountain and rock both are natural, non-living things.

24. **(c)** Boy is a living thing. Plant is also a living thing.

25. **(d)** Chair, table and train are man-made non-living things.

26. **(c)** Advise her to keep the flower pots in the open garden as plants need sunlight to make their food.

27. **(b)** Ship is a man-made, non-living thing.

28. **(d)** River is a non-living thing.

29. **(a)** There are 2 natural, non-living things in the diagram-River and rock.

30. **(b)** Tree makes their own food. Monkey, Snake, birds eat other animals.

31. **(a)** Non-living things can be natural such as river and water. Man-made such as table, chair and so on.

32. **(c)** A cup doesn't belong to the group of living things because it is a non-living thing.

33. **(c)** Humans can grow.

34. **(c)** Man made things cannot feel the pain.

35. **(b)**

<table><tr><td>2</td><td>

# CHAPTER FOREWORD

</td></tr></table>

Plants are living things. A plant consists of different parts such as roots, stems, leaves, fruits and flowers. We see different types of plants in  our environment like herbs, shrubs, climbers, big and tall trees. We get different things from plants like food, medicine, wood, oxygen, cotton, jute, soap and perfume.

**Directions: To show how a seed becomes plant, arrange the given pictures in correct order by numbering them. Write the correct sequence of the picture in the space provided.**

(i)

(ii)

(iii)

(iv)

(v)

(vi)

(vii)

(viii)

After reading this chapter, you will know more about plants, their uses and the products derived from them.

# 2
## Chapter

# *Plants*



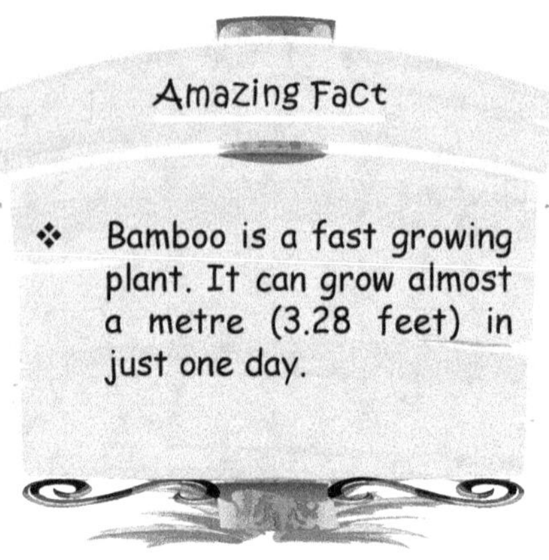



❖ Bamboo is a fast growing plant. It can grow almost a metre (3.28 feet) in just one day.

## LEARNING OBJECTIVES

**This lesson will help you to:**

❖ learn about the parts of a plants along with their functions.

❖ understand about the different types of plants on the basis of their shapes, sizes and their habitat.

❖ know about the different things we get from plants.

## INTRODUCTION

As we know plants are living things. A plant consists of different parts such as roots, shoots, stem, leaves, fruits, and flowers. Each part of a plant plays a very important role. Let us understand these roles in detail:

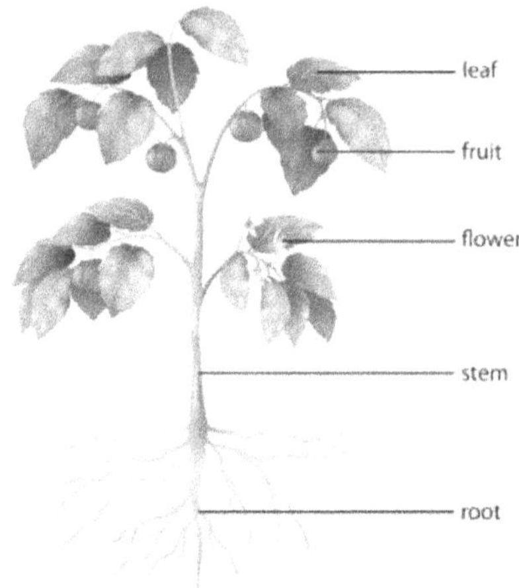


## Misconcept/Concept

❖ **Misconcept:** Seed is a non-living thing

❖ **Concept:** Seed is the dormant stage of a seedling. Seed germinates into a young plant which is a living thing

## ROOT

It is that part of the plant that develops inside the soil. Roots absorb water and minerals from soil and send them to the other parts of a plant through stem.

## STEM

Stem gives support to upper part of the plant. Water and dissolved nutrients from the soil travel up through stems. Food from leaves come down to roots by stems.

## LEAVES

Leaves of different plants can have different shapes and sizes. Generally, they are green in colour. In this part of the plant, food is produced by the help of sunlight. We eat the leaves of many plants. For example: cabbage and spinach.

## FLOWERS

They are the most colourful and beautiful part of the plant that produce fruit. Flowers attract human and insects because of their fragrance. They are the reproductive part of the plants. For example rose and sunflower.

## FRUITS

They come out from flowers. They are an edible part of a plant. We eat fruits like apple, banana, orange and grapes.

## SEEDS

They are the part of plant from which a baby plant grows. Seed contains food.

## TYPES OF PLANTS

We see many types of plants in our environment. Like, big and tall plants, herbs, shrubs and climbers. Each of these types of plants have different features. Let us study their features in detail.

### • HERBS

These are the small plants with soft stem. They have medicinal value as well.

**For example:** Mint, tulsi and coriander.

> ### Think Green
>
> ❖ 5th June is world Environment Day. Plant a few suplings in your school or at home. Look after the plant as it grows in to a tree. It may bear fruit and give shade to all.

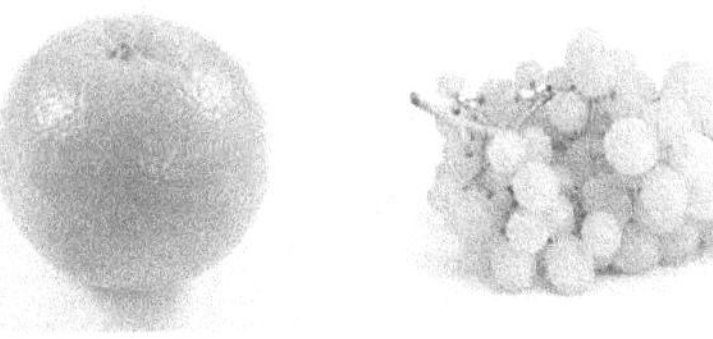

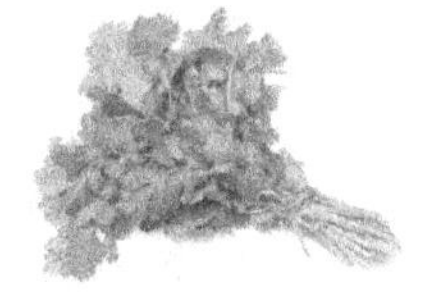

## • SHRUBS

They are smaller than trees. The stems are lower in height. Some shrubs contain flowers.

**For example:** Sunflower plant and rose plant.

## • TREES

Big plants are called trees. They are tall and have long branches. They have stronger and thicker stems in comparison to the other plants.

**For example:** Mango tree and coconut tree.

## • CLIMBERS

Plants with weak and soft stem that need support of other plants, stick or walls are called climbers.

**For example:** Money plant and grapevine.

## • CREEPERS

Plants with weak stem that grow along the ground are called creepers.

**For example:** Pumpkin, and bottle gourd.

## CLASSIFICATION OF PLANTS ON THE BASIS OF THEIR HABITAT

There are more than 3,50,000 types plant on the earth. Some plants grow on land, whereas some grows in water. We can differentiate them on the basis of their habitat.

## TERRESTRIAL PLANTS

Plants which grow on the land are called terrestrial plants.
**For example:** Papaya tree and mango tree.

## AQUATIC PLANTS

Plants which grow in water are called aquatic plants.

**For example:** Water Lily and Lotus.

## THORNY PLANTS (*Desert Plants*):

Deserts cover more than one fifth of the earth's land, and they are found on every continent. A place that receives less than 10 inches (25 centimeters) of rain per year is considered a desert. Deserts are part of a wider classification of regions called **"drylands"**. Desert plants may have to go without fresh water for years at a time. Some plants have adapted to the arid climate by growing long roots that take water from deep underground. Other plants, such as cacti, have special means of storing and conserving water. Many desert plants can live for hundreds of years. For example, a cactus grows in desert. It is a desert plant. It has thorns. These thorns keep the plant safe.

## USES OF PLANTS

Plants give us food, oil, medicines, and so on. Let us study the uses of plants:

1. Plants give us **food**. We eat leaves, stems, fruits, flowers and seeds of plants.
2. We get cereals, pulses, oil, spices, coffee, tea, sugar from plants.
3. Plants give us **medicine.**
4. Plants give us **wood, teak, bamboo.** Wood is used to make furniture, doors, tables, chairs.
5. We get oils' from some plants such as mustard, coconut and sunflower.
6. Plants give out **oxygen.** They make the air fresh and pure.
7. Plants give us **cotton and jute.**
8. Some plants are used in making **soaps and perfumes.** For example rose and jasmine.

Papaya tree

Mango tree

Real life Example

Cactus plant is found in desert

# Multiple Choice Questions

## LEVEL 1

1. **Which of the following plant is a herb?**
   (a) Mango     (b) Mint     (c) *Hibiscus*     (d) Coconut

2. **Which of these is an important function of the roots of a plant?**
   (a) To absorb oxygen from the atmosphere
   (b) To absorb carbon dioxide from the atmosphere
   (c) To absorb water and minerals from the soil
   (d) All of these

3. **Which picture shows plants commonly found in a desert?**     **[2012, Tricky]**

   (a) Mango tree     (b) Cactus     (c) Neem tree     (d) Guava Plant

4. **The leaves of _______ are used as food.**     **[2013, Tricky]**
   (a) Onion     (b) Cabbage     (c) Eggs     (d) Ginger

5. **Which of these is a creeper?**

   (a) Pumpkin        (b) Money plant

   (c) Cactus        (d) Coconut tree

6. **Which of the following statements explain about climbers?**     **[Tricky]**
   (a) Climbers are plants with weak stems
   (b) They cannot stand on their own
   (c) They climb up on support
   (d) All of the above

7. Which part of these plants given below are eaten as food?          [2014, Tricky]

(Broccoli)                    (Cauliflower)

(a)   Roots          (b)   Leaves          (c)   Flowers          (d)   Stems

8. Fruits develop from ________ .

(a)   leaves          (b)   flowers          (c)   seeds          (d)   stem

9. Observe the given picture. What would X be?          [2012]



(a)   Sweet potato          (b)   Sugarcane          (c)   Groundnut          (d)   Aloe vera

10. Small plants with weak stems are called herbs. Which of these is a herb?    [Tricky]

(a)   Tulsi          (b)   Apple          (c)   Gulmohar          (d)   Grapevine

11. Which of the following parts of a plant absorbs water from the soil?

(a)   Stem          (b)   Root          (c)   Leaves          (d)   All of these

12. Which of the following is NOT a fruit?          [2012]

(a)          (b)          (c)          (d)

13. Which of  these is NOT a plant?

(a)  Neem tree                    (b)     Mushroom

(c)  Mango tree                    (d)     Coconut tree

14. The shape of leaves of rose plant is like ______________.                    [2013]

(a)    (b)    (c)    (d)

15. Which of these is obtained from plants?

    (a)  Paper          (b)  Animals       (c)  Medicine      (d)  Both (a) and (c)

**Directions (Qs. 16 to 20): Select the odd one out**                    [Critical Thinking]

16.  (a)  money plant    (b)  grapevine    (c)  bean      (d)  pumpkin
17.  (a)  table          (b)  chair        (c)  door      (d)  medicine
18.  (a)  root           (b)  shoot        (c)  trees     (d)  leaves
19.  (a)  cactus         (b)  rose         (c)  cotton    (d)  hibiscus
20.  (a)  water          (b)  wood         (c)  pulses    (d)  medicine

21.  Oil is not obtained from which of the following plant?

    (a)  Mango plant    (b)  Sunflower plant   (c)  Mustard plant   (d)  Coconut plant

22.  Which of the following statements is/are true for a herb?                    [Tricky]

    (a)  Herbs are small plants
    (b)  Herbs have soft stem
    (c)  Herbs need the support of other plants to grow
    (d)  Both (a) and (b)

23.  Which one of the following plant comes under the category of both shrub and herb plants?                    [Tricky]

    (a)  Guava tree    (b)  Pipal tree    (c)  Banyan tree    (d)  Basil plant

24.  Which one of the following is not a shrub?                    [2016]

    (a)  Mehandi plant              (b)  Tea plant
    (c)  Coconut tree               (d)  Marigold flower plant

25.  Identify the creeper plant from the following.                    [Tricky]

(a)    (b)

(c)    (d)

26. **Which one of the following are not produced by plants?**
    (a)  Radio       (b)  Rubber       (c)  Book       (d)  Pencil

27. **Plants are responsible for the presence of ________________ in the environment.**
    (a)  Birds       (b)  Animals       (c)  Water       (d)  Oxygen

28. **Which one of the following is true?**
    (a)  Leaves are green only
    (b)  Leaves are big only
    (c)  Leaves are small only
    (d)  Leaves are generally green, but can be of different colours

29. **Which one of the following we do not get from plants?**
    (a)  Apple       (b)  Cell phone       (c)  Pear       (d)  Guava

30. **Climbers need ________________ to grow.**
    (a)  Support       (b)  Oil       (c)  Sweets       (d)  Milk

31. **Which one of the following is not true?**       **[2017, Tricky]**
    (a)  Table is made of plant wood       (b)  Chair is made of plant wood
    (c)  Doors are made of plant wood       (d)  Seeds cannot be grown into new plant

32. **The given figure shows a plant with some labelled parts P, Q, R and S.**

    Part ________ carries food from ________ to all other parts of the plant.       **[2018]**
    (a)  P, S       (b)  Q, R       (c)  R, S       (d)  S, Q

33. **Study the given flow chart and select the option which correctly identifies X, Y and Z.**       **[2018]**

|     | X | Y | Z |
|-----|-----|-----|-----|
| (a) | Creeper | Shrub | Herb |
| (b) | Herb | Creeper | Climber |
| (c) | Shrub | Climber | Herb |
| (d) | Shrub | Herb | Creeper |

34. **The three plants given in the table are grouped together because all three –** **[2018]**
    **Characteristics of three plants**

| Red barberry | Red maple | Snowball flower |
|-----|-----|-----|
| Full sun | Part shade | Full sun |

| Loses leaves | Loses leaves | Loses leaves |
| --- | --- | --- |
| Shrub | Tree | Shrub |
| Has thorn | Has no horns | Has no thorns |

(a)   Need some shade

(b)   Lose their leaves

(c)   Have thorns

(d)   Are shrubs

**35.** Select the plant that can be placed in the same group to which plant X belongs. [2018]

(a)   Watermelon plant

(b)   Pea plant

(c)   Cotton plant

(d)   Mint plant

**36. Cabbage is a** [2019]

(a)   Fruit that we eat

(b)   Leaf that we eat

(c)   Seed that we eat

(d)   Root that we eat

**37. Refer to the given figure of a plant. Which of the following plant parts transports water, minerals and food to all plant parts?** [2020]

(a) P

(b) Q

(c) R

(d) S

**38. What will happen to a plant if we remove all the flowers from it?**

(a) It will not produce fruits. [2020]

(b) It cannot stand upright on the ground.

(c) It will stop transporting food and water to all other parts.

(d) It will stop absorbing nutrients and waer from the soil.

**39. Refer to the given relationship.** [2020]

**Creeper : Watermelon**

**Select the pair with similar type of relationship.**

(a) Climber : pea

(b) Shrub : Spinach

(c) Herb : Money plant

(d) Tree : Pumpkin

**40. Which of the following is a many seeded fruit?** [2021]

 (a)

 (b)

 (c)

 (d)

**41. Select the option that completes the given analogy.** [2021]

Energy-giving food : Rice :: Body-building food : __________

(a)   (b) (c)  (d)

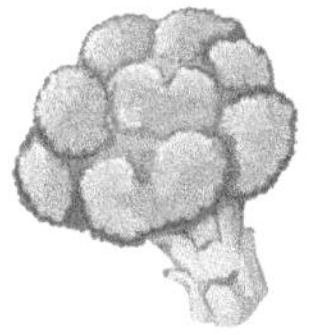

**42.** Wool is obtained from ____________.  [2021]

(a)  (b)  (c)  (d)

**43.** We get gum from the __________ tree.  [2022]
(a) Acacia  (b) Oak  (c) Bamboo  (d) Jasmine

**44.** Select the option which correctly shows the relationship between number of seeds in different fruits.  [2022]
(a) Mango = Litch  (b) Watermelon < Cherry
(c) Papaya = Peach  (d) Pear > Pomegranate

**45.** Which among the following plants has the longest life span?  [2022]
(a) Coriander  (b) Wheat
(c) Jasmine  (d) Banyan

**46.** Stem and root are important parts of which of the following organisms?  [2022]

(a)  (b)  (c)  (d)

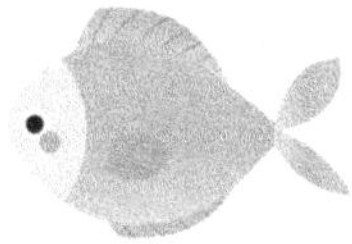

**47.** What has been shown in the following figures?  [2022]

(a) Leaves of different plants  (b) Flowers of different plants
(c) Seeds of different plants  (d) Roots of different plants

## LEVEL 2

**1.** Study the given flowchart and select the correct option to fill the empty spaces 'x' and 'y'.  [Critical Thinking]
(a)  Mint and Clove  (b)  Clove and Neem
(c)  Tulsi and Cocoa  (d)  Cardamon and Almond

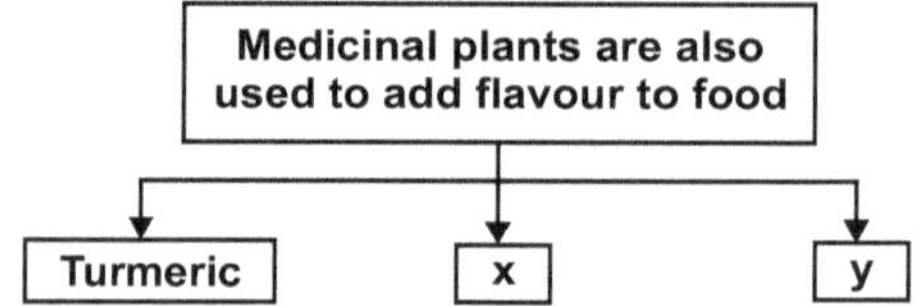


2. **What will happen to a plant if all its flowers are removed from it?** [2013, Tricky]
   (a) The plant will stop making food.
   (b) The plant will stop transporting water to all other parts.
   (c) The plant will not produce any seeds or fruits.
   (d) The plant will eventually die

3. **Study the given figure. Which of the following best represents X and Y?**
   [Critical Thinking]

   (a) X — Mustard, Y — Sunflower
   (b) X — Coconut, Y — Sunflower
   (c) X — Sunflower, Y — Groundnut
   (d) X — Groundnut, Y — Mustard



4. **Plants give us foodgrains. What are the examples of such grains?**
   (a) Wheat and Rice
   (b) Maize and Barley
   (c) Gram and Pulses
   (d) All of these

5. **Read the given features of a plant and identify it.** [2013, Tricky]
   (A) It is a small plant with soft stem.
   (B) Its leaves are used to make medicine.
   (C) It is used to add flavour to food.
   (a) Tulsi     (b) Hibiscus     (c) Rose     (d) Both (a) and (c)

6. **What are the similarities between the plants bearing the flowers as shown?**

   [Critical Thinking]

   (a) They have weak stems
   (b) Woody plants have hard stems
   (c) They have woody stems
   (d) They grow along the ground

7. **Study the flow chart and choose the correct statement.** [Critical Thinking]

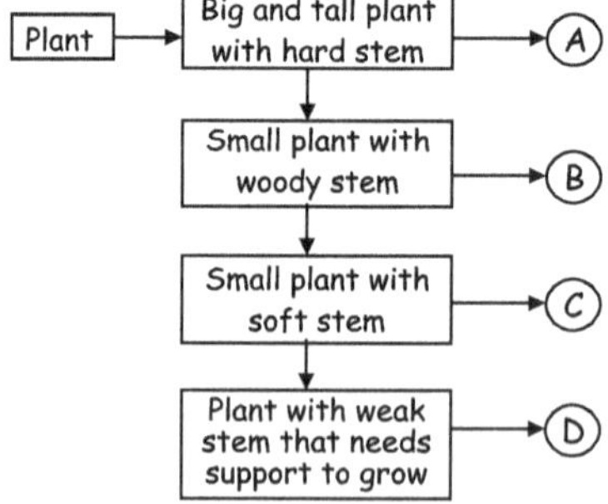

(a)   A is a rose plant          (b)   B is a hibiscus plant
(c)   C is a banyan tree         (d)   D is a shrub

8.   Match column (I) with column (II).                    [2014, Tricky]

| Column (I) | | Column (II) | |
|---|---|---|---|
| A. | Roots | 1. | supports the plant |
| B. | Stem | 2. | reproductive part of plant |
| C. | Leaves | 3. | absorb water from soil |
| D. | Flower | 4. | food production |

|     | A | B | C | D |     | A | B | C | D |
|-----|---|---|---|---|-----|---|---|---|---|
| (a) | 1 | 2 | 3 | 4 | (b) | 2 | 3 | 4 | 1 |
| (c) | 3 | 1 | 4 | 2 | (d) | 2 | 1 | 3 | 4 |

**Directions (Qs. 9 to 15): Fill in the blanks in the passage given below.**          [Tricky]

Plants are the living things. They consist of different parts. Roots, _________ (9) stem, flower and fruits are the main parts of plant. Each of these part has a specific function. Some plants are very tall and big known as _________ (10) Banyan tree and _________ (11) tree are big trees. Some plants grow in water and are known as _________ (12) plants. For example _________ (13) is an aquatic plant. Plants are very useful for us. They give us food and medicines. They also gives us _________ (14) to make doors, table, chair and furniture. Plants give out _________ (15) which make the air fresh and pure.

9.   (a)   air          (b)   leaves        (c)   trees        (d)   trunk
10.  (a)   herbs        (b)   shrubs        (c)   trees        (d)   roots
11.  (a)   cactus       (b)   mango         (c)   rose         (d)   lotus
12.  (a)   terrestial   (b)   aquatic       (c)   desert       (d)   cactus
13.  (a)   rose         (b)   lotus         (c)   hibiscus     (d)   marigold
14.  (a)   wood         (b)   water         (c)   air          (d)   food
15.  (a)   water        (b)   oxygen        (c)   nitrogen     (d)   both (a) and (b)
16.  **Rose : Shrub :: Pumpkin: _________?**                    **[2015, Tricky]**
     (a)   Tree         (b)   Herb          (c)   Creeper      (d)   Bud
17.  **Which of the following is NOT matched correctly?**
     (a)   Root — Absorb water from soil      (b)   Leaf — Prepares food
     (c)   Fruit — Protect seeds             (d)   Flower — Carries food
18.  **Which of the following shows the correct match of plant types along with their examples?**                    **[2012]**

|     | **Tree** | **Shrub** | **Herb** |
|-----|----------|-----------|----------|
| a.  | Banyan   | Coriander | Hibiscus |
| b.  | Rose     | Hibiscus  | Marigold |
| c.  | Coconut  | Rose      | Coriander |
| d.  | Coconut  | Marigold  | Rose |

19.  **Which of the following is an aquatic plant?**
     (a)   Bottle gourd    (b)   Water lily    (c)   Mint    (d)   Pumpkin

20. Read the given features of a plant and identify it. [2013]
    - A. It is a small plant with soft stem.
    - B. Its leaves are used to make medicine.
    - C. It is used to make food tasty.
    - (a) Coriander     (b) Hibiscus     (c) Aloe vera     (d) Either A or C

21. The rose and hibiscus plants can be placed in the same group because both of them are ________ . [Tricky]
    - (a) Trees     (b) Shrubs     (c) Herbs     (d) Annuals

22. I am a fast growing plants and can grow almost 1 metre in a day. Who am I?
    - (a) Rose     (b) Cactus     (c) Money plant     (d) Bamboo

23. Which among the following is a thorny plant that provides us perfumes?

    (a)     Rose             (b)     Cactus

    (c)     Sunflower        (d)     Mushroom

24. Study the given flow chart and select the correct option that fills the spaces d, e, f, and g. [2013]

    Parts of Plants → Flower, e, Stem, g
    Flower → d; e → Spinach; Stem → f; g → Radish

| | d | e | f | g |
|---|---|---|---|---|
| (a) | Broccoli | Leaf | Onion | Root |
| (b) | Cabbage | Root | Potato | Leaf |
| (c) | Coconut | Leaf | Cinnamon | Root |
| (d) | Cauliflower | Root | Cardamon | Leaf |

25. Which one of the following is correct? [Tricky]
    - (a) Every plant has medicinal value
    - (b) No plant has medicinal value
    - (c) Small plants have medicinal value
    - (d) Some plants have medicinal value

26. Pooja places a black plastic tape over the blade of a leaf as shown in the given diagram. She expected that the plant would die after a few days but it did not because ____________. [2013]

(a) Air is absorbed by the other leaves.

(b) Water reaches all the leaves from the roots through the stem.

(c) Food can be transported from the other leaves to the leaf covered with tape through the stem.

(d) All of these.

27. **Read the following statements and choose the correct option.** (Critical Thinking)

**Statement 1:** Trees have stronger stem than herbs and shrubs.

**Statement 2:** Cactus is an aquatic plant.

(a) Statement A is true, Statement B is false.

(b) Statement A is false, Statement B is true.

(c) Both the Statements are true.

(d) Both the statement are false

28. **'X' is a stem that grows above the ground while 'Y' is a stem that grows under the ground. What are 'X' and 'Y'?** [2013]

| | X | Y |
|---|---|---|
| (a) | Potato | Ginger |
| (b) | Sugarcane | Carrot |
| (c) | Carrot | Radish |
| (d) | Sugarcane | Potato |

29. **Which of the following option will replace 'X' and 'Y' in the table.**

| Plants | Names | |
|---|---|---|
| Aquatic | Lily | 'X' |
| Desert plant | Cactus | Opuntia |
| Herb | 'Y' | Coriander |

(a) X = Lotus, Y = Banyan      (b) X = Rose, Y = Mint

(c) X = Lotus, Y = Mint      (d) X = Opuntia, Y = Cotton

30. **Which of these is the stage of the plant before bearing the fruits?** [2013]

(a) 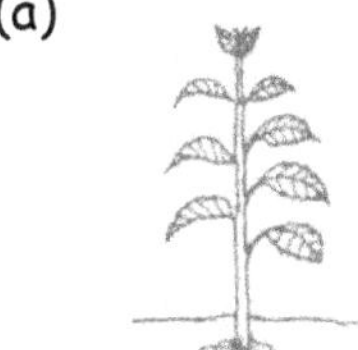      (b) 

(c)       (d) 

**31.** What could be the reason for the poor growth of the plant in pot C?

[Critical Thinking]

(a) It was not given water regularly.      (b) It is filled with cement.

(c) It was placed in dark.      (d) Both (a) and (c).

**32.** Read the following characteristics of 'X' plant and identify it.     [2015]

1. It is a small plant that grows close to the ground.

2. The stem is thin, hard and woody.

3. Thread for cloth fabric is obtained from it.

(a) Hibiscus       (b) Bougainvillea

(c) Cotton       (d) Jute

**Directions (Qs. 33 to 35):** Read the rhyme carefully and answer the following questions.

> I see you are a seed
> Tell me what you need
> I need soil to grow
> I can grow in water too
> Water makes me wet
> Air for my leaves to get
> Space for my roots to spread
> Now I grow into a green plant.

**33.** Plants can grow in ________

(a) soil      (b) air      (c) water      (d) both (a) and (c)

**34.** What is the colour of the plant described in the rhyme?

(a) Red      (b) Green'      (c) Black      (d) Blue

**35.** Which of the following helps a plant to grow?

(a) Air      (b) Water      (c) Space      (d) All of these

**36.** Which of the following is a stem?   [2016, Tricky]

(a)   Beetroot          (b)   Carrot          (c)   Turnip          (d)   Ginger

**37.** Which of the following activities you should NOT do in the park?   [Tricky]
(a)   Throw stones on the plants.
(b)   Pluck flowers and leaves from the plants
(c)   Grow more and more plants
(d)   Both (a) and (b)

**38.** What is "Q"?   [2017, Tricky]

(Q)

(a)   Flower          (b)   Root          (c)   stem          (d)   Fruit

**39.** Which of the following is an edible root?   [2021]

(a) 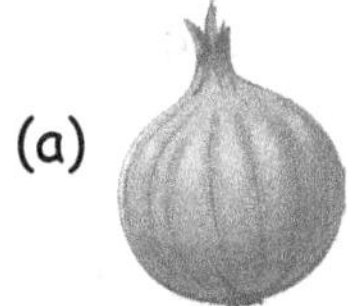   (b)    (c) 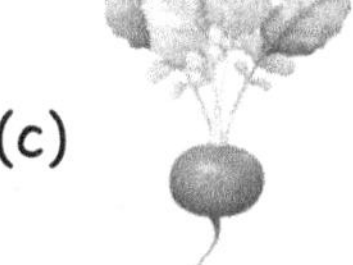   (d) 

**40.** Match the columns and select the correct option.   [2021]

|    | Column I | | Column II |
|----|----------|---|-----------|
| A. | Seed | 1. | Fixes the plant to the ground |
| B. | Root | 2. | Makes food for the plant |
| C. | Fruit | 3. | Grows into a new plant |
| D. | Leaf | 4. | Grows from the flower |

(a) A-4, B-2, C-3, D-1          (b) A-3, B-1, C-4, D-2
(c) A-1, B-2, C-3, D-4          (d) A-2, B-1, C-4, D-3

**41.** Which of the following is hidden in the given word grid?   [2021]

(a) A herb from which paper is made.

(b) A climber that gives bunches of tiny juicy fruits.

(c) A shrub that is used to make clothes.

(d) A water plant with big pink-coloured flowers.

| D | Y | G | S | J | A |
|---|---|---|---|---|---|
| Z | L | C | P | p | O |
| N | T | O | V | M | V |
| O | F | T | K | W | E |
| B | W | T | U | R | S |
| Y | Q | O | U | X | C |
| I | X | N | T | H | R |

42. Refer to the given diagram and select the option that correctly identifies X, Y and Z. **[2022]**

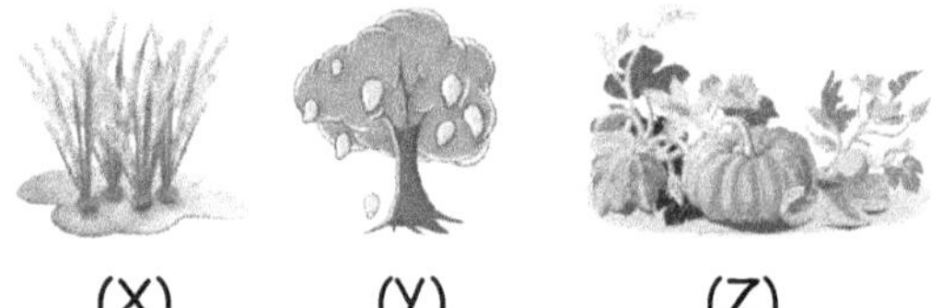

|     | X      | Y       | Z        |
|-----|--------|---------|----------|
| (a) | Teak   | Mustard | Banyan   |
| (b) | Coconut| Jasmine | Mango    |
| (c) | Mustard| Neem    | Sheesham |
| (d) | Cotton | Peepal  | Deodar   |

43. Three different types of plants have been shown below. Choose the correct option with respect to the plants and types of food they produce. **[2022]**

(X)　　　(Y)　　　(Z)

(a) X-cereals; Y- fruits; Z-vegetables　(b) X-pulses; Y-fruits; Z-cereals

(c) X-cereals; Y-vegetables; Z-fruits　(d) X-pulses; Y-vegetables; Z-fruits

## RESPONSE GRID

### LEVEL 1

1. a b c d　2. a b c d　3. a b c d　4. a b c d　5. a b c d
6. a b c d　7. a b c d　8. a b c d　9. a b c d　10. a b c d
11. a b c d　12. a b c d　13. a b c d　14. a b c d　15. a b c d
16. a b c d　17. a b c d　18. a b c d　19. a b c d　20. a b c d
21. a b c d　22. a b c d　23. a b c d　24. a b c d　25. a b c d
26. a b c d　27. a b c d　28. a b c d　29. a b c d　30. a b c d
31. a b c d　32. a b c d　33. a b c d　34. a b c d　35. a b c d
36. a b c d　37. a b c d　38. a b c d　39. a b c d　40. a b c d
41. a b c d　42. a b c d　43. a b c d　44. a b c d　45. a b c d
46. a b c d　47. a b c d

### LEVEL 2

1. a b c d　2. a b c d　3. a b c d　4. a b c d　5. a b c d
6. a b c d　7. a b c d　8. a b c d　9. a b c d　10. a b c d
11. a b c d　12. a b c d　13. a b c d　14. a b c d　15. a b c d
16. a b c d　17. a b c d　18. a b c d　19. a b c d　20. a b c d
21. a b c d　22. a b c d　23. a b c d　24. a b c d　25. a b c d
26. a b c d　27. a b c d　28. a b c d　29. a b c d　30. a b c d
31. a b c d　32. a b c d　33. a b c d　34. a b c d　35. a b c d
36. a b c d　37. a b c d　38. a b c d　39. a b c d　40. a b c d
41. a b c d　42. a b c d　43. a b c d

# Answers with Explanations

## LEVEL 1

1. **(b)** Mint is a herb.
2. **(c)** Roots absorb water and minerals from the soil.
3. **(b)** Cactus plant is found in a desert.
4. **(b)** The leaves of cabbage are used as food.
5. **(a)** Pumpkin is a creeper.
6. **(d)** All the statements are correct about climbers.
7. **(c)** Flowers of broccoli and cauliflower are eaten as food.
8. **(b)** Fruits develop from flower.
9. **(c)** Groundnut is a source of cooking oil.
10. **(a)** Tulsi is a herb.
11. **(b)** Roots absorb water from the soil.
12. **(c)** Option (c) is turnip, which is a vegetable. All others pomegranate, watermelon and muskmelon are fruits.
13. **(b)** Mushroom is not a plant.
14. **(d)** The shape of rose leaves is shown in option (d). They are small leaves with zigzag margin.
15. **(d)** Both paper and medicines are obtained from plants.
16. **(d)** Pumpkin is a creeper. Money plant, grapevine and bean are climbers.
17. **(d)** Table, chair and doors are obtained from wood.
18. **(c)** Root, shoot and leaves are the part of plant; tree is a type of plants.
19. **(a)** Rose, cotton and hibiscus are shrubs; cactus is a desert plant.
20. **(a)** Wood, pulses and medicines are obtained from plants. Water is a natural thing.
21. **(a)** Oil is not obtained from mango plant.
22. **(d)** Herbs are the small plants with soft stem.
23. **(d)** A basil plant is smaller than a tree and has medicinal value as well.
24. **(c)** Coconut tree is not a shrub.
25. **(a)** It grows along the wall or ground.
26. **(a)** Radio cannot be produced by plants.
27. **(d)** Plants give out oxygen.
28. **(d)** Leaves are generally green, but can be of different colours as well.
29. **(b)** We do not get cell phone from plants as it is an electronic device.
30. **(a)** The stems of creepers are weak. They need support to grow.
31. **(d)** Seeds grow into new plants.
32. **(b)** Stems (Q) carry food from leaves (R) to all the other parts of the plants.
33. **(c)** Cotton is a shrub, Betel is a climber and Coriander is a herb.
34. **(b)** All the three plants lose their leaves in autumn season.
35. **(c)** Cotton plant is a shrub. The shown image is of rose plant, that is also a shrub.
36. **(b)** Cabbage is a leafy vegetable that we eat.
37. **(c)** Stem transports water, mineral and food to all parts of the plant.
38. **(a)** Because flowers produce fruits.
39. **(a)** pea - climber, spinach – herb, money plant – climber, pumpkin – creeper.
40. **(a)** Pomegranate
41. **(c)** Milk is a body building food.
42. **(b)** Sheep
43. **(a)** Acacia
44. **(a)** Both mango and litchi contains one seed.
45. **(d)** Banyan tree
46. **(c)**                 47. **(a)**

## LEVEL 2

1. **(a)** Mint and clove are the medicinal plants used to add flavour to food and have medical value as well.
2. **(c)** If all the flowers of a plant are removed, then the plant will not produce any seeds or fruits.
3. **(b)** X- Coconut, Y-Sunflower.

4. **(d)** All of these are food grains.
5. **(a)** Tulsi is a herb, which is a small plant with soft stem and its leaves are used to make medicine. It adds flavour to food.
6. **(c)** Rose and hibiscus plants have woody stem.
7. **(b)** 'B' is a hibiscus plant which is a small plant with woody stem.
8. **(c)** Roots absorb water from soil, stem supports the plants. Leaves are responsible for food production, flower is the reproductive part of plant.
9. **(b)** leaves
10. **(c)** trees
11. **(b)** mango
12. **(b)** aquatic
13. **(b)** lotus
14. **(a)** wood
15. **(b)** oxygen
16. **(c)** Rose is a shrub and pumpkin is a creeper.
17. **(d)** Flower is the reproductive part of plant.
18. **(c)** Coconut is a tree, rose is a shrub and coriander is a herb.
19. **(b)** Waterlily is an aquatic plant.
20. **(a)** Coriander is a small seasonal herb with soft stem. Its leaves are used to make medicines. Its seeds and leaves are used to make food tasty.
21. **(b)** Both rose and hibiscus plants are shrubs.
22. **(d)** Bamboo is a fast growing plant and grows almost a metre (3-28 feet) in 1 day.
23. **(a)** Rose is a thorny plant that provides perfume.
24. **(a)** We eat different parts (stems, roots, leaves and flowers) of different plants. Flowers of broccoli, leaves of spinach, underground stems of onion and roots of raddish are edible parts of these plants.
25. **(d)** Some plants have medicinal value.
26. **(b)**

27. **(a)** Statement A is correct. Trees have stronger stem than herbs and shrubs and cactus is not an aquatic plant, it is a desert plant.
28. **(d)** Sugarcane is a stem that grows above the ground. Ginger and patoato are stems that grow under the ground. Carrot and radish are roots that grow underground.
29. **(c)** 'X' is lotus which is an aquatic plant. 'Y' is mint which is a herb.
30. **(b)** Before bearing fruits, plants bear flowers. These flowers turn into fruits.
31. **(d)** It is not given water regularly and placed in dark.
32. **(c)** Cotton is a small plant which grows close to the ground and has a thin, hard and woody stem. The seeds of cotton have fibres attached to it. These cotton fibres are used to make cotton yarn which is used for making cloth fabric.
33. **(d)** Plants can grow in water and soil.
34. **(b)** Green
35. **(d)** Plants need air, water and space to grow.
36. **(d)** Ginger is a stem.
37. **(d)** You should not throw stones on the plants and do not pluck flowers and leaves from the plants.
38. **(a)** Cauliflower is a flower.
39. **(d)** Turnip
40. **(b)** (a) – 3, (b) – 1, (c) – 4, (d) – 2
41. **(c)** Cotton is used to make clothes.

| D | Y | G | S | J | A |
|---|---|---|---|---|---|
| Z | L | C | P | P | O |
| N | T | O | V | M | V |
| O | F | T | K | W | E |
| B | W | T | U | R | S |
| Y | Q | O | U | X | C |
| I | X | N | T | H | R |

42. (X = Mustard, Y = Neem, Z = Sheesham)

43. **(a)**

# 3 | CHAPTER FOREWORD

Plants and animals both are living things. Plants can prepare their food but animals depend on humans and plants for their food and shelter. The animals which depend on humans for their food and shelter are called domestic animals. Animals that live independently in the forest are known as wild animals. Animals that live in water are called aquatic animals. Insects are small animals. They have six legs and some of them have wings to fly. Birds can fly like hen, sparrow and pigeon, but some birds can't fly like ostrich and penguin. This is the world of different types of animals.

**Directions: Look at the kinds of animals given below and colour the ring blue for aquatic animals, green for amphibians (that can live on land and in water both) and red for terrestrial animals.**

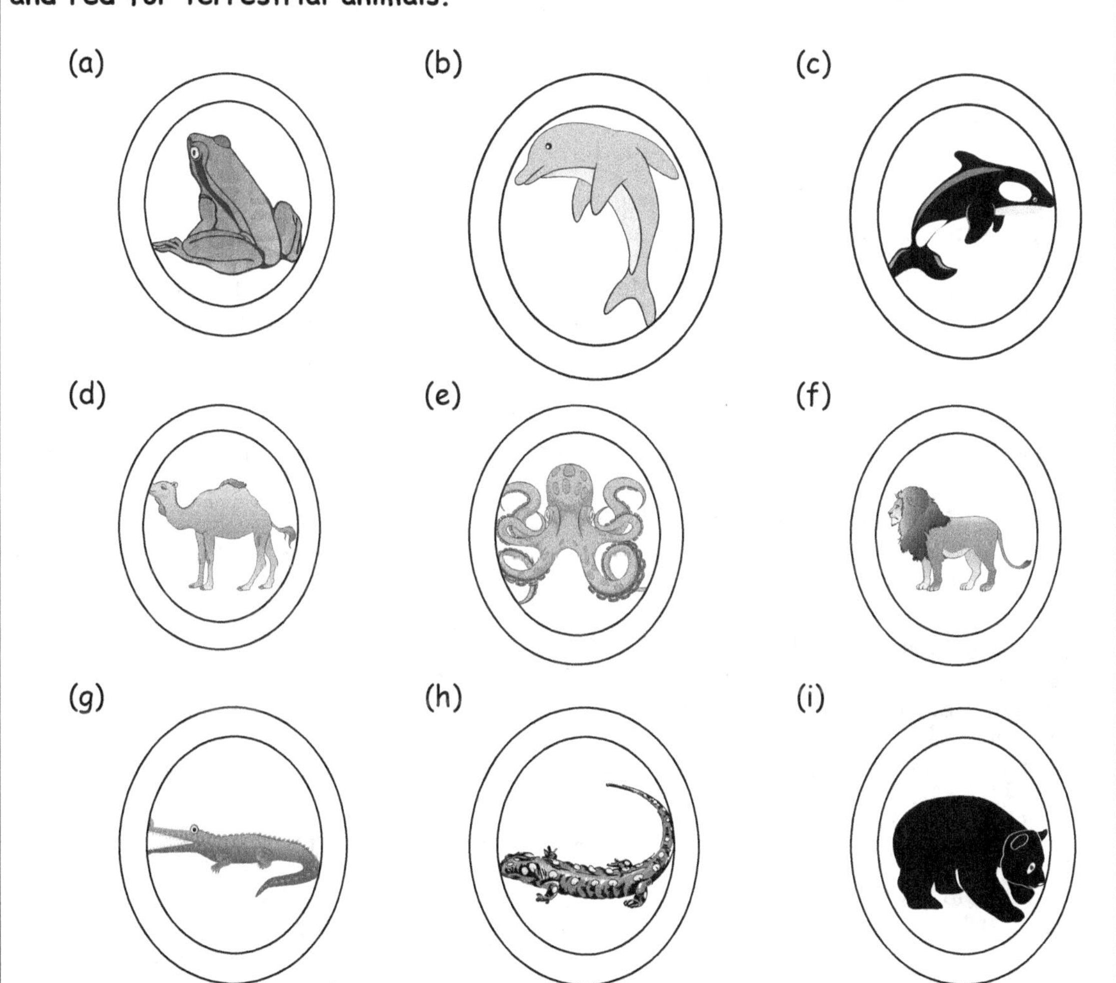

After reading this chapter, you will be able to know more about different types of animals and their habitat.

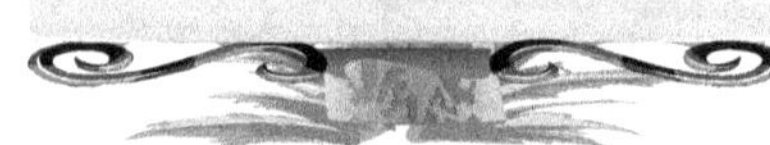

# 3
## Chapter

# Animals



- ❖ Ostrich can run faster than horse and the male ostrich can roar like lion.
- ❖ The stomach of cow is divided into 4 parts.

### Desert Animal Facts

- ❖ Desert animals eat plants filled with water. They often wait until night time to dine because this is when the water content is the highest in the plants. Predators obtain water from their prey's meat and blood.
- ❖ Animals that survive in the desert are also very efficient at storing and conserving water.
- ❖ Small desert animals dig burrows to live in. These burrows become cooler during the hot days and warmer during the cold desert nights.
- ❖ To protect themselves from the heat many desert animals, especially rodents, become inactive in the hot summer months.

## LEARNING OBJECTIVES

**This chapter will help you to:**

- ❖ study the habitat of animals.
- ❖ know about the different eating habits of animals.
- ❖ understand the importance and uses of animals.
- ❖ learn about insects and birds.

## INTRODUCTION

We all know that, plants and animals both are living things. The only difference between plants and animals is that plants can prepare their own food, but animals depend on humans and plants for their food and shelter.

Some animals live only on land, some on trees, some in water and some can live on land and in water both.

Let us study these animals and their habitat in detail.

## DOMESTIC ANIMALS

The animals which depend on humans for their food and shelter are called domestic animals. Cow is a domestic animal. It give us milk. Horse is also a domestic animal and is used for travelling from one place to another.

Domestic animals give us many useful things. For example:

- We get **milk** from cows and buffaloes.

- We get **eggs** from hens and ducks. Some people eat **flesh** of animals like fish, goat, sheep and chicken.

- We get **silk** from silkworms.
- The skin of animals like snakes and crocodiles is used to make **leather**.
- Animals like oxes, horses, donkeys, elephants and camels are used to carry heavy loads.
- Camels are also known as "Ship of the desert". They are used as the transport system in a desert or an arid region.

## WILD ANIMALS

Animals which live independently in the forest are called wild animals. Wild animals are dangerous.

For example: Lion, tiger, wolf, fox, deer, giraffe, leopard and cheetah.

## AQUATIC ANIMALS

Animals such as fish and dolphin live in water and are called aquatic animals.

Frog, crocodiles and turtles can live on land and as well as in water.

## FOOD OF ANIMALS

Different animals have different food habits.

For example: Cow, buffalo and goat eat grass. Lion and tiger eat flesh of other animals. Let us study different eating habits of animals.

Real Life examples

❖ Horses, Donkeys and Oxes are used for transportation

Historical Preview

❖ Cow has been considered as a symbol of worship, since ancient times.

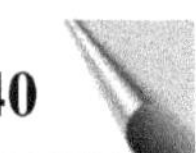



- ❖ Crocodiles are blind in water, but can see on the land.
- ❖ A cockroach can survive without its head for nine days.
- ❖ An ant can lift a weight of 50 times of its own weight.

## 1. Herbivorous Animals

Those animals which eat grass and other plants are called herbivorous animals. For example: Cow, buffalo, goat, deer, giraffe, donkey and elephant.

## 2. Carnivorous Animals

Those animals that eat only the flesh of other animals are known as carnivorous animals. For example: Lion, tiger, leopard, hawk and whale.

## 3. Omnivorous Animals

Some animals like crows, bear, jackal and gorilla eat both plants as well as flesh of other animals. These type of animals are known as Omnivorous animals.

## INSECTS

Insects are small animals. They have six legs. Some insects have wings. Wings help them to fly.

Examples of insects are butterfly, housefly and mosquito.

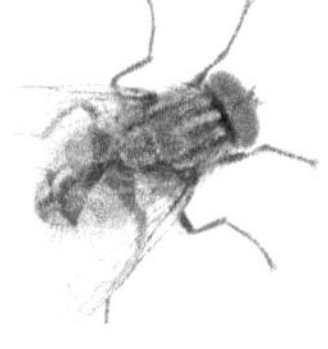

## BIRDS

Most birds can fly such as hen, crow and parrot. Some of the birds cannot fly such as ostrich, penguin and emu. These are known as **flightless birds**. They can walk and run. Birds have two wings which help them to fly. Birds have legs that help them to walk. Some birds like ducks and swans can swim.

# Multiple Choice Questions

## LEVEL 1

1.  **Which of the following is a domestic animal?**

    (a)  Tiger          (b)  Parrot          (c)  Bear          (d)  Cow

2.  **Domestic animals depend on _________ for their food and shelter.**

    (a)  wild animals                    (b)  birds

    (c)  humans                          (d)  All of these

3.  **Which of the following animal is used for carrying load?**

    (a)  Lion          (b)  Donkey          (c)  Monkey          (d)  Cow

4.  **Which of the following statement is true for a wild animal?**          [2012, Tricky]

    (a)  Wild animals depend on humans for food and shelter

    (b)  Wild animals are not dangerous for living organisms

    (c)  Wild animals live independently in the forest

    (d)  Wild animals cannot live without humans

5.  **Which of the following is not a wild animal?**

    (a)  Tiger          (b)  Deer          (c)  Fox          (d)  Goat

6.  **Find the incorrect match**          [Tricky]

    (a)  Cow — herbivorous              (b)  Tiger — omnivorous

    (c)  Leopard — carnivorous          (d)  Giraffe — herbivorous

7.  **Which of the following animal provides us leather?**          [2012]

    (a)                                  (b)

    (c)                                  (d)

8.  **Carnivorous animals eat _________.**

    (a)  cereals                         (b)  fruits

    (c)  flesh of other animals          (d)  grass

9. Which of the following eat both plants and other animals?
   (a) Herbivorous    (b) Omnivorous    (c) Carnivorous    (d) Both (a) and (c)

10. Which of the following animals live on land only?    **[2013, Tricky]**
    (a) Cow    (b) Crocodile    (c) Frog    (d) All of these

11. Choose odd one out
    (a) Giraffe    (b) Horse    (c) Donkey    (d) Tiger

12. Amongst the given animals which does/do NOT help us in carrying our load? **[2014]**
    (a) 1, 2 and 3    (b) 3 and 4    (c) 4 only    (d) 2, 3 and 4

13. Which of the following bird/s cannot fly?    **[Tricky]**

    (a)      (b)

    (c)      (d) Both (b) and (c)

14. Which of the following is not a bird?
    (a) Peacock    (b) Owl    (c) Bat    (d) Ostrich

15. _______ animals help in maintaining ecological balance.
    (a) Wild      (b) Domestic
    (c) Both wild and domestic      (d) None of these

16. Which of the following food we get from animals?    **[2014, Tricky]**
    (a) Meat    (b) Apple    (c) Mushroom    (d) Pulse

17. Which of the following animals is NOT a 'farm animal'?    **[2015]**

    (a)      (b)

    (c)      (d) None of these

18. Which of the following is a wild as well as a carnivorous animal?    **[Tricky]**
    (a) Goat    (b) Leopard    (c) Crow    (d) Horse

19. Which of the following statement is true?    **[Tricky]**
    (a) Wolf is a domestic animal      (b) Owl is an animal
    (c) Horse is used for house keeping      (d) Rabbit is a herbivorous animal

**20.** Whale is an _________ animal and is a _________ animal

    (a)   domestic, carnivorous        (b)   aquatic, carnivorous

    (c)   aquatic, omnivorous         (d)   domestic, herbivorous

**21.** Which one of the following is true?                             [Tricky]

    (a)   Lion is a domestic animal

    (b)   Lion is the another name of cow

    (c)   Horse is a domestic animal

    (d)   Lion is not dangerous for other living organism

**22.** Which of the following animal is NOT an insect?                [2015]

    (a)                      (b)

    (c)                      (d)

**23.** Which one of the following is a wild animal?

    (a)  Dog        (b)  Cat        (c)  Hyena        (d)  Donkey

**24.** Which one of the following animal is wild and carnivorous both?    [2017, Tricky]

    (a)                      (b)

    (c)                      (d)

**25.** _______________ is a herbivorous animal.

    (a)  Rabbit       (b)  Dog       (c)  Cat       (d)  Bear

**26.** Which one of the following option is the food of omnivorous animal?

    (a)   Only meat             (b)   Only fruit

    (c)   Only vegetables       (d)   Plants and flesh both

**27.** Which one of the following is true?

    (a)   Tiger is a domestic animal      (b)   Camel is a wild animal

    (c)   Horse is a wild animal          (d)   Wolf is a wild animal

**28.** _______________ is both herbivorous and domestic animal.                    **[Tricky]**
   (a)  Goat　　　　(b)  Leopard　　　　(c)  Hyena　　　　(d)  Bear

**29.** Which one of the following is not the product of animals?
   (a)  Meat　　　　(b)  Pulse　　　　(c)  Egg　　　　(d)  Fish

**30.** Herbivorous animals eat __________.
   (a)  plants and plant products　　　　(b)  flesh
   (c)  flesh and plants　　　　(d)  none of these

**31.** A nest is a home of __________.
   (a)  Snake　　　　(b)  Sparrow　　　　(c)  Lizard　　　　(d)  Hamster

**32.** Which of the following animals give us milk ?
   (a)  Cow　　　　(b)  Goat　　　　(c)  Buffalo　　　　(d)  All of these

**33.** Identify the wild animal given in the picture.                    **[2016]**

   (a)  This is chimpanzee　　　　(b)  This is bear
   (c)  This is wolf　　　　(d)  This is whale

**34.** Select the option that correctly fills the blank in the given riddle.                    **[2018]**
   Bleat, Bleat !! I say,
   eat grass and hay.
   I give you milk to drink,
   My baby is called __________.
   (a)  Kid　　　　(b)  Calf　　　　(c)  Cub　　　　(d)  Joey

**35.** Refer to the given flow chart and select the option which correctly identifies animal X.                    **[2018]**



   (a)　　　(b)　　　(c)　　　(d)

**36.** Which of these belongs to the centre ?                    **[2018]**

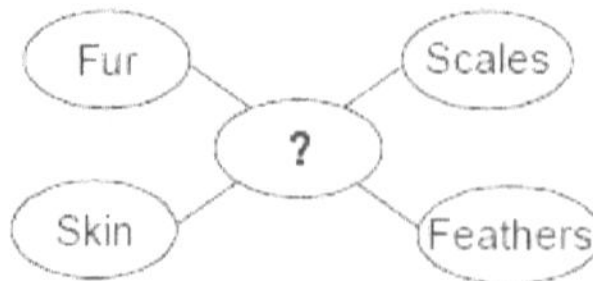

(a)  Things that cover animal bodies
(b)  Things that help animal bodies get oxygen
(c)  Things that make the animal smaller
(d)  Things that keep animal bodies cool

37. Which animal probably made this foot mark    ?    [2018]

(a)     (b)     (c)     (d)

38.  Select the option that correctly completes the given table.    [2018]

| Animal | Sound |
| --- | --- |
| Tiger | Growl |
| Donkey | X |
| Y | Trumpet |

|  | X | Y |
| --- | --- | --- |
| (a) | Quack | Pig |
| (b) | Neigh | Duck |
| (c) | Chatter | Horse |
| (d) | Bray | Elephant |

39.  Which of the following is obtained from sheep?    [2019]

(a)     (b)     (c)     (d)  All of these

40.  Read the given riddle and idenfity the animal.    [2020]

> - I can hop.
> - I have a pouch.
> - I have a long tail.
> - My baby is called joey.
> - Who am I?

(a) Camel    (b) Rabbit
(c) Bear    (d) Kangaroo

41.  Baby of the animal shown in the given picture is called a ________ .    [2020]
(a) Lamb
(b) Fawn
(c) Foal
(d) Joey

**42.** Which of the following is/are domestic animal(s)?    [2021]

1          2          3          4

(a) 1 and 4 only    (b) 1 and 2 only    (c) 3 and 4 only    (d) 3 only

**43.** Foal is the baby of __________.    [2021]

(a) Sheep    (b) Horse    (c) Kangaroo    (d) Cow

**44.** Wax is obtained from __________.    [2021]

(a) Honey bee    (b) Cow    (c) Snake    (d) Hen

**45.** Select the correct match of animal and the thing we get from it.

(a) Sheep - Honey    (b) Cow – Silk    [2022]

(c) Horse – Eggs    (d) Goat – Milk

**46.** In the given diagram, what would deer be called?    [2022]

(a) Prey animal

(b) Pet animal

(c) Domestic animal

(d) None of these



**47.** A carnivorous animal eats __________ only.    [2022]

(a) cereal    (b) fruit    (c) vegetable    (d) flesh

**48.** How many legs does the organism shown below has?    [2022]

(a) 4    (b) 6    (c) 8    (d) 10

## LEVEL 2

**1.** Study the given classification chart carefully.    [2012]

What could X be?

(a)  Cow

(b)  Tiger

(c)  Frog

(d)  Bear

| Animals | | |
|---|---|---|
| Plant-eater | Plant-eater | Plant-eater |
| Bee<br>Goat | Wolf<br>Lion | Pig<br>X |

2.  Match the list I with list II.                                    [2012, Tricky]

    |     | List I    |     | List II          |
    |-----|-----------|-----|------------------|
    | (A) | Hen       | 1.  | Bird             |
    | (B) | Cow       | 2.  | Insect           |
    | (C) | Camel     | 3.  | Lives in desert  |
    | (D) | Butterfly | 4.  | Domestic animal  |

    |     | A | B | C | D |     |     | A | B | C | D |
    |-----|---|---|---|---|-----|-----|---|---|---|---|
    | (a) | 2 | 3 | 4 | 1 |     | (b) | 1 | 2 | 4 | 3 |
    | (c) | 1 | 4 | 3 | 2 |     | (d) | 2 | 3 | 4 | 1 |

3.  An _______ has six legs, and a bird have _______ wings.          [Tricky]
    (a) bird, six          (b) insect, two          (c) bird, two          (d) crow, two

4.  Group 1: Lion, bear, tiger, elephant
    Group 2: Ox, cow, horse
    Which of the following is correct about the given groups of animals ? [2013, Tricky]
    (a)  Group 1: Domestic animals; Group 2: Wild animals
    (b)  Group 1: Wild animals; Group 2: Domestic animal
    (c)  Both Group 1 and Group 2 have Domestic animal
    (d)  None of these.

5.  Study the given diagram and select the correct option that can fill spaces 'X', 'Y'
    and 'Z'.                                                          [2013]

    |     | X          | Y       | Z       |
    |-----|------------|---------|---------|
    | (a) | Wolf       | Giraffe | Crow    |
    | (b) | Rhinoceros | Lion    | Hyena   |
    | (c) | Crocodile  | Bear    | Vulture |
    | (d) | Bat        | Deer    | Lion    |

6.  Match the following animals with their uses.                     [Tricky]

    |     | Animals |     | Uses          |
    |-----|---------|-----|---------------|
    | (A) | Horse   | 1.  | House keeping |
    | (B) | Dogs    | 2.  | Wool          |
    | (C) | Sheep   | 3.  | Mutton        |
    | (D) | Goat    | 4.  | Travelling    |

    |     | A | B | C | D |     |     | A | B | C | D |
    |-----|---|---|---|---|-----|-----|---|---|---|---|
    | (a) | 1 | 3 | 2 | 4 |     | (b) | 2 | 1 | 3 | 4 |
    | (c) | 4 | 1 | 2 | 3 |     | (d) | 3 | 2 | 1 | 4 |

7.  Look at the diagram shown below and mark the correct option. (Critical Thinking)

**A** : represents animals that live in water.

**B** : represents animals that live on land.

**Which of these animals best represent 'X' ?**

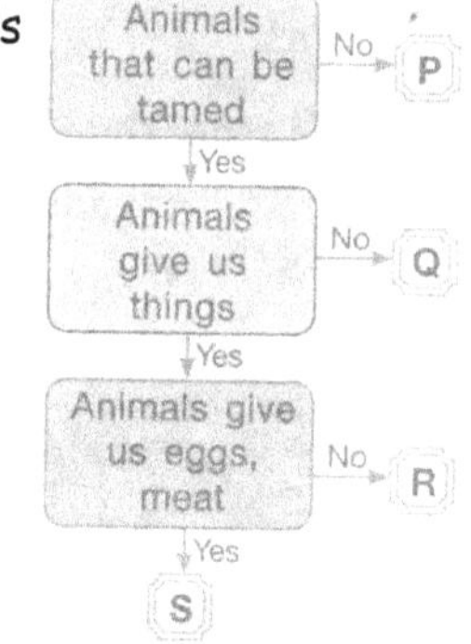



(i)    Tortoise      (ii)    Crocodile

(iii)    Shark      (iv)    Star fish

(a)    Only (i)      (b)    Only (ii)

(c)    Both (i) and (ii)    (d)    All of these

**8. Read the following statements and choose the correct answer.** [2015, Tricky]

**Statement 1:** Leather can be made from rabbit.

**Statement 2:** Cows, pigs, goats and sheep are wild animals.

(a)    Statement 1 is correct, statement 2 is incorrect

(b)    Statement 1 is incorrect, statement 2 is correct

(c)    Statement 1 and statement 2 are incorrect

(d)    Statement 1 and statement 2 are correct

**9. Study the given flow chart. Identify one example of the following and select the correct option.** [2013, Critical Thinking]

(a)    'P' animals that eat the flesh of dead animals and 'R' animals that give wax.

(b)    'Q' and 'S' animals.

| | P | Q | R | S |
|---|---|---|---|---|
| (a) | Crocodile | Horse | Giraffe | Chicken |
| (b) | Hyena | Donkey | Honeybee | Hen |
| (c) | Jackal | Elephant | Silkworm | Goat |
| (d) | Vulture | Camel | Sheep | Snake |



**Directions (Qs. 10 to 12): Read the passage carefully and answer the questions.**

Wild animal is a term that refers to animals that are not normally domesticated. The wild animals provide useful products like ivory, honey and tusk, whereas, domestic animals provide products like milk, meat and wool. Domestic animals do very useful jobs for human beings. On the other hand, wild animals help to maintain the ecological balance of nature and maintain the food chain. **[Critical Thinking]**

**10. Which of the following statement is true?**

(a)    Wild animals are friendly.

(b)    Wild animals are dangerous.

(c)    Wild animals can be domesticated easily

(d)    Wild animals include cow, deer and ox.

**11.** **Which of the following product is not provided by wild animals?**

(a)    Ivory     (b)    Honey     (c)    Tusk     (d)    Mutton.

**12.** **Which of the following is/are obtained from animal?**

(a)    Milk     (b)    Tusk     (c)    Wool     (d)    All of these

**13.** **What is similar among the given animals?** [2013]

[Crow,    Frog,    Lizard]

(a)    They live in burrow

(b)    They give meat and eggs

(c)    They live both on land and water

(d)    They eat insects and worms

**14.** **Identify X and Y.** [Critical Thinking]

| Animals | Uses | Eating habits |
| --- | --- | --- |
| X | Carry load | Herbivorous |
| Elephant | Tusk | Y |

(a)    X = Pig    Y = Carnivorous

(b)    X = Donkey    Y = Herbivorous

(c)    X = Monkey    Y = Herbivorous

(d)    X = Deer    Y = Omnivorous

**15.** **Read the following statements.** [Tricky]

**Statement 1:** Both carnivorous and herbivorous animals, maintain balance in nature.

**Statement 2:** Only herbivorous animals maintain balance in nature.

Which of the following is correct about the above statements ?

(a)    Statement 1 is true and 2 is false     (b)    Statement 1 is false and 2 is true

(c)    Both statements are false     (d)    Both statements are true

**16.** **Study the given word grid and answer the questions:** [2013]

(A)    How many names of animals who carry heavy loads are hidden in the word grid?

(B)    How many animal products are hidden in the word grid?

| | **A** | **B** |
| --- | --- | --- |
| (a) | Two | Three |
| (b) | Two | Two |
| (c) | Four | Two |
| (d) | Four | One |

**17.** **Different animals provide different products. Each of the following groups contains animals providing similar products, except one. Select this odd group out.** [2015]

(a)    Cow, Buffalo, Goat     (b)    Camel, Snake, Crocodile

(c)    Hen, Duck, Honey bee     (d)    Sheep, Yak, Rabbit

**18.** **Which of the following statement/s is/are true?**                                    [Tricky]

    (i)     Whale is an aquatic animal

    (ii)    Seahorse is a terrestrial animal

    (iii)   Crocodile is both aquatic as well as terrestrial animal

    (iv)   Goat is omnivorous

    (a)    (i)       (b)    (i) and (iii)    (c)    (ii) and (iv)    (d)    All

**19.** **Which of the following is true about crocodiles?**                                    [Tricky]

    (a)    Crocodiles are blind in water, but can see on the land.

    (b)    Crocodiles are carnivorous animals.

    (c)    Crocodile lives on land as well as water.

    (d)    All the above statement are true.

**20.** **Complete the series**                                    [Critical Thinking]

    (a)    Deer       (b)    Grass       (c)    Tiger       (d)    Leopard

**21.** **Identify the animal whose sound is hidden in the given group of letters by crossing out every alternate letter starting from first.**                                    [2015]

M T Q R G U E M S P U E V T N

    (a)    Monkey       (b)    Lion       (c)    Elephant    (d)    Giraffe

**22.** **Which of these on unscrambling gives the name of a wild animal that does NOT live in a hole in the ground?**                                    [2014]

    (a)    BRIATB      (b)    LRIGLAO     (c)    OSONGEMO  (d)    KNESA

**23.** **Which of the following can not be considered as the beast of burden?**

    (a)    Buffalo      (b)    Cow       (c)    Donkey      (d)    Camel

**24.** **Match the following.**                                    [Tricky]

|  | Column (I) |  | Column (II) |
|---|---|---|---|
| (A) | Monkey | 1. | Grass |
| (B) | Snake | 2. | Rat |
| (C) | Deer | 3. | Flesh |
| (D) | Lion | 4. | Banana |

|  | A | B | C | D |  |  | A | B | C | D |
|---|---|---|---|---|---|---|---|---|---|---|
| (a) | 1 | 3 | 4 | 2 | | (b) | 3 | 4 | 2 | 1 |
| (c) | 4 | 2 | 1 | 3 | | (d) | 2 | 3 | 4 | 1 |

**25.** **Which type of living organisms forms a food chain ?**

    (a)    Plants only           (b)    Animals only

    (c)    Both plants and animals    (d)    None of these

**26.** Study the given diagram. Which of the following animal can be placed at the place X? **[2015]**

(a) Frog

(b) Woodpecker

(c) Spider

(d) Grasshopper

**27.** The given groups of animals were formed on the basis of feeding habits, each with one odd member. Ravi was asked to encircle the odd one in each group, but he made one mistake. Select the group in which he encircled a wrong animal. **[2015]**

(a) Frog, Lizard, (Sheep)

(b) Tiger, (Hen), Cat

(c) Rabbit, Squirrel, (Spider)

(d) (Cow), Lion, Buffalo

**28.** Which of the following animals's sound is NOT hidden in the word grid? **[2015]**

(a) Tiger

(b) Elephant

(c) Monkey

(d) Frog

| A | G | Q | Y | J | U | Q |
|---|---|---|---|---|---|---|
| T | R | U | M | P | E | T |
| C | O | T | M | O | R | R |
| E | W | C | R | O | A | K |
| F | L | V | S | T | N | P |

**29.** Read the following statements and guess who I am ? **[Tricky]**

(i) I am not dangerous for human

(ii) I do not eat animal flesh

(iii) I give milk to prepare paneer

(a) Rat     (b) Cow     (c) Giraffe     (d) Peacock

**30.** Which of the following is true ?

(a) Horse is called the 'ship of the desert'   (b) Horse kills the domestic animals

(c) Horse is an insect     (d) Horse is a domestic animal

**31.** Which of the following is a group of wild animals only. **[Tricky]**

(a) Owl, lion, whale and cat     (b) Lion, whale, tiger and horse

(c) Rhinoceros, wolf, deer and lion     (d) Fox, leopard, pig and hen

**32.** Which of the following animal is known as 'Ship of the desert'? **[Tricky]**

(i) Camel     (ii) Buffalo     (iii) Donkey     (iv) Rhinoceros

(a) only (i)     (b) (i), (ii) and (iii)     (c) only (ii)     (d) none

**33.** Match the column (I) with the column (II) **[2017, Tricky]**

| Column (I) | Column (II) |
|---|---|
| (A) Lion | 1. Desert |
| (B) Whale | 2. Forest |
| (C) Camel | 3. Water |
| (D) Crow | 4. Nest |

|  | A | B | C | D |  | A | B | C | D |
|---|---|---|---|---|---|---|---|---|---|
| (a) | 1 | 2 | 3 | 4 | (b) | 2 | 3 | 1 | 4 |
| (c) | 4 | 3 | 2 | 1 | (d) | 3 | 4 | 2 | 1 |

34. Amit's father purchased a cow so that he gets pure milk everyday. After a few days, the cow got ill and could not give milk. Amit's father started beating the cow. What will you suggest them ?
    (a)   Tell him to beat the cow everyday
    (b)   Tell him to give proper food, water and medicines to the cow.
    (c)   Give injection to the cow everyday
    (d)   Both (b) and (c)

35. Match the column I with the column II.                                              [Tricky]

| Column-I | | Column-II |
|---|---|---|
| (A) | Camel | 1. King of the jungle |
| (B) | Cheetah | 2. Tallest land animal |
| (C) | Giraffe | 3. Largest land animal |
| (D) | Elephant | 4. Ship of the desert |
| (E) | Lion | 5. Fastest land animal |

|   | A | B | C | D | E |   |   | A | B | C | D | E |
|---|---|---|---|---|---|---|---|---|---|---|---|---|
| (a) | 2 | 1 | 5 | 4 | 3 | | (b) | 2 | 5 | 1 | 3 | 4 |
| (c) | 4 | 5 | 2 | 3 | 1 | | (d) | 4 | 5 | 2 | 1 | 3 |

36. Ramesh went to the forest with his uncle. His uncle loves hunting deers. He started hunting. What should Ramesh suggest to his uncle?
    (a)   Deer is a food for lion so, he should not kill deers
    (b)   Number of deers will decrease
    (c)   Deer is an important animal so, you can kill some other animal
    (d)   both (a) and (b)

37. Study the given classification chart. Where should (1) peacock and (2) louse be placed?                                              [Tricky]

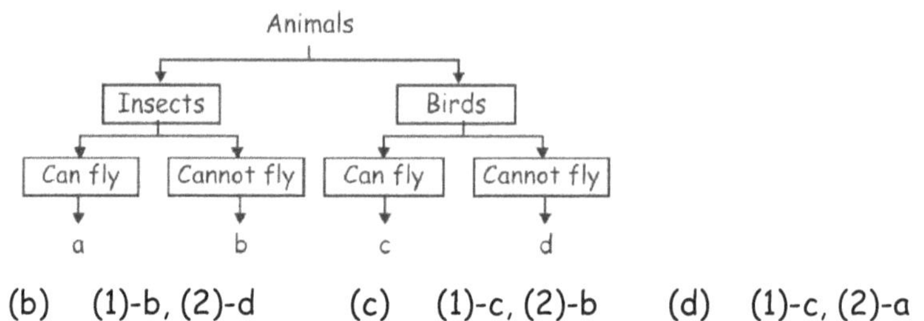


    (a)   (1)-d, (2)-b      (b)   (1)-b, (2)-d      (c)   (1)-c, (2)-b      (d)   (1)-c, (2)-a

38. Study the given figure and select the correct option regarding it.                                              [Tricky]

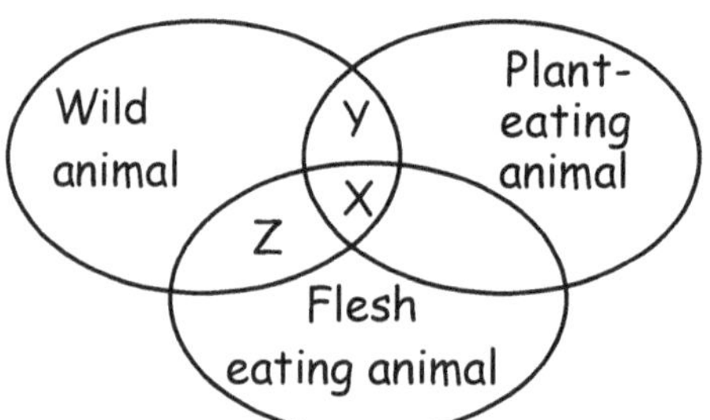


    (a)   X represents bear                    (b)   Y represents zebra
    (c)   Z represents lion                    (d)   All of these

**39.** **In the diagram as shown here, what would giraffe be called?**   **[Critical Thinking]**



(a)   Prey animal
(b)   Endangered animal
(c)   Home animal
(d)   Domestic animal

**Directions (Qs. 40 to 45): Fill in the blanks:**   **[Critical Thinking]**

Domestic animals are those which depend on _________ (40) for their survival. Goat, ox, buffalo and _________ (41) are examples of domestic animals. Cow, goat and buffalo give us _________ (42) which is used to prepare food items like _________ (43) paneer and ghee. Horse is used for _________ (44) and _________ (45) is used for carrying load.

**40.** (a)   air     (b)   water     (c)   humans     (d)   wild animals
**41.** (a)   horse     (b)   lion     (c)   fox     (d)   giraffe
**42.** (a)   butter     (b)   milk     (c)   meat     (d)   pulse
**43.** (a)   curd     (b)   pulse     (c)   mango     (d)   meat
**44.** (a)   measurement     (b)   house keeping     (c)   cultivation     (d)   transportation
**45.** (a)   donkey     (b)   monkey     (c)   wolf     (d)   hyena

**46.** **The given leather items can be made from the skin of which of these animals?**
   **[Tricky]**

(a)   (b)   (c)   (d)   (a) and (c)

**47.** **What are 'X' and 'Y' in the given rhyme?**   **[Tricky]**



|     | X | Y |
|-----|-----|-----|
| (a) | Hen | Horse |
| (b) | Camel | Rabbit |
| (c) | Fish | Kangaroo |
| (d) | Duck | Monkey |

**48.** Match the columns and select the correct option.      [2020]

| Column I | Column II |
|---|---|
| (A) Herbivore | 1. Crow |
| | 2. Giraffe |
| (B) Carnivore | 3. Zebra |
| | 4. Bear |
| (C) Omnivore | 5. Deer |
| | 6. Tiger |

|  | (A) | (B) | (C) |  | (A) | (B) | (C) |
|---|---|---|---|---|---|---|---|
| (a) | 1, 6 | 2. 5 | 3, 4 | (b) | 2, 5 | 3, 4 | 1, 6 |
| (c) | 1, 3 | 2, 4 | 5, 6 | (d) | 2, 3, 5 | 6 | 1, 4 |

**49.** Refer to the given diagram and identify X, Y and Z.      [2021]

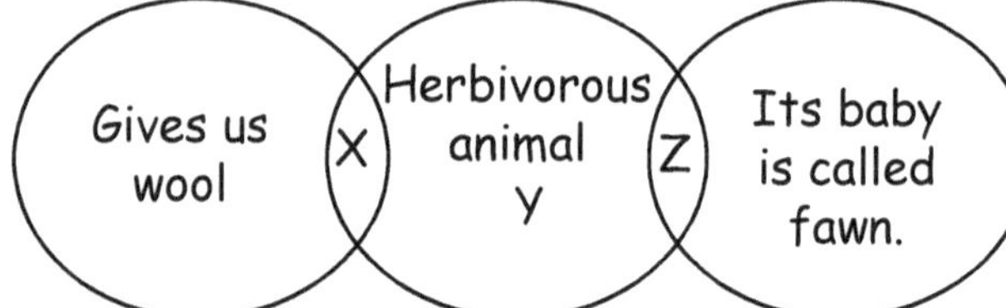


|  | X | Y | Z |
|---|---|---|---|
| (a) | Silkworm | Sheep | Cow |
| (b) | Rabbit | Wolf | Kangaroo |
| (c) | Sheep | Elephant | Deer |
| (d) | Yak | Snake | Monkey |

**50.** Refer to the given classification table and select the option that correctly identifies P and Q.      [2021]

|  | P | Q |
|---|---|---|
| (a) | Sugarcane | Sweet potato |
| (b) | Chilli | Carrot |
| (c) | Garlic | Brinjal |
| (d) | Gourd | F Lady's finger |

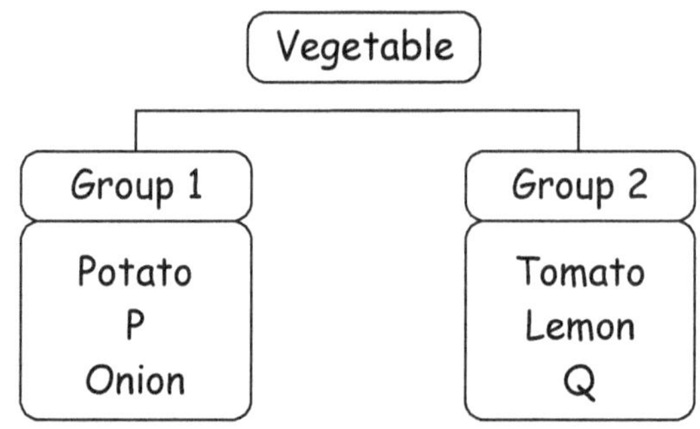


**51.** Refer to the given classification chart and select the correct option about P, Q, R and S.      [2022]

(a) P can be adult frog and R can be hawk.
(b) Q can be bear and S can be kingfisher.
(c) R can be sparrow and S can be vulture.
(d) P can be rhinoceros and Q can be zebra.

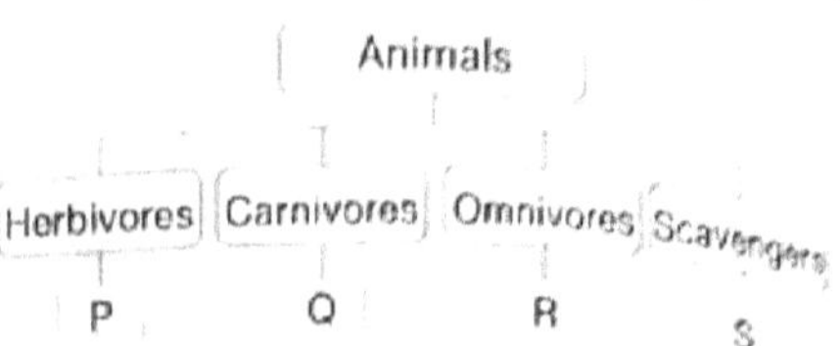

**52.** Which of the following statements is/are correct for\the given animal?

[2022]

(i)   It has four legs and one sticky tongue.
(ii)  It eats small insects and fruits.
(iii) It can live both on land and in water.

(a) Only (i) and (ii)
(b) Only (ii) and (iii)
(c) Only (i) and (iii)
(d) All (i), (ii) and (iii)

**53.** M, N and O are three types of animals. M is an arboreal, N is an aquatic and O is an aerial animal. Choose the correct options from the following for M, N and O.                                    [2022]

(a) M-Squirrel, N-Monkey, O-Peacock
(b) M-Pigeon, N-Lion, O-Duck
(c) M-Elephant, N-Monkey, O-Lion
(d) M-Monkey, N-Dolphin, O-Pigeon

**54.** Which combination of statements is correct about the animal shown below?

[2022]

1.  It is a herbivorous animal.
2.  It kills other animals for its food.
3.  It is the largest land animal.
4.  It does not lay eggs to reproduce.

(a) Only 1 and 2
(b) Only 1 and 4
(c) Only 2 and 3
(d) All 1, 2, 3 and 4

RESPONSE GRID

## LEVEL 1

1. a b c d     2. a b c d     3. a b c d     4. a b c d     5. a b c d
6. a b c d     7. a b c d     8. a b c d     9. a b c d     10. a b c d
11. a b c d    12. a b c d    13. a b c d    14. a b c d    15. a b c d

16. a b c d   17. a b c d   18. a b c d   19. a b c d   20. a b c d
21. a b c d   22. a b c d   23. a b c d   24. a b c d   25. a b c d
26. a b c d   27. a b c d   28. a b c d   29. a b c d   30. a b c d
31. a b c d   32. a b c d   33. a b c d   34. a b c d   35. a b c d
36. a b c d   37. a b c d   38. a b c d   39. a b c d   40. a b c d
41. a b c d   42. a b c d   43. a b c d   44. a b c d   45. a b c d
46. a b c d   47. a b c d   48. a b c d

## LEVEL 2

1. a b c d   2. a b c d   3. a b c d   4. a b c d   5. a b c d
6. a b c d   7. a b c d   8. a b c d   9. a b c d   10. a b c d
11. a b c d   12. a b c d   13. a b c d   14. a b c d   15. a b c d
16. a b c d   17. a b c d   18. a b c d   19. a b c d   20. a b c d
21. a b c d   22. a b c d   23. a b c d   24. a b c d   25. a b c d
26. a b c d   27. a b c d   28. a b c d   29. a b c d   30. a b c d
31. a b c d   32. a b c d   33. a b c d   34. a b c d   35. a b c d
36. a b c d   37. a b c d   38. a b c d   39. a b c d   40. a b c d
41. a b c d   42. a b c d   43. a b c d   44. a b c d   45. a b c d
46. a b c d   47. a b c d   48. a b c d   49. a b c d   50. a b c d
51. a b c d   52. a b c d   53. a b c d   54. a b c d

# Answers with Explanations

## LEVEL 1

1. **(d)** Cow is a domestic animal. Tiger and bear are wild animals and parrot is a bird.

2. **(c)** Domestic animals depend on humans for food and shelter.

3. **(b)** Donkey is used for carrying load.

4. **(c)** A wild animal lives independently in the forest. A wild animal does not depend on human for food and shelter. A wild animal is dangerous for human and living organism.

5. **(d)** Goat is not a wild animal. Tiger, Deer, and Fox are wild animals.

6. **(b)** Tiger is a carnivorous animal.

7. **(a)** Leather is made from skin of the snake.

8. **(c)** Cereals, fruits and grass are all plant products and carnivorous animals eat flesh of other animals.

9. **(b)** Herbivorous animals eat only plants and plant products. Carnivorous eat only flesh of other animals. Omnivorous animals eat plants and other animals.

10. **(a)** Cow lives on land only. Crocodile and frog can live in water also.

11. **(d)** Giraffe, donkey and horse are herbivorous animals. Tiger is a carnivorous animal.

12. **(c)** Pig is a farm animal and is mainly used for obtaining meat.

13. **(d)** Crow can fly. Penguin and ostrich are flightless bird.

**14.** **(c)** Peacock, owl and ostrich are birds. Bat is not a bird.

**15.** **(c)** Wild animals and domestic animals help is maintaining ecological balance.

**16.** **(a)** Meat is obtained from animals.

**17.** **(a)** Sheep and cow (Options b and c) are kept in a farm and are useful to us in many ways. Hence, they are farm animals. Whereas, a langoor (in option a) is a wild animal.

**18.** **(b)** Leopard is both wild as well as carnivorous animal.

**19.** **(d)** Rabbit is a herbivorous animal.

**20.** **(b)** Whale is an aquatic animal and it is a carnivorous animal.

**21.** **(c)** Horse is a domestic animal.

**22.** **(c)** Animal in option 'c' is a spider which is not an insect as it has eight legs. Whereas, butterfly, dragonfly and ladybird are grouped under insects as they have six legs.

**23.** **(c)** Hyena is a wild animal.

**24.** **(a)** Lion is a wild and a carnivorous animal.

**25.** **(a)** Rabbit is a herbivorous animal.

**26.** **(d)** An omnivorous animal eats both plants and flesh of other animals.

**27.** **(d)** Wolf is a wild animal

**28.** **(a)** Goat is both herbivorous and domestic animal.

**29.** **(b)** Pulses refer to the dried seeds and can't be obtained from animals.

**30.** **(a)** Herbivorous animals eat only plants and plants products.

**31.** **(b)** Sparrow is a bird. Only birds live in nest. Snake, lizard and hamster are not birds.

**32.** **(d)** We get milk from cow, goat and buffalo.

**33.** **(a)** Chimpanzee

**34.** **(a)** Kid is the baby of goat. Goat says bleet, bleet. It eats grass and hay and gives us milk.

**35.** **(c)** 'X' is a snake. It lives in hole and wriggles on the ground. It is a source of leather and it lays eggs.

**36.** **(a)** All the things shown are found on animal bodies.

**37.** **(c)** The shown footprints is of a sheep. The footprints of other animals are tiny.

**38.** **(d)** The sound of donkey is bray, the sound of elephant is trumphet.

**39.** **(a)** We get wool from sheep. We make woollen clothes from wool.

**40.** **(d)** Kangaroo

**41.** **(a)** Baby of sheep is called lamb.

**42.** **(b)** 1 and 2 only

**43.** **(b)** Foal is the baby of horse.

**44.** **(a)** Honey bee

**45.** **(d)** Milk can be obtained from goat.

**46.** **(d)** None of these

**47.** **(d)**          **48.** **(b)**

# LEVEL 2

**1.** **(d)** X could be bear because it is both plant and animal eater. Cow eats only plants while tiger and frog eat only animals.

**2.** **(c)** Hen is a bird, cow is a domestic animal, camel lives in desert and butterfly is an insect.

**3.** **(b)** An insect has six legs and a bird has two wings.

**4.** **(b)** Lion, bear, tiger, elephant are wild animals. Ox, cow, and horse are domestic animals.

**5.** **(a)** In the given venn diagram, 'X' represents animal-eater animals, 'Y' represents plant-eater animals and 'Z' represents animals that eat both animals and plants. From the given options, option a is correct, in which X is wolf (animal eater), Y is giraffe (plant eater) and Z is crow (which eats both plants and animals).

6. **(c)** Horse is used for transportation, dog is used for house keeping, sheep is used for wool and goat is used for mutton.

7. **(c)** Both (i) and (ii) represent 'X'. Tortoise and crocodile can live both on land as well water.

8. **(c)** Statement 1 and 2 both are incorrect. Leather is made from the skin of goat, sheep, pig and alligator. Pigs, cows, goats and sheep are domestic animals.

9. **(b)** Hyena (P) eats the flesh of dead animals, is a wild animal and cannot be tamed. Honeybee (R) gives honey and wax, hen (S) is tamed to give us eggs and meat. Donkey (Q) is tamed for carrying loads, it does not give us things.

10. **(b)** Wild animals are dangerous.
11. **(b)** Honey is obtained from honeybee.
12. **(d)** All of these obtain from animals.
13. **(d)** Crow, frog and lizard all eat insects and worms.
14. **(b)** X - Donkey which carries load, Y - Herbivorous (elephant is a herbivorous animal).
15. **(a)** Both Carnivorous and herbivorous animals maintain balance in nature.

16. **(b)**

| M | L | I | O | N |
|---|---|---|---|---|
| O | S | T | X | S |
| H | O | N | E | Y |
| O | P | D | N | U |
| R | A | T | H | A |
| S | I | L | K | V |
| E | M | U | N | T |

Two animals who carry heavy loads are hidden in this word grid are ox and horse.

Two animal products are hidden in this word grid are honey and silk.

17. **(c)** Hen and duck provide us eggs whereas, honey bee provides honey. Cow, buffalo and Goat are milk-giving animals. Camel, snake and crocodiles give us leather to make shoes, bags, suitcase, and sheep, yak and rabbit give us wool to make woollen clothes.

18. **(b)** Seahorse is a marine animal, goat is herbivorous.

19. **(d)** All the statements are true.

20. **(a)** A deer eats plants and deer is eaten by a tiger.

21. **(c)**

M T O R G U E M S P M E X T N

The word obtained from the given group of letters by crossing out every alternate letter starting from first is TRUMPET, which is a sound of an elephant.

22. **(b)** GORILLA does not live in a hole. RABBIT, MONGOOSE and SNAKE live in a hole,

23. **(b)** Cow is not considered as a beast of burden. Buffalo, donkey and camel are working animals, hence called beasts of burden.

24. **(c)** Monkey eats banana, snakes eat rat, cow eats grass, lion eats flesh.

25. **(c)** Both plants and animals form food chain.

26. **(d)** According to the given diagram, a grasshopper can be placed at the place 'X' as it has wings and six legs. Woodpecker is a bird with two legs and has wings for flying. Frog and spider have four

and eight legs respectively, and they do not possess wings. So, these three cannot be placed at the X.

27. **(d)** Cow has been wrongly encircled in the group (d). Lion is the odd one in the group. Cow and buffalo both are plant-eaters (herbivorous) and eat grass and leaves of plants. Lion is a flesh-eater (carnivorous) and eats flesh of other animals.

28. **(c)** Words hidden in the word grid are GROWL, TRUMPET, CROAK. A growl is the sound of a tiger. The sound of an elephant is called a trumpet. The sound of a frog is called croak. Cry of monkey is chatter.

| A | G | Q | Y | J | U | Q |
|---|---|---|---|---|---|---|
| T | R | U | M | P | E | T |
| C | O | T | M | O | R | R |
| E | W | C | R | O | A | K |
| F | L | V | S | T | N | P |

29. **(b)** Cow is a domestic animal and is therefore, not dangerous for human being. Cow do not eat animal flesh and gives milk to produce paneer.

30. **(d)** Horse is a domestic animal.

31. **(c)** Rhinoceros, wolf, deer and lion represent a group of wild animals.

32. **(a)** Camel is known as the 'ship of the desert'.

33. **(b)** Lion lives in forest, whale lives in water, camel lives in desert and crow lives in nest.

34. **(b)** Tell him to give proper food, water and medicines to cow.

35. **(c)** Camel is a ship of the desert, cheetah is the fastest land animal, giraffe is the tallest land animal, elephant is the largest land animal, lion is the king of jungle.

36. **(d)** Ramesh should tell his uncle that deer is a food for lion so, he should not kill deers and also its number will decrease.

37. **(c)** Peacock is a bird that can fly. Louse is an insect that cannot fly.

38. **(d)** Bear is a wild animal, zebra is a herbivorous and lion is a flesh-eating animal.

39. **(a)** Prey animal

40. **(c)** humans

41. **(a)** horse

42. **(b)** milk

43. **(a)** curd

44. **(d)** transportation

45. **(a)** donkey

46. **(d)** The skin of crocodiles and snakes is used to make leather items.

47. **(c)** 'X' is Fish and 'Y' is Kangaroo.

48. **(d)** Giraffe, zebra and deer are herbivore; crow and bear are omnivore; tiger is a carnivore.

49. **(c)** X – Sheep, Y – Elephant, Z – Deer

50. **(c)** P – Garlic, Q – Brinjal

51. **(c)** As sparrows are omnivores and vultures are scavengers.

52. **(c)**

53. **(d)**

54. **(b)**

<table><tr><td>**4**</td><td></td></tr></table>

# CHAPTER FOREWORD

The basic organs of the body are eyes, ears, nose, skin and tongue. Our body is made up of cells which combine together to form tissue. Tissues join together to form organ. A number of organs in our body connect together to do a particular work. This process is known as organ system. Human body consists of different organ system like  digestive system, circulatory system, respiratory system, excretory system, skeletal system, muscular system, nervous system and reproductive system.

**Directions: Find out the relation between the unknown and the known and fill in the blanks with the help of the given analogy in each question. Choose your answer from the clues.**

**Bones, Skin, Skeletal, Muscles, Respiratory, Chest, Oxygen,**

**Heart, Digestive system, Smell**

1.  Food : Digestive system : : Air : _____________________ System.

2.  Nervous system : Brain : : Circulatory system : _____________________.

3.  Lungs : Respiratory system : : Bones : _____________________ system.

4.  Eye : See : : Nose : _____________________.

5.  Head : Brain : : _____________________ : Heart.

6.  _____________________ : Feel pain : : Ears : Listen.

7.  Muscles : Movement : : _____________________ : Support.

8.  Breathe-out : Carbon dioxide : : Breathe-in : _____________________.

9.  Sprain : _____________________ : : Dandruff : scalp.

10. Diarrhoea : _____________________ : : Asthama : Respiratory system.

After reading this chapter, you will be able to know more about our body parts.

# 4 Chapter

# Human Body and their Needs





## LEARNING OBJECTIVES

**This lesson will help you to:**

- ❖ study about human body and its parts.
- ❖ learn different functions performed by human body.
- ❖ understand the importance of organ system in our body.
- ❖ learn the function of every organ system of our body.

## INTRODUCTION

In the previous class, you have learnt about the basic organs of the body that are eyes, ears, nose, skin and tongue. Let us study them in detail.

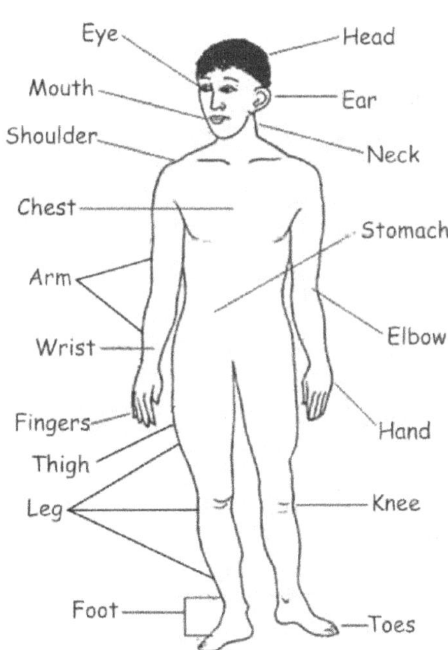


Parts of a Body

## 1. EYES

Eyes are the sense organs of the human body. They are located on the face. Every human being has two eyes.

We see different things around us with the help of our eyes. Without eyes, we cannot see anything.

## 2. EAR

Ears are the sense organs of the human body. They are located one on each side of the head part of the body. Every human being has two ears.

We can hear different types of sounds with the help of ear. Without ear, we cannot hear anything.

## 3. NOSE

Nose is a sense organ. It is also located on the face. Nose helps us to breathe and smell. Every human being has one nose.

## 4. TONGUE

Tongue is the sense organ of the human body. It is present inside the mouth. Every human being has one tongue. Tongue helps us to taste different food items.

## 5. SKIN

Skin is the sense organ of the human body. Skin is present all over the body. It protects us from the external environment and germs. Skin gives us the sense of touch.

## ORGAN SYSTEM

Our body is made up of cells which combine together to form tissue. Tissues join to form organs. Organs do not work alone. A number of organs in our body are connected together to do a particular kind of work. This is known as **organ system**.

1. The **digestive system** helps in breakdown of food from complex to simpler form and being utilized by the body.

2. The **circulatory system** is made up of heart, blood and blood vessels. It carries blood to all parts of the body.

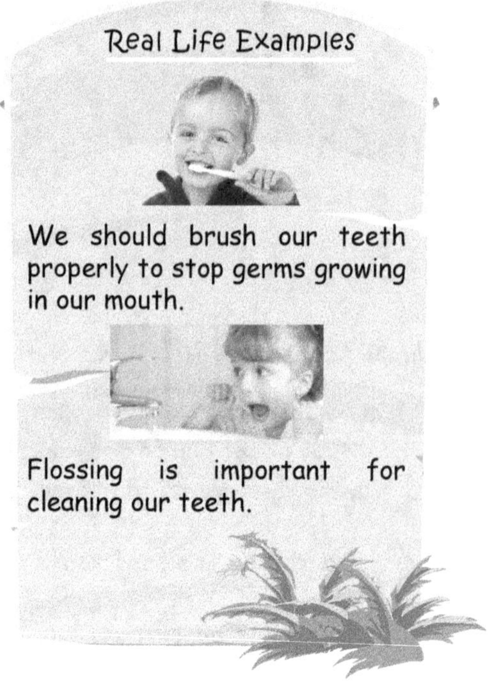



We should brush our teeth properly to stop germs growing in our mouth.

Flossing is important for cleaning our teeth.

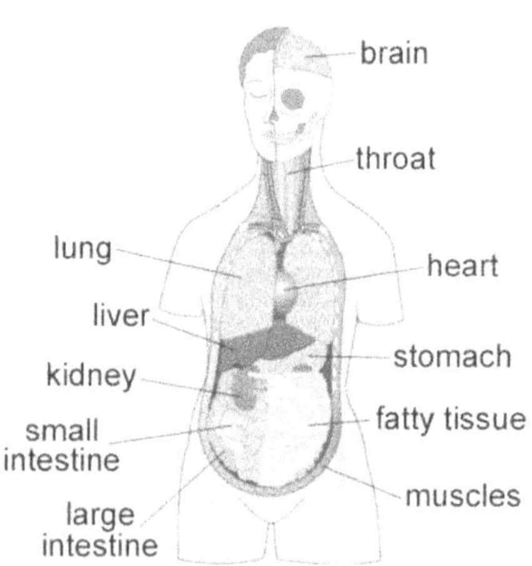

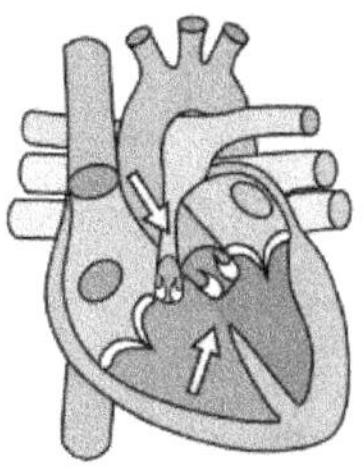

3.  The **respiratory system** helps us in breathing. It includes lungs and windpipe, provides us oxygen that our body needs and removes the harmful carbon dioxide from our body.

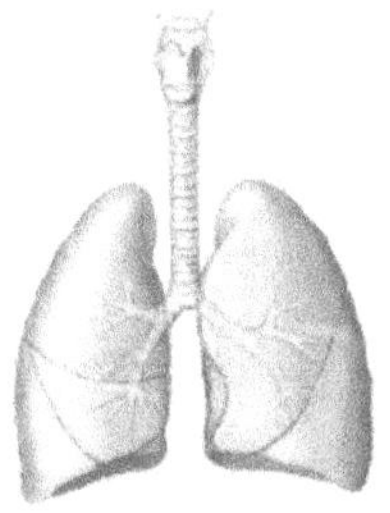

❖  Nervous system consists of special type of cell called nerve cell which is the largest cell in the human body.

❖  There are 100 billion nerve cells in human brain

4.  The **excretory system** consists of kidneys and ureters. It removes the waste products from the body.

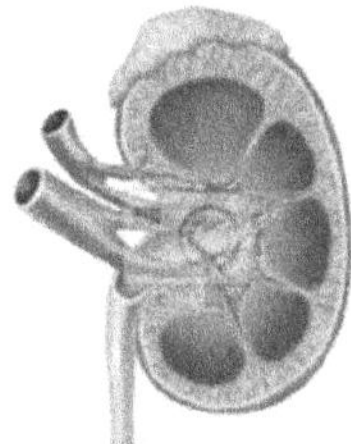

5.  **Skeletal system** is made up of bones. It provides shape and support to the body.

    An adult body has 206 bones while newborn babies have 300 small, soft bones. As the baby grows, the bones join together.

6.  **Muscular system** is made up of muscles. Most of the muscles are fixed with the bones. Bones and muscles work together and help in movement.

7.  The **nervous system** consists of brain and nerves. Brain is the **storehouse of knowledge.** It is protected by skull. It receives messages from the sense organs and other parts of the body and sends order for the action. For instance, when we touch a hot cup of coffee nerves take the message to brain where hotness is sensed and message is sent back to hand and we put our hands off.

8.  The **reproductive system** helps to produce the young ones.

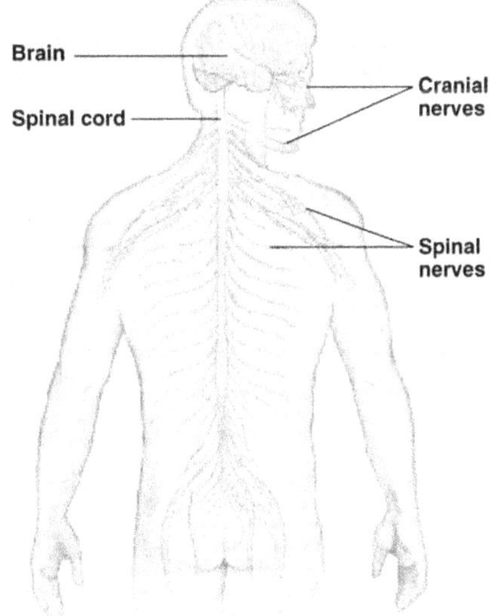

# Multiple Choice Questions

## LEVEL 1

1. Which of the following is not a sense organ?
   (a) Ear     (b) Hair     (c) Nose     (d) Tongue

2. The _______ system helps us to take air from outside.    [2012]
   (a) Respiratory    (b) Circulatory    (c) Digestive    (d) Excretory

3. Which of the following make muscular system?    [Tricky]
   (a) Bones     (b) Arms     (c) Muscles     (d) Hair

4. Which of the following body parts is called 'storehouse of knowledge'.    [Tricky]
   (a) Hands     (b) Eyes     (c) Brain     (d) Nose

5. Priya is blind- folded as shown in the picture. Which senses would help her to recognise things?    [2012]
   (a) Hearing, Taste, Smell
   (b) Hearing, Touch, Sight
   (c) Hearing, Touch, Smell
   (d) Hearing, Taste, Touch and Smell

6. Which of the following organ is located in chest?    [Tricky]
   (a) Lungs     (b) Kidney     (c) Stomach     (d) Brain

7. Which of the following organ is not present in our body in a pair?
   (a) Ears     (b) Tongue     (c) Hands     (d) Kidneys

8. How many bones are present in our body?    [2013]
   (a) 200     (b) 208     (c) 206     (d) 306

9. Unscramble the given words and select the correct option which is associated with 'taste sense'.    [2013]
   (a) SECIIUDOL
   (b) ROTSEPU
   (c) DULO
   (d) GORUH

10. Which of the following is the sense organ?
    (a) Hair     (b) Tail     (c) Nail     (d) Eye

11. Which of the following organ in our body is used to smell?
    (a) Teeth     (b) Nose     (c) Palm     (d) Sole

12. Which of the following is not a part of the human body?
    (a) Nails     (b) Knee     (c) Nose     (d) None of these

13. Select the correct match.    [2013]
    (a) Singing - Sense of sight
    (b) Eating - Sense of hearing
    (c) Painting - Sense of smell
    (d) Rubbing - Sense of touch

14. Our skin gives us the sense of __________.
    (a)   taste          (b)   touch          (c)   smell          (d)   movement
15. Which part of our body can be moved?
    (a)   Knee          (b)   Elbow          (c)   Neck          (d)   All of these
16. Which of the following controls the body function?                    [Tricky]
    (a)   Heart          (b)   Lung          (c)   Brain          (d)   Retina
17. The smallest particle which constitutes to form a human body is called __________?
    (a)   tissue          (b)   cell          (c)   nerve          (d)   organ
18. Our sense of _________ and _________ tell us that soya sauce is dark and salty. [2014]
    (a)   smell, hearing    (b)   smell, taste    (c)   sight, taste    (d)   sight, smell
19. How many holes are there in an ear?
    (a)   One          (b)   Three          (c)   Two          (d)   None
20. The function of the organ system given below is to                    [2015, Tricky]

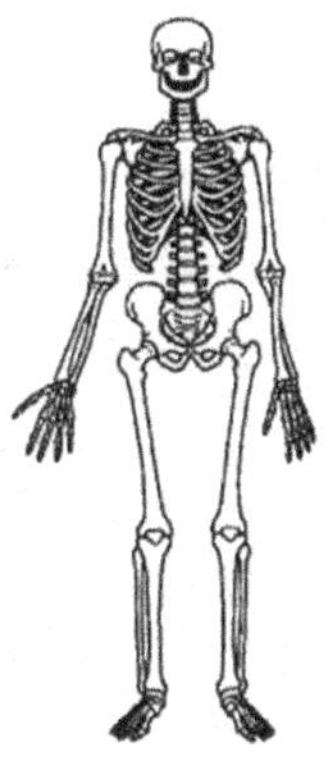

    (a)   enable the organism to make food
    (b)   give support and shape to the body
    (c)   enable the organism to digest food
    (d)   help in the transportation of food within the organism
21. The figure given below shows that substances.                    [Tricky]

The given food substances contain
    (a)   energy giving food          (b)   body building food
    (c)   protective food          (d)   All of these

22. Which of the following organ system gives shape and support to our body?    [Tricky]

    (a)   Muscular system          (b)   Nervous system

    (c)   Skeletal system           (d)   Circulatory system

23. Observe the figure given below and identify X.       [Tricky]

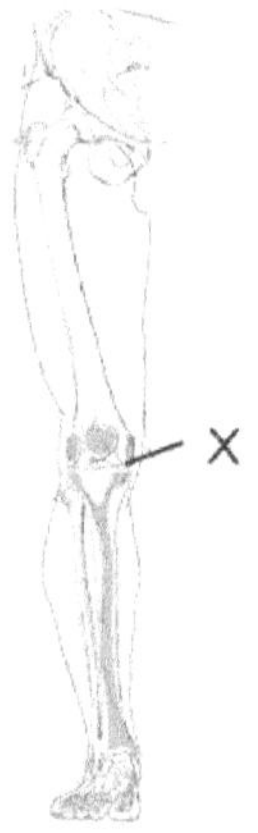


    (a)   Joint        (b)   Muscle        (c)   Blood vessel    (d)   Nerve

24. Which of the food items shown in the given picture are called protective foods?

                                                 [Critical Thinking]

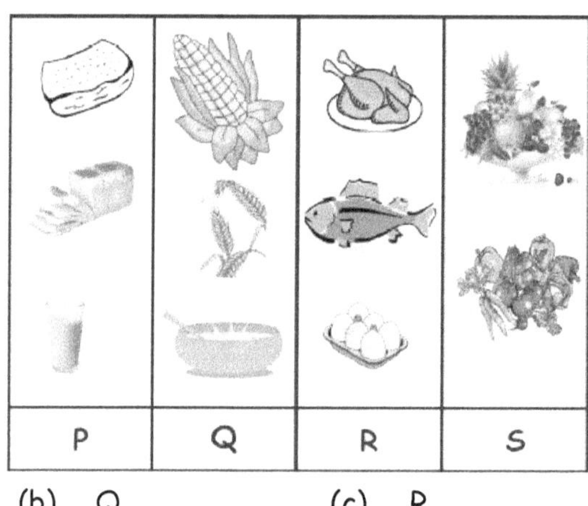


    (a)   P          (b)   Q          (c)   R          (d)   S

25. The diagram below shows a part of the skeletal system.      [2016]

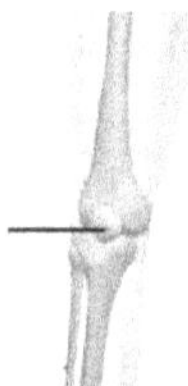

    In which part of the body does this joint present?

    (a)   Ankle        (b)   Wrist        (c)   Knee        (d)   Elbow

26. In the figure given below, **Q** is a chemical substance that can be detected by sensory organs **P** and **R**.  [Critical Thinking]

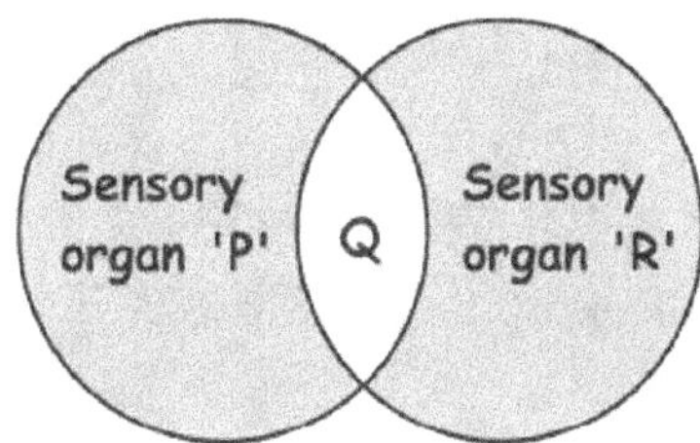


Which of the following most probably represent P and R?

(i)   The nose      (ii)   The ear      (iii)   The tongue

(a)   Only (i) and (ii)      (b)   Only (i) and (iii)

(c)   Only (ii) and (iii)      (d)   (i), (ii) and (iii)

27. Observe the figure given below.

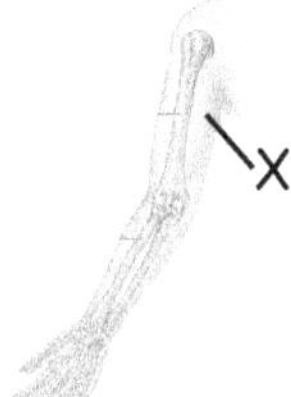


Identify 'X'.

(a)   Blood      (b)   Bone      (c)   Organ      (d)   Muscle

28. Look at the figure below carefully.  [2017, Tricky]

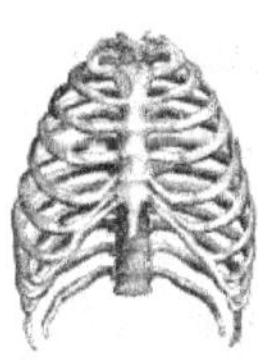

Which organs are protected by these bones?

P – Stomach      Q – Lungs      R – Liver      S - Heart

(a)   P and Q      (b)   P and R      (c)   Q and R      (d)   Q and S

29. Which of the following organ of body is protected by skull?  [Tricky]

(a)   Stomach      (b)   Lungs      (c)   Brain      (d)   Heart

30. If you have taken a shower, which organ of your body part is wet?

(a)   Lungs      (b)   Liver      (c)   Knee      (d)   None

31. Which of the following is the external part of the body?

    (a)  Brain            (b)  Nerves          (c)  Skin            (d)  Bones

32. Which organ is responsible for walking?

    (a)  Fingers          (b)  Legs            (c)  Arms            (d)  Shoulders

33. Select the option that will complete the word in the given statement.

    Our body has a framework of bones called S____E____E____O____ for support.
    [2018]

    (a)  W, D, N, L       (b)  O, P, L, M       (c)  K, L, T, N       (d)  K, L, E, N

34. Which sense is used to tell if there is sugar in a glass of tea ?          [2018]

    (a)  Touch            (b)  Hearing          (c)  Taste           (d)  Smell

35. Which of the following organs is NOT protected by ribcage?          [2018]

    (a)                   (b)                   (c)                   (d)  Both (a) and (b)

36. The ________ controls our body. It receives, analyzes and stores information.
    [2019]

    (a)  Heart            (b)  Brain            (c)  Stomach         (d)  None of these

37. Which of the following vegetables is rich in iron?          [2019]

    (a)                   (b)                   (c)                   (d)

    Peas                 Potato               Spinach              Red Chilli

38. Anuj goes to the gym every day. After coming back from the gym, the eats eggs and fish at home. How do you think they help him?          [2020]

    (a)  They give him energy to do workout.

    (b)  They protect him from diseases.

    (c)  They help him in building muscles and bones.

    (d)  They help him in preventing constipation.

39. Refer to the statement given by Pawan.          [2020]



Pawan

Which of the following sense organs is he using?

    (a)  Eyes            (b)  Nose            (c)  Ears            (d)  Tongue.

40.  is an internal organ of the body. It helps to __________.  [2020]

(a) Think and work
(b) Digest the food
(c) Breathe air
(d) Pump the blood to all parts of the body

41. Which of these children will NOT be able to differentiate between (1) Vinegar and sugar solution and (2) Red pen and blue pen?  [2020]

(a) 1 - Aman, 2 - Nakul      (b) 1 - Puneet, 2 - Sumit
(c) 1 - Puneet, 2 - Aman     (d) 1 - Nakul, 2 - Sumit

42. The words in the given box are associated with which of the following sense organs?  [2021]

Sour, Sweet, Salty, Bitter

(a)       (b) 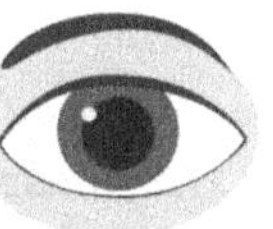      (c) 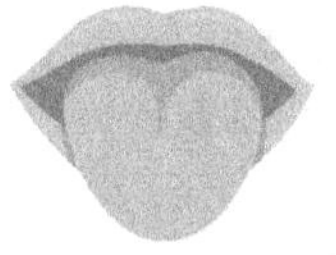      (d) 

43. Which of the following is used in winter season to stay warm?  [2022]

(a)       (b) 

(c)       (d) Both A and B

44. Select the INCORRECT statement(s).  [2022]
(a) There are about 300 muscles in our body.
(b) Facial expressions are controlled by muscle movements.
(c) Heart does not have any muscles.
(d) Both a and c

**45.** Which clothe is worn specifically in winter? [2022]

 (a)    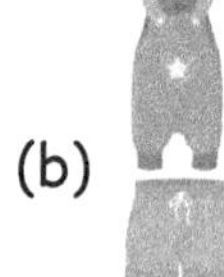 (b)     (c)    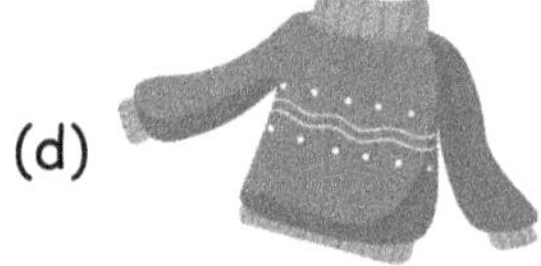 (d)

**46.** Which part of our body helps us to know the taste of the food that we eat?

[2022]

(a) Tongue     (b) Lips     (c) Palm     (d) Teeth

**47.** Identify the organ shown below. [2022]

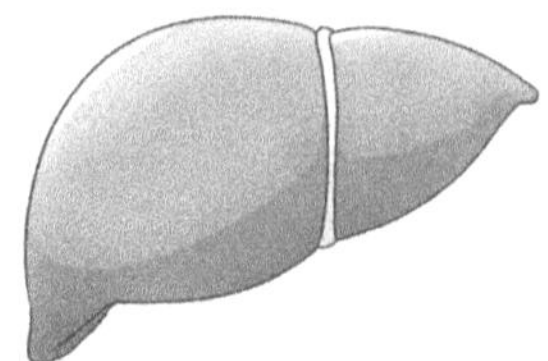

(a) It is a lung.          (b) It is a stomach.
(c) It is a liver.          (d) It is a kidney

## LEVEL 2

**1.** Which of the following is/are true about skin? [Critical Thinking]
   A.    Skin is the internal part of the body.
   B.    It is a sense organ because it gives us the sense of taste.
   C.    Skin covers the whole body.
   D.    Skin can be white, black or wheatish in colour.
   (a)    Both (A) and (B)          (b)    Both (C) and (D)
   (c)    Both (B) and (C)          (d)    All are true

**2.** Match the columns and select the correct option. [2013]

| | Column-I | | Column-II |
|---|---|---|---|
| A. | Brain | 1. | Helps us to breathe |
| B. | Heart | 2. | Helps us to think and remember |
| C. | Lung | 3. | Helps us in the digestion |
| D. | Stomach | 4. | Pumps blood to all parts of the body |

   (a)    A -2, B - 1, C - 4, D - 3        (b)    A -2, B - 4, C - 1, D - 3
   (c)    A -4, B - 2, C - 3, D - 1        (d)    A -3, B - 4, C - 1, D - 2

**3.** Match the column (I) with the column (II). [Critical Thinking]

| | Column I | | Column II |
|---|---|---|---|
| A. | Brain | (1) | Hear |
| B. | Eye | (2) | Hand |
| C. | Ear | (3) | Head |
| D. | Fingers | (4) | Vision |

|     | A | B | C | D |     |     | A | B | C | D |
|-----|---|---|---|---|-----|-----|---|---|---|---|
| (a) | 1 | 2 | 4 | 3 | (b) | 2 | 3 | 3 | 1 |
| (c) | 3 | 4 | 1 | 2 | (d) | 4 | 1 | 2 | 3 |

4. **Read the following statements and choose the correct answer.**  **[Critical Thinking]**
   **Statement 1:** Nerves transfer senses from the various places of the body to brain.
   **Statement 2:** Brain is the main organ of the nervous system.
   (a)    Statement 1 is true and Statement 2 is false.
   (b)    Statement 1 is false and Statement 2 is true.
   (c)    Both Statement 1 and Statement 2 are true.
   (d)    Both Statement 1 and Statement 2 are false.

5. **Read the sentences carefully and find out True/False (T/F)**      **[Critical Thinking]**
   (a)    Your heart pumps blood throughout your body.
   (b)    Brain is the thinking part of the body.
   (c)    The smallest particle which constitutes to form a human body is called 'Tissue'.
   (a)    TTT          (b)    TFT          (c)    FTF          (d)    TTF

6. **The given diagram shows shadow puppets which are supported and controlled by sticks attached to their bodies, legs and feet. They can be moved by adjusting the sticks attached to them.**
   **Which two human body systems work in the same way as the shadow puppet to help in movement?**          **[2014, Tricky]**
   (a)    Nervous system and Circulatory system   (b)    Digestive system and Skeletal system
   (c)    Skeletal system and Muscular system     (d)    Excretory system and Nervous system

7. **Which one of the following activity is performed by the main body part that has knee, ankle and thigh as its sub-parts?**          **[2015]**

   (a)          (b)          (c)          (d)

8. **Identify X and Y**          **[Critical Thinking]**

|  |  |  |
|---|---|---|
|  | 'X' | Organ of respiratory system. |
|  | Intestine | Organ of 'Y' system |

|     |            |                 |
|-----|------------|-----------------|
| (a) | X = Heart  | Y = Circulatory |
| (b) | X = Knee   | Y = Respiratory |
| (c) | X = Lungs  | Y = Digestive   |
| (d) | X = Kidney | Y = Excretory   |

**Directions (Qs. 9 to 11): Read the following passage carefully and answer the following.**

The human body includes head, neck, arms, hands, legs and feet. The human body consists of organ systems like digestive, respiratory and nervous system. Nervous system controls and regulates the activity of all other systems of body. Skeletal system frames the overall shape of the body. **[Critical Thinking]**

9. **The human body consists of which of the following?**

    (a)  Head and neck       (b)  Legs and feet

    (c)  Arms and hands      (d)  All of the above

10. **Which of the following system controls the activity of all other systems of body?**

    (a)  Digestive system      (b)  Nervous system

    (c)  Reproduction system      (d)  Respiratory system

11. **Which system gives the shape to the body?**

    (a)  Cell    (b)  Skeletal    (c)  Tissue    (d)  Nerves

12. **Four different questions were asked to the pupil as shown below. Which pupil will not be able to answer?** **[2014, Critical Thinking]**

(a)


(b)


(c)


(d)


13. **Match the following.** **[2013, Tricky]**

| List I       | List II         |
|--------------|-----------------|
| (A)  Brain   | (1)  Breathe    |
| (B)  Heart   | (2)  Taste      |
| (C)  Tongue  | (3)  Pumps blood|
| (D)  Lungs   | (4)  Think      |

|     | A | B | C | D |     |     | A | B | C | D |
|-----|---|---|---|---|-----|-----|---|---|---|---|
| (a) | 1 | 2 | 4 | 3 |     | (b) | 4 | 3 | 2 | 1 |
| (c) | 3 | 2 | 4 | 1 |     | (d) | 1 | 3 | 2 | 4 |

**Directions (Qs. 14 to 20): Fill in the blanks in the passage given below:**

The skeletal system of human being is made up of _________ (14) bones. Bones are the _________ (15) part of the body. They make _________ (16) of the body. Bones help in _________ (17) of the body. They are of _________ (18) shapes and sizes. Bones are covered with _________ (19) Bones protect various _________ (20) of the body. **[Tricky]**

| | | | | | | | |
|---|---|---|---|---|---|---|---|
| **14.** | (a) 200 | (b) 206 | (c) 250 | (d) 300 |
| **15.** | (a) smallest | (b) internal | (c) external | (d) soft |
| **16.** | (a) length | (b) skin | (c) framework | (d) size |
| **17.** | (a) movement | (b) sleeping | (c) bathing | (d) all of this |
| **18.** | (a) same | (b) equal | (c) different | (d) soft |
| **19.** | (a) germs | (b) organs | (c) cells | (d) muscles |
| **20.** | (a) organs | (b) pain | (c) muscles | (d) Cell |

**21.** **Maya's teacher asked her to fill up the blanks in the sentences which are given in the column I. The words which Maya filled in, are given in the column II.**  [2014, Tricky]

|   Column I | Column II |
|---|---|
| 1.  My_______ help me to breath. | Eyes |
| 2.  My_______ beats like a drum | Stomach |
| 3.  The food I eat goes to my_______. | Stomach |
| 4.  My _______ pumps blood to all parts of my body. | Brain |

However, Maya filled up some blanks with incorrect words. Select the sentences which she incorrectly filled up.

    (a)  1 and 4      (b)  2 and 3      (c)  1, 2 and 4      (d)  1, 2 and 3

**22.** **Identify the organ shown in the following figure.**

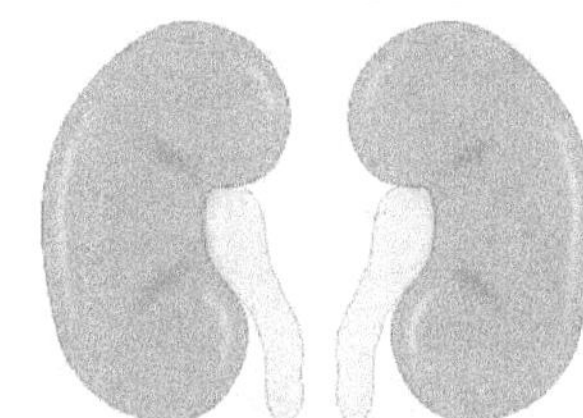

    (a)  Heart      (b)  Stomach      (c)  Brain      (d)  Kidneys

**23.** **Look at the given figure and recognise which organ this figure illustrates?**

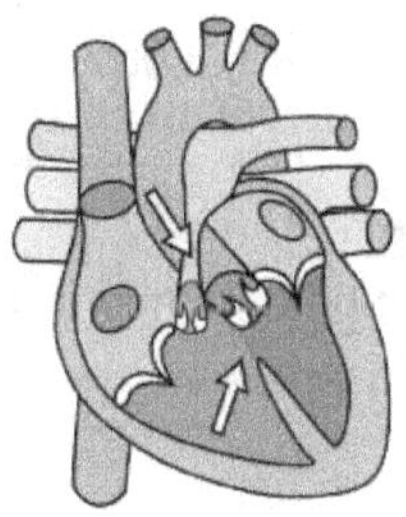

    (a)  Lung      (b)  Liver      (c)  Brain      (d)  Heart

**24.** **Which of the following activity can be done with the help of hands?**

    (a)  Playing cricket  (b)  Watching movie  (c)  Writing poem  (d)  Cooking food

**25.** **Ram is a brilliant student of class II. He comes regularly to the school. But, he feels weak after going back home. Feeling weak is not common in his age group. As a friend what will you suggest to him?**

    (a)  Ram should exercise regularly to build strong bones and muscles.

    (b)  Ram should stop coming to school.

    (c)  Ram should eat healthy food.

    (d)  Both (a) and (c)

**26.** Match the column (I) with the column (II)  [Tricky]

| | Column I | | Column II |
|---|---|---|---|
| (A) | Digestive system | 1. | removes waste material |
| (B) | Respiratory system | 2. | carries blood |
| (C) | Circulatory system | 3. | helps in digesting food |
| (D) | Excretory system | 4. | helps to take air |

|  | A | B | C | D |  |  | A | B | C | D |
|---|---|---|---|---|---|---|---|---|---|---|
| (a) | 1 | 2 | 4 | 3 | | (b) | 2 | 3 | 4 | 3 |
| (c) | 4 | 3 | 1 | 2 | | (d) | 3 | 4 | 2 | 1 |

**27.** Which of the following system helps to produce the young ones?  [2014]
(a) Respiratory system  (b) Nervous system
(c) Digestive system  (d) Reproductive system

**28.** Your heart beats faster, when which of the following activity is performed?
(a) When you are eating  (b) When you are reading
(c) When you are sitting  (d) When you are running

**29.** Which one of the following is true.  [2015, Tricky]
(a) An adult heart beats 70-72 times per minute.
(b) Leg is a part of nervous system.
(c) There are 600 bones in our body.
(d) Nose has one hole only.

**30.** Which of the following organ is present in the head part and is used to hear the sound of ringing bell?
(a) Bones  (b) Fingers  (c) Legs  (d) Ears

**31.** Which of the following are sense organs?  [Tricky]
(a) Cells and tissues  (b) Bones and teeth
(c) Ears and eyes  (d) All of these

**32.** Rahul loves to study till late night. At night, there is very dim light in his room. He gets very less marks in his class tests because he is not able to read properly and he makes many spelling mistakes. His mother is worried about Rahul. As a friend what will you suggest to his mother?
(a) His eye sight is weak so she should take him to eye doctor.
(b) He should not study in dim light.
(c) He should stop studying.
(d) Both (a) and (b)

**33.** Which of the following organ can sense taste?

(a)  tongue  (b) eye

(c) 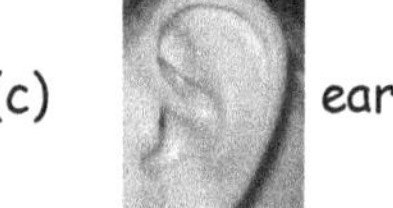 ear  (d) 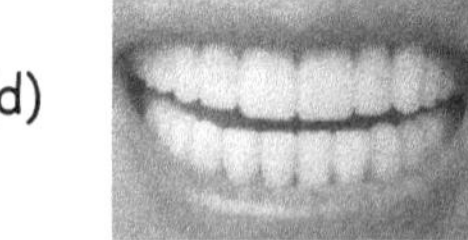 mouth

**34.** Which of following is necessary for human survival?    [Tricky]

    (a)   Air, water and bones
    (b)   Bones, muscles, and blood

    (c)   Food, blood and heart
    (d)   All of these

**35.** Which of the following is INCORRECT regarding body posture?    [Tricky]

    (a)   We should always sit with the back straight

    (b)   We should lie down while reading

    (c)   We should always stand with the back straight

    (d)   We must sit straight when we work on a computer

**36.** During camping, Rohit and his family burnt a campfire at the night time. The campfire was completely burnt in the morning. Rohit's father told others that the campfire is still warm. Which of these sense organs did Rohit's father use? [Tricky]

    (a)       (b)       (c)       (d)

**37.** 'X' is inside the chest. It pumps blood to all parts of the body. What is X?

    (a)   Lung
    (b)   Brain
    (c)   Stomach
    (d)   Heart

**38.** When a baby is born, it has about _______________.    [Tricky]

    (a)   230 bones
    (b)   300 bones
    (c)   150 bones
    (d)   450 bones

**39.** In which of the following activity, bones and muscles are being used the least?    [Tricky]

    (a)       (b)

    (c)       (d)

**40.** Which senses are being used by the girl as shown?    [Tricky]

Oh God! Someone broke the oil jar. But, why is it smelling awful?

|     |                  |     |                 |
|-----|------------------|-----|-----------------|
| (a) | Sight and Touch  | (b) | Sight and Smell |
| (c) | Smell and Hearing| (d) | Smell and Taste |

41. **Unscramble the given names of the bones and select the correct match of the bone with its fuction.** **[Tricky]**

| Word to unscramble | Function | | Word to unscramble | Function |
|---|---|---|---|---|
| (a) LUKLS | Encloses heart | (b) | SIBR | Enclose lungs |
| (c) KEEN | Encloses leg | (d) | NICH | Encloses brain |

42. **Sonu is blind-folded and she is asked to differentiate some pairs of items. Which of the following pairs of items can she differentiate?** **[Tricky]**

(i)   A glass of wine and a glass of plain water.
(ii)  A piece of red and a piece of blue cloth.
(iii) A round ball and a rectangular box.
(iv)  An empty piggy bank and a piggy bank with some coins in it.

|     |                  |     |                       |
|-----|------------------|-----|-----------------------|
| (a) | (i) and (ii)     | (b) | (ii) and (iii)        |
| (c) | (i), (iii) and (iv)| (d) | (i), (ii), (iii) and (iv) |

43. **The body part which helps Binny to lift a bag will also help her to ______________.** **[Tricky]**

| (a) Throw | (b) Jump | (c) Hop | (d) Kick |
|---|---|---|---|

44. **Hearing disability may happen due to which of these?** **[Tricky]**

| (a) | (b) | (c) | (d) All of these |
|---|---|---|---|

45. **For which of these activity, sense of sight is the least important?** **[2016]**

| (a) | (b) | (c) | (d) |
|---|---|---|---|

46. **Match the given eatables with their supposed tastes.**

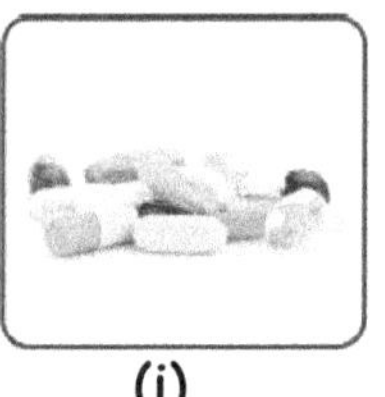 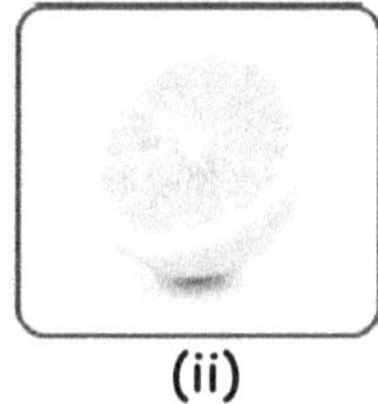  

| (i) | (ii) | (iii) | (iv) |
|---|---|---|---|

   (a)   (i)-Salty, (ii)-Sour, (iii)-Sweet, (iv)-Bitter

   (b)   (i)-Sweet, (ii)-Sweet, (iii)-Salty, (iv)-Bitter

   (c)   (i)-Sour, (ii)-Bitter, (iii) -Salty, (iv)-Sweet

   (d)   (i)-Bitter, (ii)-Sour, (iii)-Sweet, (iv)-Salty

**47. Which of these is an internal organ?**

(a)   (b)   (c)   (d)

**48. Read the given conversation of Ms. Sheena's pupils.**   **[Critical Thinking]**

Sneha : Priya, your hair is so silky!

Pooja : Sneha, I like the fragrance of your perfume.

Harshita : Why you both are making noise?

Tripti : Let them talk, we will watch this video.

Sense used by which pupil will also help her in differentiating hot coffee and cold drink?

(a) Harshita   (b) Sneha   (c) Tripti   (d) Pooja

**49. Which of these is an INCORRECT manner of cleanliness of our body?**

(a) Clean your nails with a pin   (b) Rinse your mouth after every meal

(c) Cover your mouth when you cough   (d) Clean your ears with a cotton bud

**50. What gives support and shape to our body?**   **[Tricky]**

(a) Joints   (b) Skeleton   (c) Muscles   (d) Posture

**51. What is the correct posture for reading?**

(a)   (b)

(c)   (d) All of these

**52. Unscramble the letters given in the options and select the one that gives the name of a body part that is used for identifying red colour.**   **[2021]**

(a) DAHN   (b) OOTF   (c) INFRGE   (d) YESE

**53. Starting from the first letter, strike out every alternate letter in the given box to obtain the name of a body part.**   **[2021]**

**DSNKRUWLTLC**

Now, select the option that correctly shows the organ that it protects.

(a)   (b)   (c)   (d)

**Directions (Q. No. 54 and 55):** Refer to the given word grid and answer the following questions. [2022]

| | | | | | | | | | | |
|---|---|---|---|---|---|---|---|---|---|---|
| A | Z | R | L | L | M | K | K | M | T | S |
| S | O | I | P | U | C | A | D | G | P | P |
| T | A | B | L | E | T | E | N | N | I | S |
| K | I | C | H | O | C | K | E | Y | L | H |
| E | F | A | T | R | I | L | U | D | O | L |
| G | A | G | N | P | F | U | M | E | Q | O |
| C | H | E | S | S | Q | Q | B | J | I | R |

54. Which of the following can you find in the given word grid?
    (a) Internal organ that forms the urine
    (b) Name for the framework of bones
    (c) Bony structure that protects the lungs
    (d) Sense organ that helps us to feel

55. Select the name of a game that CANNOT be found in the given word grid.
    (a) A two player indoor game that is played on a board with 64 black and white squares.
    (b) A multiplayer outdoor game played between two teams with a ball and wooden sticks curved at the striking end.
    (c) A two to four player indoor game played on a table with a ball and small rackets.
    (d) A multiplayer game played with a rope.

RESPONSE GRID

## LEVEL 1

| | | | | |
|---|---|---|---|---|
| 1. a b c d | 2. a b c d | 3. a b c d | 4. a b c d | 5. a b c d |
| 6. a b c d | 7. a b c d | 8. a b c d | 9. a b c d | 10. a b c d |
| 11. a b c d | 12. a b c d | 13. a b c d | 14. a b c d | 15. a b c d |
| 16. a b c d | 17. a b c d | 18. a b c d | 19. a b c d | 20. a b c d |
| 21. a b c d | 22. a b c d | 23. a b c d | 24. a b c d | 25. a b c d |
| 26. a b c d | 27. a b c d | 28. a b c d | 29. a b c d | 30. a b c d |
| 31. a b c d | 32. a b c d | 33. a b c d | 34. a b c d | 35. a b c d |
| 36. a b c d | 37. a b c d | 38. a b c d | 39. a b c d | 40. a b c d |
| 41. a b c d | 42. a b c d | 43. a b c d | 44. a b c d | 45. a b c d |
| 46. a b c d | 47. a b c d | | | |

## LEVEL 2

| | | | | |
|---|---|---|---|---|
| 1. a b c d | 2. a b c d | 3. a b c d | 4. a b c d | 5. a b c d |
| 6. a b c d | 7. a b c d | 8. a b c d | 9. a b c d | 10. a b c d |

11. [a] [b] [c] [d]    12. [a] [b] [c] [d]    13. [a] [b] [c] [d]    14. [a] [b] [c] [d]    15. [a] [b] [c] [d]
16. [a] [b] [c] [d]    17. [a] [b] [c] [d]    18. [a] [b] [c] [d]    19. [a] [b] [c] [d]    20. [a] [b] [c] [d]
21. [a] [b] [c] [d]    22. [a] [b] [c] [d]    23. [a] [b] [c] [d]    24. [a] [b] [c] [d]    25. [a] [b] [c] [d]
26. [a] [b] [c] [d]    27. [a] [b] [c] [d]    28. [a] [b] [c] [d]    29. [a] [b] [c] [d]    30. [a] [b] [c] [d]
31. [a] [b] [c] [d]    32. [a] [b] [c] [d]    33. [a] [b] [c] [d]    34. [a] [b] [c] [d]    35. [a] [b] [c] [d]
36. [a] [b] [c] [d]    37. [a] [b] [c] [d]    38. [a] [b] [c] [d]    39. [a] [b] [c] [d]    40. [a] [b] [c] [d]
41. [a] [b] [c] [d]    42. [a] [b] [c] [d]    43. [a] [b] [c] [d]    44. [a] [b] [c] [d]    45. [a] [b] [c] [d]
46. [a] [b] [c] [d]    47. [a] [b] [c] [d]    48. [a] [b] [c] [d]    49. [a] [b] [c] [d]    50. [a] [b] [c] [d]
51. [a] [b] [c] [d]    52. [a] [b] [c] [d]    53. [a] [b] [c] [d]    54. [a] [b] [c] [d]    55. [a] [b] [c] [d]

# Answers with Explanations

## LEVEL 1

1. **(b)** Hair is not a sense organ.
2. **(a)** The respiratory system helps us to take air from outside.
3. **(c)** Muscles make muscular system.
4. **(c)** Brain is the store house of knowledge.
5. **(d)** Out of five sense organs of Priya, namely eyes, ears, tongue, nose and skin, only eyes are covered and all other organs are free to work. Hence, Priya can hear, touch, taste and smell to recognise things.
6. **(a)** Lungs are present in chest.
7. **(b)** Tongue is not present in pair.
8. **(c)** There are 206 bones in our body.
9. **(a)** The given word is delicious. This word is related to sense of taste. Tongue, 'the taste sensing organ' tells us whether a food is delicious or tasteless. Other words obtained after uscrambling posture (related to sight), loud (related to hearing) and rough (related to touch).
10. **(d)** Eye is a sense organ.
11. **(b)** Nose is used to smell.
12. **(d)** All of these are a part of human body.
13. **(d)** Singing – Sense of hearing
    Eating – Sense of taste
    Painting – Sense of sight
    Rubbing – Sense of touch
14. **(b)** Our skin gives us the sense of touch.
15. **(d)** All these parts can be moved.
16. **(c)** Brain controls all body functions.
17. **(b)** The smallest particle which constitutes to form a human body is called cell.
18. **(c)** Our sense of sight tells us that soya sauce is dark and sense of taste tells us that it is salty.
19. **(a)** In one ear, one hole is present.
20. **(b)** The given figure is that of a skeleton. The skeleton gives support and shape to the body.
21. **(d)** Honey, eggs, milk and sunlight are a good source of vitamins and proteins that help us grow.
22. **(c)** Skeletal system gives shape and support to our body.
23. **(a)** In the given figure, part 'X' is a joint.
24. **(d)** Fruits and vegetables are called protective food.
25. **(c)** The given joint is present at the knee.
26. **(b)** In the given figure 'P' and 'R' represent the nose and the tongue.
27. **(d)** In the given figure part X is muscles.
28. **(d)** Rig cage protects lungs and heart.
29. **(c)** Brain is protected by skull.
30. **(c)** Lungs and liver are inside the body so, they can not get wet.

31. **(c)** Brain, bones and nerves are internal parts of the body. While, Skin is external part of the body

32. **(b)** Legs are responsible for walking.

33. **(c)** The word is skeleton. It provides shape and support to the body.

34. **(c)** The sense of taste is used to tell if sugar is in the tea or not.

35. **(a)** The option (a) is a brain. It is in a head. It is not protected by rib cage as it protects heart and lungs.

36. **(b)** The brain controls our body. It receives, analyzes and stores information.

37. **(c)** Spinach is rich in iron. Leafy vegetables are rich is iron.

38. **(a)** They give him energy to do workout.

39. **(c)** Ears

40. **(d)** Heart pumps the blood to all parts of the body.

41. **(b)** Vinegar and sugar solution are differentiated by using tongue while red pen and blue pen are differentiated by using eyes.

42. **(c)** Tongue

43. **(b)** Heater is used in winter season to stay warm.

44. **(d)** There are about 640 muscles in an adult human body. Also, heart is a muscular organ. So, both A and C options are incorrect.

45. **(d)**    46. **(a)**       47. **(c)**

## LEVEL 2

1. **(b)** Skin Covers the whole body and it can be white, black or wheatish in colour.

2. **(b)** Brain – Helps us to think and remember
Heart – Pumps blood to all parts of the body
Lung – Helps us to breathe
Stomach – Helps us in digestion

3. **(c)** Brain is present in the head of the body, eye is used for vision (to see), ear is used to hear, fingers are present in hand.

4. **(c)** Both statement 1 and statement 2 are true

5. **(d)** Smallest particle of body is called cell.

6. **(c)** Skeletal system and muscular system help in the movement of the various parts of our body.

7. **(c)** Activity in option (c) that is sack race is performed by legs as main body part and also involves knee, ankle and thigh as sub-parts.

8. **(c)** Lungs are respiratory organ and intestine is a digestive organ

9. **(d)** Human body consists of head, neck, arms, legs, hands and feet.

10. **(b)** Nervous system controls the activity of all other systems of body.

11. **(b)** Skeletal system gives shape to the body.

12. **(c)** In option (c) the mouth of the pupil is covered, so she cannot tell about the taste of the coffee. In option (a), the eyes of the pupils are covered, so he cannot see, but can smell the soap with his nose. In option (b), the nose of the pupil is clipped, so he cannot smell, but can hear the ticking of watch with his ears. In option (d), the ears of the pupils are covered with headphones so, he cannot listen to any sound from outside, but can tell the colour of the orchid by seeing with his eyes.

13. **(b)** Brain helps in thinking. Heart pumps blood. Tongue helps in tasting, lungs help in breathing.

14. **(b)** 206

15. **(b)** internal

16. **(c)** framework

17. **(a)** movement

18. **(c)** different

19. **(d)** muscles

20. **(a)** Organs

21. **(c)** Lungs help us to breathe, heart beats like a drum and it also pumps blood to all parts of the body.

22. **(d)** These are kidneys.

23. **(d)** This is a heart.

24. **(b)** We watch movie with the help of eyes.

25. **(d)** Ram should exercise daily and eat healthy food.

26. **(d)** Digestive system helps in digesting food, respiratory system helps to take air, circulatory system carries blood and excretory system removes waste.

27. **(d)** Reproductive system helps to produce young ones.

28. **(d)** Heart beats faster when you are running.

29. **(a)** An adult heart beats 70-72 times per minute.

30. **(d)** Ears are present in the head part and are used to hear sound of ringing bell.

31. **(c)** Ears and eyes are sense organs.

32. **(d)** Get his eyesight checked and also study in bright light.

33. **(a)** Tongue can sense taste.

34. **(d)** All the things are essential for human survival.

35. **(b)** We shouldn't lie down while reading.

36. **(d)** By feeling the heat on his hands.

37. **(d)** Heart

38. **(b)** 300 bones

39. **(b)** Skipping

40. **(b)** Sight and Smell

41. **(b)** Ribs-Lungs

42. **(c)**

43. **(a)** Throw

44. **(d)** All of them

45. **(a)** Playing Tabla

46. **(d)**

47. **(d)** Heart

48. **(b)** Pooja

49. **(a)**

50. **(b)** Skeleton

51. **(a)** Sit straight and study

52. **(d)** Given options are: HAND, FOOT, FINGER and EYES. Eyes are used for identifying red colour.

53. **(c)** SKULL protects the brain.

54. **(c)** RIB CAGE

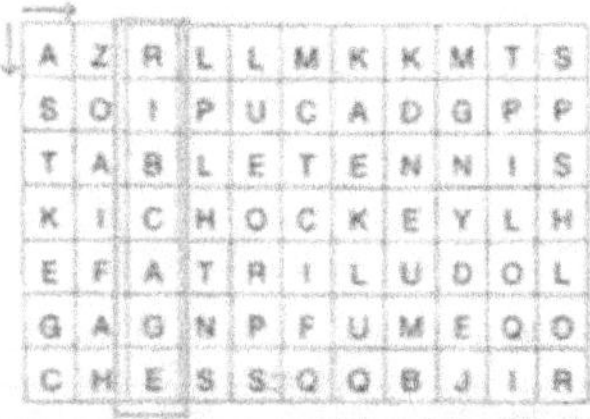

55. **(d)** Multiplayer game played with a rope is tug of war which is not present in the given grid.

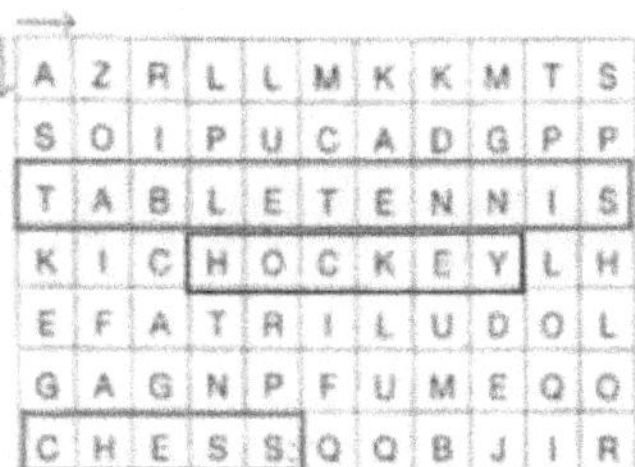

# 5 CHAPTER FOREWORD

India is one of the most beautiful country in the world. In India, there are several mountains, hills, rivers, seas and oceans. Our country is the seventh largest country in the world. There are 29 states in India. Delhi is the capital of India. There are many famous places in India. There are so much of variations in the climate of different places. Every country has national symbols which represent the country.

These are some interesting facts about our country.

(i)   Our National flag         _________________________

(ii)   Our National animal       _________________________

(iii) Our National fruit          _________________________

After reading this chapter, you will know more interesting facts like climate of different places and national monuments.

# 5
## Chapter

# Our Country India

## LEARNING OBJECTIVES

**This lesson will help you to:**

* know about the famous places of India.
* study about the climate of different places of India.
* learn about the national symbols of India.

## INTRODUCTION

India is the most beautiful country in the world. In India, there are mountains, hills, rivers and seas. India is the seventh largest country in the world.

Let us learn more about our country.

## FAMOUS PLACES IN INDIA

There are many famous places in India. There are 29 states in India and **Delhi** is the capital of India. Delhi is very hot in summer and cold in winter. Delhi is one of the four metro cities of India.

Qutub Minar

* Before independence, Kolkata was the capital of India. But, later on Delhi became the capital of India.

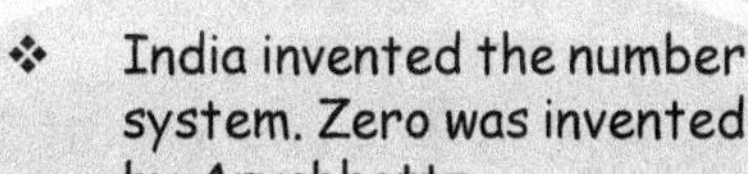


* India invented the number system. Zero was invented by Aryabhatta.
* Chess was invented in India
* India is the world's largest, oldest and continuous civilization.
* India has the largest postal network in the world.

* The Dal Lake floating post office was inaugurated in August 2011.

## DELHI

Tourists from all over the world come every year to visit places like **Qutub Minar, India Gate, Jantar Mantar, Red Fort, International Museums**. There are many places of worship in Delhi such as **Akshardham Temple, Lotus Temple, Birla Mandir** and many more. Delhi has an extreme climate condition. It is very hot in summer (April-July) and cold in winter (December-January). The average temperature of Delhi can vary from 25°C to 45°C during summers.

## OTHER METRO CITIES IN INDIA

### MUMBAI

Mumbai is one of the four metro cities in India. Mumbai is warm and humid in summer. It is not very cold in winter. People who live in Mumbai speak **'Marathi'**.

**Ganesh Chaturthi** is the most popular festival celebrated here.

The most famous tourist spots in Mumbai are **Gateway of India, Marine Drive** and the most popular **Essel World**.

Famous cricketer and filmstars live in Mumbai. Mumbai is also famous for beaches such as **Juhu Chaupati, Marine Drive** and **Versova**.

### KOLKATA

Kolkata is known as the **"city of joy"**. Kolkata is situated along the bank of river 'Hugli'. The main festival of Kolkata is 'Durga Puja'. The climate of Kolkata is neither too hot nor too cold. People of Kolkata speak **'Bengali'**. The famous places of Kolkata are **Victoria Memorial, Birla Planetarium, Rabindra Sarovar** and **Science City**.

Rice and fish is the main food of Kolkata. **'Rasogulla'** is the famous bengali sweet.

**Historical Preview**

❖ The first train in India ran from Mumbai to Thane in **1853**.

❖ The first metro rail in India started in Kolkata.

Akshardham

Gateway of India

Victoria Memorial

## CHENNAI

Chennai is known as the "city of temples". Chennai is warm throughout the year. 'Pongal' is the main festival celebrated here. Chennai is an important tourist centre. The main attraction of the city is the **Marina Beach, War Memorial, Gandhi Mandapam** and **Vivekanand Museum.**

**Bharatnatyam** is a famous dance of Chennai. Chennai has a tropical wet and dry climate. There are extreme variation in seasonal temperature. This means the day temperature is at 34°C and the night temperature is 27°C.

## NATIONAL SYMBOLS OF INDIA

Every country has national symbols which represent the country. Our country also has some symbols. Let us study the symbols of India.

## 1. NATIONAL FLAG

The flag of India is a tricolour flag with deep saffron at the top, white in the middle and green at the bottom. In the centre, navy blue wheel with **twenty four spokes** called **Ashok Chakra** is present.

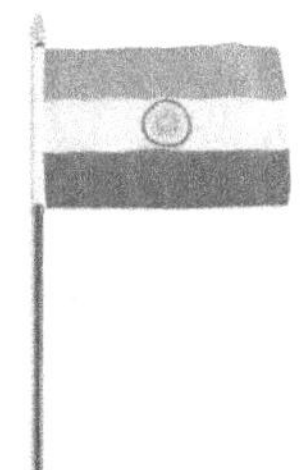

## 2. NATIONAL EMBLEM

It consists of 4 lions standing back to back. At the bottom, it has horse, bull, lion and elephant separated by a wheel.

## 3. NATIONAL ANTHEM

**'Jana Gana Mana'** is the national Anthem of India written by **"Rabindra Nath Tagore"**.

## 4. NATIONAL SONG

**'Vande Mataram'** is the national song of India.

## 5. NATIONAL FLOWER

**'Lotus'** is the national flower of India.

## 6. NATIONAL ANIMAL

**Tiger** is the national animal of India.

## 7. NATIONAL BIRD

**'Peacock'** is the national bird of India.

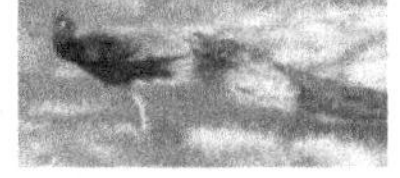

# Multiple Choice Questions

## LEVEL 1

1. Which of the following is the national bird of India? **[2012]**
   (a) Parrot    (b) Peacock    (c) Pigeon    (d) Penguin

2. How many states are there in India? **[2013, Tricky]**
   (a) 29    (b) 26    (c) 24    (d) 32

3. Which of the following is the Capital of India?
   (a) Mumbai    (b) Delhi    (c) Chennai    (d) Bangalore

4. The people of Mumbai speak which of these languages?
   (a) Marathi    (b) Bengali    (c) Tamil    (d) None of these

5. Akshardham Temple is situated in __________
   (a) Chennai    (b) Delhi    (c) Mumbai    (d) Goa

6. Which of the following state is warm throughout the year? **[2015, Tricky]**
   (a) Bangalore    (b) Chennai    (c) Delhi    (d) Mumbai

7. Red fort is situated in __________
   (a) Mumbai    (b) Chennai    (c) Delhi    (d) Tamil Nadu

8. Which of the following city is known as the 'city of temples'. **[Tricky]**
   (a) Delhi    (b) Mumbai    (c) Chennai    (d) Nainital

9. Which of the following festival is celebrated in Chennai?
   (a) Durga Puja      (b) Pongal
   (c) Eid      (d) Ganesh Chaturthi

10. Marine Drive is situated in __________ **[Tricky]**
    (a) Delhi    (b) Mumbai    (c) Kolkata    (d) Goa

11. Gateway of India is situated in __________
    (a) Delhi      (b) Mumbai
    (c) Jammu and Kashmir      (d) None of these

12. Identify the monument. **[2016]**

    (a) Red fort      (b) Akshardham Temple
    (c) Gateway of India      (d) Qutub Minar

13. The most popular festival celebrated in Mumbai is __________. **[Tricky]**
    (a) Durga Puja      (b) Pongal
    (c) Ganesh Chaturthi      (d) None of these

14. The national flower of India is __________.
    (a) Rose    (b) Lotus    (c) Lily    (d) Sunflower

15. Which of the following is the famous food of 'Kolkata'?  [Tricky]
    (a)  Rice and fish          (b)  Rasogulla
    (c)  Kheer                  (d)  Both (a) and (b)
16. How many colours are present in the Indian flag (including the Ashok Chakra)?
    (a)  3          (b)  2          (c)  1          (d)  4          [Tricky]
17. Which of the following is the national animal of India?
    (a)  Lion          (b)  Tiger          (c)  Giraffe          (d)  None of these
18. Which of the following place/s is/are situated in Mumbai?
    (a)  Essel World          (b)  Versova Beach
    (c)  Marina Beach          (d)  Both (a) and (b)
19. Which of the following is/are the national symbol/s of India?
    (a)  National flower          (b)  National flag
    (c)  National emblem          (d)  All of these
20. Which of the following is the main festival of Kolkata?
    (a)  Onam          (b)  Pongal          (c)  Durga Puja          (d)  Bharat natyam
21. Which of the following is the capital of our country?
    (a)  Mumbai          (b)  Kolkata          (c)  Delhi          (d)  Kerala
22. _______________is the national song of India.  [2017]
    (a)  Jana Gana Mana          (b)  Vande Mataram
    (c)  Hum honge Kamyab          (d)  Mera Bharat Mahaan

23. What is the name of the Samadhi of our Rashtrapita?  [2018]

    (a)  Raj Ghat          (b)  Vijay Ghat

    (c)  Shaheed Sthal          (d)  Shakti Sthal

24. Select the INCORRECT match regarding the festivals celebrated in India.

    [2018]

|      | Festival | Celebrated in |
|------|----------|---------------|
| (a)  | Lohri | Winter |
| (b)  | Holi | Autumn |
| (c)  | Eid-ul-Fitr | Summer |
| (d)  | Good Friday | Spring |

25. We sing ............. songs on the Republic Day and Independence Day.  [2019]

    (a)  Sad          (b)  Bad          (c)  Film          (d)  Patriotic

26. Which of the following is called the 'Ship of desert' ?  [2019]

    (a)          (b)          (c)          (d)

## LEVEL 2

**Directions (Qs. 1 to 10): Read the given passage carefully and answer the following question.**

There are many famous places in India. _________ (1) is the capital of India. It is hot in summer and _________ (2) in winters. Tourists from all over the world visit Delhi every year. _______

(3) is situated in Delhi. There are many places of worship in Delhi. For example _________ (4) Mumbai is also the most popular city. People living in Mumbai speak _________ (5) _________ (6) is the most famous tourist spot in Mumbai. The main festival celebrated in Mumbai is (7) Kolkata is also known as the city of _________ (8) People of Kolkata speak _________ (9) language. The famous places in Kolkata are _________ (10) Science city and Birla Planeterium.

**[Critical Thinking]**

1. (a) Mumbai      (b) Kolkata
   (c) Delhi      (d) Chennai
2. (a) humid      (b) cold
   (c) rainy      (d) none of these
3. (a) Red fort      (b) Marine drive
   (c) Birla Planetorium      (d) Versova Beach
4. (a) Essel world      (b) Science city
   (c) Victoria Memorial      (d) Akshardham Temple
5. (a) Tamil      (b) Hindi
   (c) Marathi      (d) Bengali
6. (a) Gateway of India      (b) Lotus Temple
   (c) Marina Beach      (d) Both (a) and (c)
7. (a) Onam      (b) Pongal
   (c) Ganesh Chaturthi      (d) Id
8. (a) colours      (b) temples
   (c) joy      (d) festivals
9. (a) Marathi      (b) Bengali
   (c) Tamil      (d) Hindi
10. (a) Victoria Memorial      (b) India Gate
    (c) Lotus temple      (d) Marina Beach

11. **Match the columns (I) with the column (II).** [2012, Tricky]

| | Column (I) | | Column (II) |
|---|---|---|---|
| (A) | New Delhi | (1) | Marathi |
| (B) | Chennai | (2) | City of joy |
| (C) | Mumbai | (3) | Pongal |
| (D) | Kolkata | (4) | Red Fort |

|  | A | B | C | D |  | A | B | C | D |
|---|---|---|---|---|---|---|---|---|---|
| (a) | 1 | 3 | 4 | 2 | (b) | 4 | 3 | 1 | 2 |
| (c) | 2 | 3 | 4 | 1 | (d) | 3 | 2 | 4 | 1 |

12. **Read the following statements and choose the correct answer.** [Critical Thinking]
    **Statement A:** There are total 23 states in India.
    **Statement B:** Victoria Memorial is situated in Mumbai.
    (a) Statement A is true, Statement B is false.
    (b) Statement B is true, Statement A is false.
    (c) Both the statement are true.
    (d) Both the statement are false.

13. Renuka lives in a city which is hot and humid in summers. Versova beach and Juhu chaupati are situated here. In which city, Renuka is living? **[Critical Thinking]**
    (a) Delhi     (b) Goa     (c) Mumbai     (d) Tamil Nadu

14. This city is located along the bank of the river, Hugli. Identify the city.
    (a) Jammu and Kashmir    (b) Kolkata    **[2014, Tricky]**
    (c) Punjab    (d) Chennai

15. How many lions are present in the national emblem?
    (a) 2     (b) 3     (c) 4     (d) 5

16. Read the following statements and choose True/False (T/F). **[Tricky]**
    A. Mumbai is warm and humid in summer.
    B. People of Mumbai celebrate Pongal.
    C. Gateway of India is situated in Mumbai
    (a) TTF     (b) TFT     (c) TTT     (d) FTF

17. Rashi lives in Delhi, which of the following place/s you will find in this city?
    (a) Jantar Mantar    (b) Akshardham Temple
    (c) Science City    (d) Both (a) and (b)

18. Sachin Tendulkar, Amitabh Bachchan and Shahrukh Khan all live in the same city. In which city, they are living? **[2016]**
    (a) Delhi     (b) Mumbai     (c) Bangalore     (d) Shimla

19. My uncle lives in the city of joy, where rice and fish are the famous food. In which city my uncle lives? **[Tricky]**
    (a) Gujrat     (b) Kolkata     (c) Mumbai     (d) Pune

20. Vivekanand Museum is situated in the city which is also known as the city of temples. Identify the city. **[2015, Tricky]**
    (a) Chennai     (b) Delhi     (c) Mumbai     (d) Pune

21. _____ is located in which of the following city?
    (a) Chennai     (b) Delhi     (c) Mumbai     (d) None of these

**Directions (Qs. 22 to 26):** Read the following passage carefully and answer the following questions. **[Critical Thinking]**

In every summer vacation, we visit our grandmothers house. She lives in the city of joy, Kolkata which is situated along the banks of river 'Hugli'. A bridge known as Rabindra Setu is built over this river. The weather here is very pleasent. People use to travel in Kolkata by bus, train and underground metro. People of Kolkata are fond of rice, fish and Rasogulla. People use to celebrate Durga Puja. They wear colourful clothes and exchange gifts on this occasion.

22. Which festival is celebrated in my grandmother's city?
    (a) Diwali     (b) Dussehra     (c) Durga Puja     (d) Holi

23. Which type of weather is there in Kolkata?
    (a) Very hot    (b) Very cold
    (c) Humid    (d) Neither hot nor cold

**24.** In which city my grandmother lives?

    (a) Delhi      (b) Kolkata      (c) Chennai      (d) Gujarat

**25.** Which river is present in Kolkata?

    (a) Ganga      (b) Yamuna      (c) Hugli      (d) Sutlej

**26.** What is the main sweet of Kolkata?

    (a) Ladoo      (b) Burfi      (c) Rasogulla      (d) Milk cake

**27.** Raju had studied about many places in India in his books. But, he was unaware of the cultures and festivals of these places. As a parent, what would you do to make him aware?

    (a) Tell his teacher to make him aware of these.

    (b) Tell him about the culture of different places by the help of internet.

    (c) Take him to visit different cities to know their culture in summer vacations.

    (d) Tell him to watch television to know more about culture and festivals of different places.

**28.** 'Bharatnatyam' is the famous dance of the city in which marine beach is present. Identify the city.

    (a) Mumbai              (b) Kolkata

    (c) Chennai            (d) Bangalore

**29.** Your summer vacations are going on and you have finished all your holiday homework and now you are getting bored at home. Which of these is the best way to spend your holidays.

    (a) Watch cartoons on T.V.

    (b) Request your parents to visit different historical places

    (c) Read books of the topic of your interest.

    (d) Both (b) and (c).

**30.** Rabindra Sarovar is located in _______________

    (a) Delhi      (b) Mumbai      (c) Kerala      (d) Kolkata

**31.** Which of the following state has extreme weather conditions?

    (a) Kolkata      (b) Goa      (c) Delhi      (d) Chennai

### RESPONSE GRID

### LEVEL 1

| | | | | |
|---|---|---|---|---|
| 1. a b c d | 2. a b c d | 3. a b c d | 4. a b c d | 5. a b c d |
| 6. a b c d | 7. a b c d | 8. a b c d | 9. a b c d | 10. a b c d |
| 11. a b c d | 12. a b c d | 13. a b c d | 14. a b c d | 15. a b c d |
| 16. a b c d | 17. a b c d | 18. a b c d | 19. a b c d | 20. a b c d |
| 21. a b c d | 22. a b c d | 23. a b c d | 24. a b c d | 25. a b c d |
| 26. a b c d | | | | |

## LEVEL 2

1. [a] [b] [c] [d]    2. [a] [b] [c] [d]    3. [a] [b] [c] [d]    4. [a] [b] [c] [d]    5. [a] [b] [c] [d]
6. [a] [b] [c] [d]    7. [a] [b] [c] [d]    8. [a] [b] [c] [d]    9. [a] [b] [c] [d]    10. [a] [b] [c] [d]
11. [a] [b] [c] [d]    12. [a] [b] [c] [d]    13. [a] [b] [c] [d]    14. [a] [b] [c] [d]    15. [a] [b] [c] [d]
16. [a] [b] [c] [d]    17. [a] [b] [c] [d]    18. [a] [b] [c] [d]    19. [a] [b] [c] [d]    20. [a] [b] [c] [d]
21. [a] [b] [c] [d]    22. [a] [b] [c] [d]    23. [a] [b] [c] [d]    24. [a] [b] [c] [d]    25. [a] [b] [c] [d]
26. [a] [b] [c] [d]    27. [a] [b] [c] [d]    28. [a] [b] [c] [d]    29. [a] [b] [c] [d]    30. [a] [b] [c] [d]
31. [a] [b] [c] [d]

# Answers with Explanations

## LEVEL 1

1. **(b)** Peacock is the national bird of India.
2. **(a)** 29 states are there in India including, Telangana. Remark: Presently there are 28 states and 8 UTs in India.
3. **(b)** Delhi is the Capital of India.
4. **(a)** The people of Mumbai speak Marathi.
5. **(b)** Akshardham temple is situated in Delhi.
6. **(b)** Chennai is warm throughout the year.
7. **(c)** Red fort is situated in Delhi.
8. **(c)** Chennai is known as the city of temples.
9. **(b)** Pongal is celebrated in Chennai.
10. **(b)** Marine drive is situated in Mumbai.
11. **(b)** Gateway of India is situated in Mumbai.
12. **(d)** This is Qutub Minar.
13. **(c)** The most popular festival celebrated in Mumbai is **Ganesh Chaturthi**.
14. **(b)** Lotus is the national flower of India.
15. **(d)** Rice, fish and rasogulla are the famous food of Kolkata.
16. **(d)** There are total **4 colours** in the Indian flag (saffron, white and green) and blue in Ashok Chakra.
17. **(b)** Tiger is the national animal of India.
18. **(d)** Essel World and Versova beach both are situated in Mumbai.
19. **(d)** All these are the national symbols of India.
20. **(c)** Durga Puja is the main festival of Kolkata.
21. **(c)** Delhi is the capital of India.
22. **(b)** Vande Mataram is the national song of India.
23. **(a)** Our Rashtrapita Mahatma Gandhi's samadhi is known as Raj Ghat
24. **(b)** Holi is celebrated at the end of winter.
25. **(d)** We sing patriotic songs on the Republic Day and Independence Day.
26. **(c)** A camel is known as ship of desert.

# LEVEL 2

1.  (c)  Delhi
2.  (b)  cold
3.  (a)  Red fort
4.  (d)  Akshardham Temple
5.  (c)  Marathi
6.  (a)  Gateway of India
7.  (c)  Ganesh Chaturthi
8.  (c)  joy
9.  (b)  Bengali
10. (a)  Victoria Memorial
11. (b)  Red Fort is situated in New Delhi, Pongal is celebrated in Tamil Nadu. In Mumbai people speak marathi. Kolkata is known as the city of joy.
12. (d)  Both the statements are false. As there are total 29 states in India and Victoria Memorial is situated in Kolkata.
13. (c)  Renuka is living in Mumbai which is hot and humid in summers.
14. (b)  Kolkata is located along the bank of river 'Hugli'.
15. (c)  There are 4 lions present in the national emblem.
16. (b)  People of Mumbai celebrates 'Ganesh Chaturthi'.
17. (d)  Jantar Mantar and Akshardham Temple both are situated in Delhi.
18. (b)  Sachin Tendulkar, Amitabh Bachchan and Shahrukh Khan all live in Mumbai.
19. (b)  My uncle lives in Kolkata.
20. (a)  Vivekanand Museum is situated in Chennai.
21. (b)  This is the lotus temple situated in Delhi.
22. (c)  Durga Puja
23. (d)  Neither hot nor cold.
24. (b)  Kolkata
25. (c)  Hugli river is present in Kolkata.
26. (c)  'Rasogulla' is the main sweet of Kolkata.
27. (c)  Take him to the places where he can learn about different cultures.
28. (c)  "Bharatnatyam" is the famous dance of Chennai.
29. (d)  Both (b) and (c)
30. (d)  Kolkata
31. (c)  Delhi

# 6 CHAPTER FOREWORD

Don't you love celebrating Diwali with your family? Yes, You do! You must also love going on a trip with your family. It is fun to spend time with your family as every family member shares love and respect for each other.

**Match the nationals festivals with their dates.**

| A | | B | |
|---|---|---|---|
| 1. | Independence Day | 1 | 2nd October |
| 2. | Republic Day | 2 | 15th August |
| 3. | Gandhi Jayanti | 3 | 26th January |

After reading this chapter, you will be able to know different types of festivals in India. You will also learn about different types of activities.

# 6 Chapter

# Fun and Festivals with Family

## LEARNING OBJECTIVES

**This chapter will help you to:**

❖ learn about the different types of activities i.e. indoor and outdoor activities.

❖ know about the different types of festivals celebrated in India.

❖ study the importance of national festivals in India.

## INTRODUCTION

After a long day at school, everyone wants to relax. This helps you to feel rested and happy. We do many activities that make us feel happy and refreshed. Some of the activities are outdoor and some are indoor activities.

## OUTDOOR ACTIVITIES

• The activities done outside our home or in an open space are called outdoor activities. For example: walking, jogging, swimming, bicycle riding, skating, kite flying and playing kho kho.

Outdoor activities meet the needs of physical health, self sufficiency, risk taking as well as team building.

Outdoor activities include water sports, snow sports and horse riding.

- Outdoor activities also include **outdoor games**. Games keep us fit and healthy. Outdoor games include cricket, volley ball and football.

- **Cricket:** Cricket is a bat-ball game between two teams of 11 players each on a field.

- **Volley Ball:** Volley Ball is a team in which two teams of 6 players are separated by a net.

- **Football** refers to a sport that involves kicking a ball with the foot to score a goal.

## INDOOR ACTIVITIES

The activities which are done inside our home are called indoor activities. Being stuck inside doesn't mean that you have to be bored. You can play finger game, memory game, science experiment.

Indoor activities are undertaken on the comfort of one's home. **Hobbies** are a part of indoor activities. Hobbies provide a great way to escape the pressure and the stress of the day. For example: painting, stamp collecting and book reading.

Indoor activities include indoor games such as chess, ludo and snakes and ladders.

**Chess:** It is a 2-player board game played on a chess board with 64 squares.

Kite flying is a very popular game in India. Many people fly kites on 15th August every year to celebrate independence.

**Snakes and Ladder:** Snakes and Ladder is a game played between two or more players on a game board having numbered grid square. A number of snakes and ladders are pictured on the board.

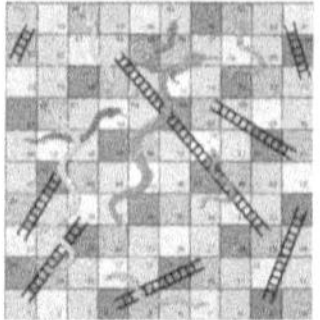

**Ludo** is a board game for 2-4 players in which the players race from start to finish according to their dice rolls.

## FESTIVALS

We have many festivals in India. We have a lot of fun during these festivals. We all get together to celebrate the festivals.

Three types of festivals are celebrated in India

    1.  Religious     2.  Harvesting     3.  National

## 1. *Religious festival*

Some of the main religious festivals that we celebrate are:

(a) **Holi:** Holi is celebrated all over India. On Holi, people put 'gulal' and throw coloured water on each other.

(b) **Diwali:** Diwali is a festival of light. People decorate their house with candles and lights. Children enjoy fireworks and crackers.

(c) **Id:** Id is the festival celebrated by Muslims. They go to mosques to do prayer which is known as 'namaz'. They offer 'Meethi Sewaian' to guests and friends.

(d) **Guruparva:** Guruparva is celebrated by Sikhs. They celebrate Guruparvas on the birthday of their ten Gurus They decorate their houses with lights. They go to gurudwara to pray and langar is served at the gurudwara.

(e) **Dussehra:** Dussehra is celebrated for 10 days. On the tenth day, the effigies of Ravan, his brother (Kumbh karan) and son (Meghnaad) are burnt with crackers.

(f) **Christmas:** Christmas is celebrated on 25th December every year. It is the birthday of Jesus Christ. On this day, Christmas tree is decorated with lights. Santa Claus comes and gives gifts to the children.

## 2. Harvesting festival

Some seasonal festivals are Lohri, Onam, Pongal, Makar Sankranti and Basant Panchmi.

## 3. National festivals

There are a few festivals that are celebrated by all Indians. These are called national festivals of India. India celebrates three national festivals.

1. **Independence Day:** Independence Day is celebrated on 15th of August every year. India got freedom on this day.

2. **Republic Day:** Republic Day is celebrated on 26th January every year. India became a republic on this day.

3. **Gandhi Jayanti:** Gandhi Jayanti is celebrated on 2nd October every year. Mahatma Gandhi was born on this day. He is known as **father of the nation.**

Apart from these festivals, we also celebrate Teacher's Day on 5th September to pay respect to our teachers and Children's Day on 14th November every year.

# Multiple Choice Questions

## LEVEL 1

1. Which of the following is an outdoor game?
   - (a) Ludo
   - (b) Chess
   - (c) Cards
   - (d) None of these

2. For which of the following game/s you need to go out of your house to play? [2012]
   - (a) Carrom
   - (b) Cycling
   - (c) Cricket
   - (d) Both (b) and (c)

3. The item shown in the picture are mainly used in which festival?    [2012]
   - (a) Holi
   - (b) Diwali
   - (c) Lohri
   - (d) Raksha Bandhan

4. Who among the following people celebrate 'Guruparva' ?
   - (a) Muslims
   - (b) Christians
   - (c) Hindu
   - (d) Sikhs

5. On which of the following festival we offer 'Meethi Sewaian' to guests and friends?    [2013]
   - (a) Holi
   - (b) Eid
   - (c) Christians
   - (d) Dussehra

6. Which of these is an indoor game?
   - (a) Kite flying
   - (b) Cycling
   - (c) Chess
   - (d) Football

7. Match the two columns and select the correct option.    [2013]

   | Column-I | | Column-II |
   |---|---|---|
   | A. Holi | (1) | Effigies burnt |
   | B. Eid | (2) | Colours |
   | C. Dussehra | (3) | Meethi sewaian |

   - (a) A - 1, B - 2, C - 3
   - (b) A - 2, B - 1, C - 3
   - (c) A - 1, B - 3, C - 2
   - (d) A - 2, B - 3, C - 1

8. Cycling and skating are _________ activities.
   - (a) Indoor
   - (b) Outdoor
   - (c) Both (a) and (c)
   - (d) None of these

9. On which of the following festival we burn the effigies of Ravana, his brother and son.    [Tricky]
   - (a) Holi
   - (b) Dussehra
   - (c) Eid
   - (d) Guruparav Eid

10. Choose the odd one out.    [Tricky]
   - (a) Jogging
   - (b) Walking
   - (c) Swimming
   - (d) Painting

11. Which among these is a family occasion?    [2013]
   - (a) Lakshmi puja
   - (b) Langar
   - (c) Gandhi Jayanti
   - (d) Christmas

12. What do we call the prayer of Muslim?
   - (a) Namaaz
   - (b) Geeta
   - (c) Mosque
   - (d) Sewaian

13.  Which of the following is celebrated on 26ᵗʰ January every year?        [2014]

(a)   Republic day                      (b)   Gandhi jayanti

(c)   Independence day                  (d)   Christians

14.  Who was born on 2ⁿᵈ october 1869?                                       [Tricky]

(a)   Amitabh Bachchan                  (b)   Sarojini Naidu

(c)   Mahatma Gandhi                    (d)   Sachin Tendulkar

15.  When do we celebrate Teacher's day?

(a)   2ⁿᵈ october    (b)   26ᵗʰ January    (c)   5ᵗʰ September (d)   15ᵗʰ August

16.  On which day, the Prime Minister of India hoists the National Flag at the Red Fort in Delhi?                                                                       [2013]

(a)   Republic Day                      (b)   Children's Day

(c)   Independence Day                  (d)   Gandhi Jayanti

17.  Which of the following is not a national festival?                      [Tricky]

(a)   Independence day                  (b)   Gandhi jayanti

(c)   Republic day                      (d)   Id

18.  Where is the Samadhi of Mahatma Gandhi situated?                        [Tricky]

(a)   Raj Ghat    (b)   Gurudwara    (c)   Mosque    (d)   Temple

19.  Which of the following is not a national holiday?                       [2014]

(a)   15ᵗʰ August                       (b)   26ᵗʰ January

(c)   2ⁿᵈ October                       (d)   14ᵗʰ November

20.  Who comes on Christmas to give gifts to the children?                   [Tricky]

(a)   Mahatma Gandhi                    (b)   Sikh guru

(c)   Santa Claus                       (d)   None of these

21.  How many players are needed in Badminton?                      [2015, Tricky]

(a)   4          (b)   3          (c)   11          (d)   2

22.  Which of these shows a festival which begins with lighting up bonfire on its eve?

[2014]

(a)                    (b)                    (c)                    (d)

23.  In which of the following festival, people decorate their house with lamps, candles, lights and rangoli?

(a)   Holi       (b)   Diwali     (c)   Eid       (d)   Teacher's day

**24.** Which of the following game/s you play in a team? [Tricky]

(a) Cricket      (b) Jogging      (c) Chess      (d) All of these

**25.** Which of the following festival CANNOT be grouped with the other three? [2015]

(a) Republic Day          (b) Independence Day

(c) Children's Day         (d) Gandhi Jayanti

**26.** Which of the following is celebrated as birthday of Jesus Christ?

(a) Diwali      (b) Holi      (c) Dussehra      (d) Christmas

**27.** How many national festivals are celebrated in India? [Tricky]

(a) 2      (b) 3      (c) 4      (d) 5

**28.** The national festivals are celebrated by _______

(a) Muslim      (b) Sikhs      (c) Hindus      (d) All Indians

**29.** Which of the following festival is commonly known as 'festival of kites'? [2015]

(a) Onam           (b) Navratra

(c) Makar Sankranti     (d) Pongal

**30.** How many harvesting festivals are celebrated in India? [2016]

(a) 1      (b) 2      (c) 3      (d) 5

**31.** Refer to the statements given by four children and find out the one who made an INCORRECT statement. [2018]

(a)


(b)


(c)


(d)


**32.** Select the odd one out among the following. [2018]

(a) Ludo      (b) Carrom      (c) Chess      (d) Football

**33.** Which of the following festivals is associated with the given picture? [2018]

(a) Pongal      (b) Eid-ul-Fitr      (c) Christmas      (d) Onam

**34.** Christians go to which of the following places on 25th December ? [2019]

(a) Temple      (b) Gurudwara      (c) Church      (d) Mosque

**35.** What do you call your mother's mother? [2019]
(a) Aunt (b) Great grandmother
(c) Maternal grandmother (d) Grand daughter

**36.** Ali is very happy today. He is wearing new clothes and enjoying meethi seviyan made by his mother. Today is _________. [2020]
(a) Christmas (b) Eid (c) Holi (d) Diwali

**37.** Which of these is a National Festival? [2020]
(a) Holi (b) Christmas (c) Gandhi Janati (d) Diwali

**38.** Refer to the given conversation between Aditya and his mother. [2020]

> Mother : Aditya, where are you?
> Aditya : Mom, I am taking bath.

In which room of the house is Aditya present?
(a) Living room (b) Kitchen (c) Dining room (d) Bathroom

**39.** A copy of Rakesh's exam answer sheet is given here. Identify the mistakes he has made and select the correct option. [2020]
Fill in the blanks.
A. __Never__ lean out of a moving bus or car.
B. __Never__ stand in a line while waiting for the bus.
C. __Never__ learn swimming in the presence of an adult.
D. __Always__ walk on the footpath.
E. __Always__ run while crossing the road.
(a) A and E (b) B, C and E (c) D and E (d) C and D

**40.** Strike out every alternate letter starting from the first one and select the option that gives the name of festival which is also called the 'festival of lights'. [2022]
(a) BWLEMDNDTIRNSGU (b) RBMAPITSLAOKRHTIN
(c) MDRISWPAOLBID (d) MHPOOLRIS.

## LEVEL 2

**1.** You have invited 3 friends at your house to play some game. Which of the following game you four can play together? [Critical Thinking]
(a) Chess (b) Carrom (c) Ludo (d) Both (b) and (c)

**2.** Match the following. [2013, Tricky]

| | List I | | List II |
|---|---|---|---|
| A | Eid | 1. | Hindu |
| B | Diwali | 2. | Sikh |
| C | Guruparav | 3. | Christian |
| D | Christmas | 4. | Muslim |

| | (A) | (B) | (C) | (D) | | (A) | (B) | (C) | (D) |
|---|---|---|---|---|---|---|---|---|---|
| (a) | 1 | 2 | 4 | 1 | (b) | 2 | 3 | 1 | 2 |
| (c) | 3 | 4 | 3 | 4 | (d) | 4 | 1 | 2 | 3 |

3. **Which of the following statement is wrong?** [Tricky]
   (a) Relaxation helps us to feel rested and happy.
   (b) Stamp collection is an outdoor activity.
   (c) Drawing is an indoor activity.
   (d) Swimming is an outdoor activity.

4. **Which of these statements are correct?** [2012]

   1. Watching television for a long time is a good way of recreation.

   2. Practising yoga is a good way of relaxing our mind.

   3. Playing indoor games helps in keeping our body fit.

   4. Going to picnic with family is a good way of spending time with family.

   (a) 1 and 2      (b) 2 and 4

   (c) 2, 3 and 4      (d) 3 and 4

5. **Read the two statements and choose the correct option.** [Critical Thinking]

   **Statement 1:** The main function of Gandhi Jayanti is held at the Raj Ghat.

   **Statement 2:** Guruparva is celebrated on the birthday of 10 Sikh Gurus.

   (a) Statement 1 is true, statement 2 is false.
   (b) Statement 1 is false, statement 2 is true.
   (c) Both the statements are true.
   (d) Both the statements are false.

6. **Which of these is a board game played by 2-4 players?** [Tricky]
   (a) Chess    (b) Ludo    (c) Table tennis    (d) Drawing

7. **Which of the following games is not played with the help of a ball?** [2014]
   (a) Cricket    (b) Volley ball    (c) Basket ball    (d) None of these

8. **________ is a game which involves two teams of 11 players each on a field.** [Tricky]
   (a) Kite-flying    (b) Volley ball    (c) Cricket    (d) Chess

9. **Which of the following statements are INCORRECT regarding the festival of Makar Sankranti?** [2014]

   1. It is commonly known as the festival of kites

   2. It is celebrated in the month of March.

   3. It is a Harvest Festival.

   4. It is celebrated in the honour of Lord Ganesha.

   (a) 1 and 2    (b) 2 and 4    (c) 2 and 3    (d) 1 and 4

10. **Hobby is ________.** [Tricky]
    (a) indoor sports      (b) indoor activity
    (c) outdoor sports      (d) None of these.

11. _________ is a game played between 2 or more players on a gameboard having number gridded square.  **[Tricky]**

    (a) Ludo                            (b) Snakes and ladder

    (c) Chess                         (d) Carrom Board

12. Which of the following is/are outdoor activity/activities?  **[2015]**

    (a) Playing chess              (b) Flying kite

    (c) Bicycle ride               (d) Both (b) and (c)

13. Which of the following is considered a hobby?  **[Tricky]**

    (a) Playing cricket           (b) Horse riding

    (c) Stamp collection         (d) None of these

14. When did India get independence?

    (a) 2 October 1957          (b) 15 August 1957

    (c) 26 January 1957        (d) 15 August 1947

15. Which of the following is considered to be the national game of India?  **[Tricky]**

    (a) Hockey     (b) Cricket     (c) Table tennis     (d) Badminton

16. Which of the following game can be played inside the house?

    (a) Ludo     (b) Carrom     (c) Table Tennis     (d) All of these

17. How many types of festivals are celebrated in India?  **[Tricky]**

    (a) 3     (b) 4     (c) 5     (d) 6

18. Which of the following festival is not a religious festival?  **[2016]**

    (a) Lohri     (b) Holi     (c) Eid     (d) Christmas

19. Which of the following is a national festival?  **[Tricky]**

    (a) Gandhi Jayanti          (b) Durga Puja

    (c) Onam                   (d) Basant Panchami

20. Which of the following festivals is/are celebrated in autumn?  **[Tricky]**

    (a) Diwali     (b) Durga puja     (c) Christmas     (d) Both (a) and (b)

21. Which of the following is/are harvesting festivals?  **[Tricky]**

    (a) Lohri                   (b) Onam

    (c) Basant Panchami       (d) All of these

**22.** Match the items of the list I with items of the list II. [Tricky]

|  | List I |  | List II |
|---|---|---|---|
| (A) | Gulal | 1. | Diwali |
| (B) | Meethi sewaian | 2. | Holi |
| (C) | Langar | 3. | Eid |
| (D) | Fireworks | 4. | Guruparva |

|  | A | B | C | D |  |  | A | B | C | D |
|---|---|---|---|---|---|---|---|---|---|---|
| (a) | 1 | 2 | 1 | 2 |  | (b) | 3 | 4 | 2 | 4 |
| (c) | 4 | 1 | 3 | 3 |  | (d) | 2 | 3 | 4 | 1 |

**23.** Find which one is an incorrect match. [Tricky]

(a) Independence day — Red fort  
(b) Gandhi Jayanti — Raj Ghat  
(c) Namaaz — Mosque  
(d) Republic day — India Gate

**24.** Your younger brother Babloo wanted to play outside, but it was very hot outside. Your mother did not let him go out to play. Babloo started crying. As his elder brother, how will you convince your younger brother?

(a) Let him play outside.  
(b) Ask him to play indoor games like carrom, chess and ludo.  
(c) Ask him to watch his favourite cartoon.  
(d) Both (b) and (c).

**25.** Onam is celebrated in which of the following state? [Tricky]

(a) Madhya Pradesh  
(b) Punjab  
(c) Kerala  
(d) Andhra Pradesh

**26.** Which of the following day is celebrated on the 5th of September?

(a) Republic day  
(b) Children's day  
(c) Independence day  
(d) Teacher's day

**27.** On which of the following days the parade is held at Kartavya Path? [Tricky]

(a) Independence day  
(b) Republic day  
(c) Dussehra  
(d) Teacher's day

**28.** Which of the following festival is celebrated as a birthday of Mahatma Gandhi ?

(a) Christians  
(b) Gandhi Jayanti  
(c) Holi  
(d) Independence Day

**29.** You and Wasim are good friends, but because of a small fight Wasim is not talking to you from last few days. Today is Eid, and you want to finish your fight with Wasim. What will you do?

(a) I will go to his house and say Eid mubarak.  
(b) I will offer him meethi sewaian.  
(c) I will say sorry to him.  
(d) All of these.

**30.** **Read the following sentences and find out true and false (T/F)?** [Tricky]

1. We offer prayer on Mahatma Gandhi's Samadhi on 2$^{nd}$ October.

2. India got independence on 15$^{th}$ January 1947

3. Dussehra is celebrated on birthday of Ravan

(a) TFF      (b) TFT      (c) FFF      (d) TTT

**31.** **Who among the following is known as the father of the nation ?** [Tricky]

(a) Mahatma Gandhi   (b) Sikh guru    (c) Santa claus    (d) Lord Ram

**32.** **Which of the fallowing game is played with a ball?**

(a) Badminton      (b) Chess      (c) Cricket      (d) Carrom

**33.** **We get plenty of fresh air when we play________________** [2017]

(a) Chess      (b) Football      (c) Ludo      (d) None of these

**34.** **Kanika and Shalini are sisters. Amyra is the daughter of Shalini.** [2021]

How are Kanika and Amyra related?

(a) Amyra is Kanika's daughter-in-law.

(b) Kanika is Amyra's aunt.

(c) Kanika is Amyra's sister-in-law.

(d) Amyra is Kanika's sibling.

**35.** **Names of four indoor games are hidden in the given puzzle. Solve the puzzle and select the game whose name is NOT hidden in it.** [2021]

(a)    (b)    (c)    (d)

RESPONSE GRID

21. a b c d  22. a b c d  23. a b c d  24. a b c d  25. a b c d
26. a b c d  27. a b c d  28. a b c d  29. a b c d  30. a b c d
31. a b c d  32. a b c d  33. a b c d  34. a b c d  35. a b c d
36. a b c d  37. a b c d  38. a b c d  39. a b c d  40. a b c d

## LEVEL 2

1. a b c d   2. a b c d   3. a b c d   4. a b c d   5. a b c d
6. a b c d   7. a b c d   8. a b c d   9. a b c d   10. a b c d
11. a b c d  12. a b c d  13. a b c d  14. a b c d  15. a b c d
16. a b c d  17. a b c d  18. a b c d  19. a b c d  20. a b c d
21. a b c d  22. a b c d  23. a b c d  24. a b c d  25. a b c d
26. a b c d  27. a b c d  28. a b c d  29. a b c d  30. a b c d
31. a b c d  32. a b c d  33. a b c d  34. a b c d  35. a b c d

# Answers with Explanations

## LEVEL 1

1. **(d)** All these games are indoor games.

2. **(d)** For cycling and cricket you need to go out of your house to play.

3. **(b)** Icons shown in the picture are crackers. We burst crackers on Diwali.

4. **(d)** Sikhs celebrate 'Guruparva'.

5. **(b)** On Eid, we offer 'Meethi Sewaian' to guests and friends.

6. **(c)** Chess is an indoor game.

7. **(d)** Holi is the festival of colours. On Eid meethi sewaian are made. On the festival of Dussehra huge effigies of Ravana with his brother kumbhkarna and his son Meghnatha are burnt.

8. **(b)** Cycling and skating are outdoor activities.

9. **(b)** On Dussehra, we burn the effigies of Ravana, his brother and son.

10. **(d)** Painting is an indoor activity. Jogging, walking and swimming are outdoor activities.

11. **(a)** Lakshmi puja is a family occasion. It is celebrated with family. Langar, a special community meal is served to all, on Guruprava in Gurudwaras. Gandhi Jayanti the birthday of Mahatma Gandhi, is a national festival. On Christmas we celebrate the birth of Jesus Christ.

12. **(a)** The prayer of Muslim is called Namaaz.

13. **(a)** Republic day is celebrated on 26th January every year.

14. **(c)** Mahatma Gandhi was born on 2nd October 1869.

15. **(c)** Teacher's day is celebrated on 5th September every year.

16. **(c)** On Independence day, Prime Minister of India hoists the National Flag at the Red Fort. On Republic Day, President of India hoists the National Flag at Rajpath. No such ceremonies are done during Gandhi Jayanti and Children's day.

17. **(d)** Eid is not a national festival.

18. **(a)** Samadhi of Mahatma Gandhi is situated at Raj Ghat.

19. **(d)** 15th August is Independence Day, 26th January is Republic Day and

2nd October is Gandhi Jayanti. All of these are national holidays. 14th November is Pandit Jawaharlal Nehru's birthday which is celebrated as Children's Day, but it is not a national Holiday.

**20. (c)** Santa claus comes during Christmas to give gifts to children.

**21. (d)** 2 players are needed for playing badminton.

**22. (a)** Option (a) shows children playing with colours, pichkaris and water balloons. It is a scene of Holi. On the eve of holi, we light a bonfire which is called 'Holika Dahan'.

**23. (b)** During Diwali, people decorate their house with lamps, candles, lights and rangoli.

**24. (a)** Cricket is played between teams.

**25. (c)** Republic day, Independence day and Gandhi Jayanti can be grouped together as these three are our national festivals while Children's Day is celebrated on birthday of Pandit Jawaharlal Nehru and is not designated as national festival.

**26. (d)** Christmas is celebrated as birthday of Jesus Christ.

**27. (b)** 3 national festivals are celebrated in India Independence Day, Republic day, Gandhi Jayanti.

**28. (d)** National festivals are celebrated by all Indians.

**29. (c)** Makar Sankranti is also known as 'festival of kites' because on this occasion most of the people fly kites and kites can be seen all over the sky.

**30. (d)** 5. Onam, Lohri, Pongal, Makar Sankranti and Basant Panchami are the harvesting festivals of India.

**31. (d)** Uncle's son is known as cousin. A nephew is son of one's brother or sister.

**32. (d)** Football is an outdoor game whereas all the other games are indoor games.

**33. (d)** The picture shown is of Onam festival. It is a harvest festival.

**34. (c)** Christians go to Church on 25th December to celebrate Christmas Day.

**35. (c)** Mother's mother is known as maternal grandmother.

**36. (b)** Meethi seviyan is offered to guest and friends on the occasion of Eid.

**37. (c)** Gandhi Jayanti is a national festival.

**38. (d)** Bathroom

**39. (b)** Always stand in a line while waiting for the bus. Always learn swimming in the presence of an adult. Never run while crossing the road.

**40. (c)** DIWALI

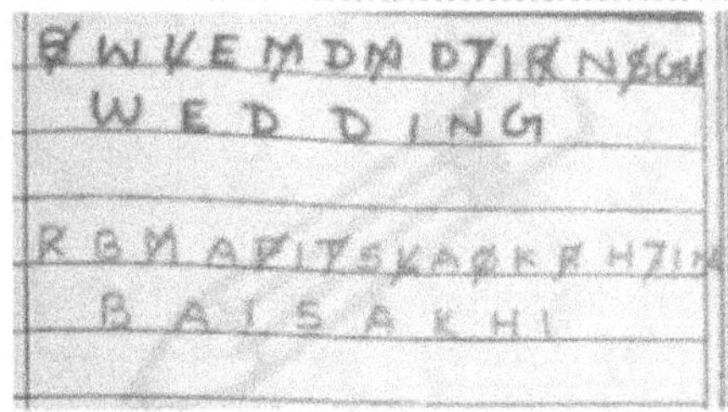

## LEVEL 2

1. **(d)** In chess, there are two players. In carrom and ludo there are 4 players.
2. **(d)** A → 4, B → 1, C → 2, D → 3. Eid is celebrated by Muslims; Diwali is celebrated by Hindus; Guruparva is celebrated by Sikhs; Christmas is celebrated by Christians.
3. **(b)** Stamp collection is an indoor activity.
4. **(b)** Watching TV for a long time is not a way of recreation as it affects our eyes badly. Playing indoor games do not provide us any physical exercise. Outdoor activities keep our body fit.
5. **(c)** Both the statement are true.
6. **(b)** Ludo is a board game played by 2-4 players.
7. **(d)** All these games are played with the help of a ball.
8. **(c)** Cricket is a game which involves two team of 11 players each on a field.
9. **(b)** Makar Sankranti is celebrated in the month of January and it is a harvest festival.
10. **(b)** Hobby is an indoor activity.
11. **(b)** Snakes and ladder is a game played between 2 or more players on a game board having number gridded square.
12. **(d)** Both flying kite and bicycle ride are outdoor activities.
13. **(c)** Stamp collection is considered as a hobby.
14. **(d)** India got independence on 15th August 1947.
15. **(a)** Hockey.
16. **(d)** Ludo, Carrom and Table tennis can be played inside the house.
17. **(a)** Three types of festivals are celebrated in India as national, religious and seasonal.
18. **(a)** Lohri is not a religious festival. It is a Harvest (sasonal) festival.
19. **(a)** Gandhi Jayanti is a national festival.
20. **(d)** Durga Puja and Diwali both are autumn festivals.
21. **(d)** All these are harvesting festivals.
22. **(d)** A → 2, B → 3, C → 4, D → 1.; Gulal is used in Holi; Meethi sewaian is served in Eid; Langar is served in Guruparva.; Fireworks are done in Diwali.
23. **(d)** Republic day function is held at Kartavya Path.
24. **(b)** Play indoor games with Babloo.
25. **(c)** Onam is celebrated in Kerala.
26. **(d)** Teacher's day is celebrated on the 5th of September.
27. **(b)** On Republic Day parade is held at Kartavya Path.
28. **(b)** Gandhi Jayanti is celebrated as birthday of Mahatma Gandhi.
29. **(d)** All of these.
30. **(a)** India got independence on 15th August 1947 and on dussehra festival effigies of raavan gets burnt.
31. **(a)** Mahatma Gandhi is known as the father of the nation.
32. **(c)** Cricket
33. **(b)** Football
34. **(b)** Kanika is Amyra's aunt.
35. **(c)** Games hidden in the given puzzle are LUDO, CARROM, CHESS and MONOPOLY.

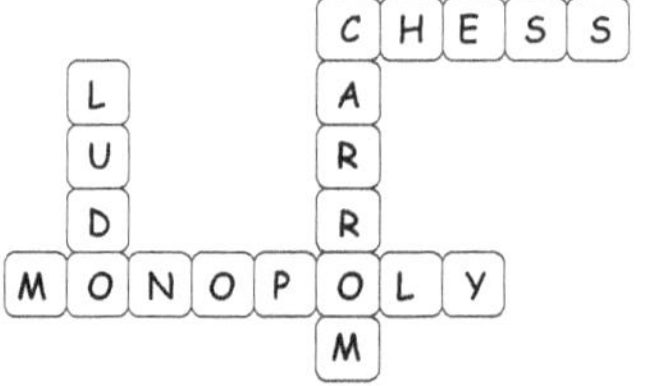

7 # CHAPTER FOREWORD

How do you go to school? How do you travel when you want to go for shopping? You can use bus or rickshaw to reach you school and taxis, cars etc. to travel from one place to another. We use different means of transport to travel. They help us to move from one place to another. Write the names of two land transports?

**Match the transports and communication devices with their names.**

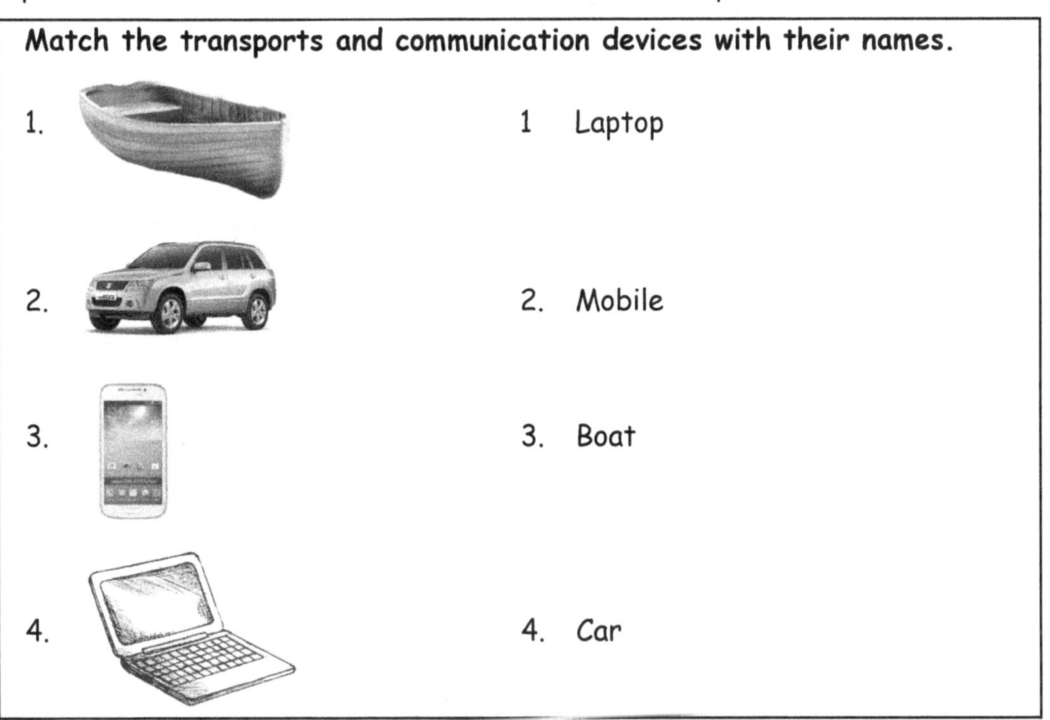

| | | |
|---|---|---|
| 1. | 1 | Laptop |
| 2. | 2. | Mobile |
| 3. | 3. | Boat |
| 4. | 4. | Car |

After reading this chapter, you will be able to know more about means of transport and communication devices.

# 7 Chapter

# Transport and Communication



## LEARNING OBJECTIVES

**This lesson will help you to:**

❖ study about different means of transport.

❖ learn about types of transport : air, land and water.

❖ study about different means of communication.

How do you come to school everyday? By bus or by rickshaw? We all travel from one place to another for different reasons such as children go to school to study and elders go to work.

## INTRODUCTION

People use different means of transport to travel. Some of them are slow and some are fast. Some move on land, some in air and some in water. Let us study these in detail.

## MEANS OF TRANSPORT

Means of transport help us to move from one place to another. There are three means of transport:

## (A) LAND TRANSPORT

Vehicles such as **cycles, rickshaws, scooters, motorcycles, cars, trucks and trains** move on land only. These are known as land transport. Land transport are used to move from one place to another or even from one city to another.

## (B) WATER TRANSPORT

Vehicles such as **boat, ship, steamer, submarine, yatch** can move in water only. These are known as water transport.

## (C) AIR TRANSPORT

Vehicles such as **aeroplane, helicopter and jet plane.** can move in air only. These are known as air transport. Air transport is the fastest means of transport. They cover long distances in a short time. This mode of transport is most expensive.

## MEANS OF COMMUNICATION

There are three main means of communication: postal communication, telecommunication and mass communication.

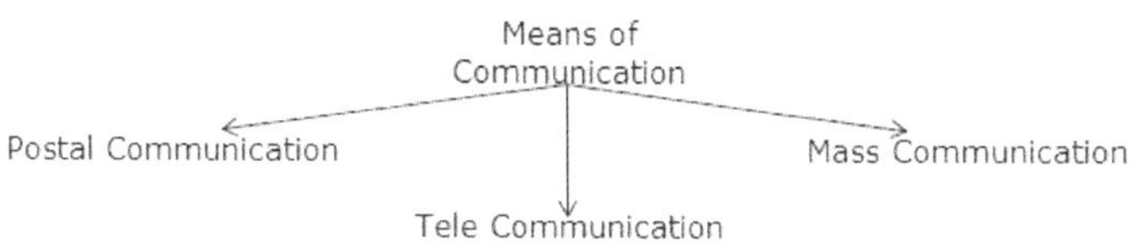


## POSTAL COMMUNICATION

Though letter writing is not very popular these days, but it been very popular means of communication in earlier days. The postal system delivers postcards, letters, and parcels physically. Let's see how our letter reaches its destination. We write letter and mention the address with PIN code (Postal Index Number), then we drop it into nearby letter box. Later, on person from postal department clears the mail box and sorts all the letter destination wise and marks its seal. After this, these letters are sent to their respective places by road, rail, air or water transport. These letters are further sorted out and sealed again at the delivery offices. Postman deputed in each area receives the letters and delivers them to the addressee.

Examples of postal communication are letter, inland letter, post card and printed post card.

### Real Life Examples

- Kolkata and Delhi have a very efficient system of metro trains that are a convenient mode of travel within the city.
- Similar system is being set up in other cities of India as well.

Letter

Inland letter

Postcard

Dr. Martin Cooper invented the first mobile phone on **3rd April 1973.**

# TELECOMMUNICATION

Telecommunication means communicating over a distance. Examples of telecommunications are telegram, mobile phones, landlines, satellite phones, radio and television.

Telegram

**Telegram** – A brief message sent over telegraph and then delivered in written or printed form to the recipient. Telegrams can also be transmitted over the phone. This service developed for urgent letters. Telegram service had been withdrawn in year 2013 in India.

Telephone

**Telephone** - Telephone was invented by Alexander Graham Bell. It is the fastest means of communication. We can make STD (Subscriber Trunk Dialing) call to talk to our family and relatives in far off cities and make ISD (International Subscriber Dialing) call in different countries.

Mobile Phone

**Mobile phone** - With mobile phone we can make call anytime. It can be used to text messages, read emails, browse the internet and do many other things. These phones are small in size and can be carried conveniently, wherever we go.

Computer (Internet)

**Computer and Internet** – Today most of us use internet to send e-mail (electronic mail) to our family and friends and to chat with our dear ones who are living very far in different country.

## MASS COMMUNICATION

Mass communication means the imparting or exchanging of information to large number of people at the same time. Various means of mass communication are newspaper, magazines, radio, television and films.

**Newspaper-** Newspaper informs us about recent happenings around the world.

**Radio and Television –** They educate, inform and entertain us. They attract large number of viewers of all age groups, literate or illiterate.

## Multiple Choice Questions

### LEVEL 1

1. **Which of the following means of transport moves on land only?**
   (a) Boat    (b) Rocket    (c) Autorickshaw    (d) None

2. **Which of the following is not a means of air transport?** [Tricky]
   (a) Helicopter    (b) Boat    (c) Airplane    (d) Rocket

3. **Which of the following is a means of water transport?** [2012]
   (a) Ship    (b) Bus    (c) Hot air balloon    (d) Cycle

4. **The object shown in the picture is a means of __________ communication.** [2015]
   (a) Mass    (b) Visual
   (c) Audio-visual    (d) Verbal

5. **Which of the following is the fastest means of transport?**
   (a) Cycle    (b) Bullock cart    (c) Aeroplane    (d) Bus

6. **Helicopter and rockets fly in the __________ only.** [2013]
   (a) Grass    (b) Water    (c) Air    (d) Land

7. **Which of the following means of transport does not produce smoke?**
   (a) Bus    (b) Cycle    (c) Car    (d) None of these

8. **To which of the given means of communication, is the symbol shown here relates?** [2015]
   (a) Fax    (b) Airmail
   (c) E-mail    (d) Video conferencing

9. **Which of the following is not a means of communication?** [Tricky]
   (a) Post Card    (b) Radio    (c) Computer    (d) Cycle

10. **Which of the following is used to carry sick people to the hospital?** [2014]
    (a) Police Van    (b) Bullock Cart    (c) Ambulance    (d) Cycle

11. **Which of the following is/are the slowest means of communication?** [Tricky]
    (a) Post card    (b) Mobile phone    (c) E-mail    (d) All of these

12. **Which of following things is/are necessary to send an e-mail to your friend?** [Tricky]
    (a) Internet              (b) Television
    (c) Computer             (d) Both (a) and (c)

13. **Choose odd one out.** [Tricky]
    (a) Radio    (b) Newspaper    (c) Television    (d) Aeroplane

14. **The fastest means of two-way communication is ___________.** [2014]
    (a) Telegram    (b) Letter    (c) Telephone    (d) Loudspeaker

15. **Which of the following transport will your mother use to buy vegetables from market?**
    (a) Rickshaw    (b) Train    (c) Aeroplane    (d) Ambulance

16. **Which of the following is/are used by a school student to go to school?**
    (a) Aeroplane    (b) School bus    (c) Boat    (d) All of these

17. **Which of the following means of transport do/does not move on water?**
    (a) Aeroplane              (b) Ship
    (c) Boat                  (d) Both (b) and (c)

18. **Some means of transport carry goods from one place to another. Goods are sent by ________.** [2013]
    (a) Ship    (b) Aeroplane    (c) Trains    (d) All of these

19. **You can make calls by which of the following means of communication?**
    (a) Post card              (b) Speed post
    (c) Telephone             (d) Telegram

20. **Which of the following is not a means of mass communication?** [Tricky]
    (a) Television             (b) Newspaper
    (c) Radio                 (d) Post card

21. **Cheapest mode of communication is _______________.** [2016]
    (a) Mobile Phone    (b) Email    (c) Letter    (d) SMS

22. **Means of communication that can give information to many people at a time is called 'X'. What is an example of 'X'?** [2013]
    (a) Telegram    (b) Radio    (c) Telephone    (d) Fax

23. **Which of the following cannot be used by people to travel from one place to another place?** [Tricky]
    (a) Train    (b) Autorickshaw    (c) Scooter    (d) Police Van

24. **Which of the following you will need to send message through post card?** [Tricky]
    (a) Internet    (b) Newspaper    (c) Stamp    (d) Radio

25. Which of the following is/are the fastest means of sending message to your friend living in America?  [2015, Tricky]

    (a)  Post card  (b)  E-mail  (c)  Telegraph  (d)  All of these

26. Which of following is the means of telecommunication?  [2017]

    (a)  Newspaper  (b)  Letter  (c)  Postcard  (d)  Telephone

27. Select the vehicle that is similar to the mode of transport shown in the given picture X.  [2018]

(a)  (b)  (c)  (d)

28. Study the given flow chart. Identify X, Y and Z and select the correct option.  [2018]

Means of transport — Yes → Moves on water — No → Runs on special track — Yes → Z

Moves on water — Yes → X

Runs on special track — No → Y

    (a)  X could be car whereas Z could be aeroplane
    (b)  Y could be ferry whereas Z could be helicopter.
    (c)  X could be boat whereas Y could be bicycle.
    (d)  Y could be ship whereas Z could be submarine.

29. You see the stars in the sky at night with an instrument called ________  [2019]

    (a)  Microscope  (b)  Stethoscope  (c)  Telescope  (d)  Miniscope

30. Full form of email is ________  [2019]

    (a)  Electronic mail  (b)  Easy mail
    (c)  Electric message  (d)  Easy message

31. Select the vehicle that has the same means of transport as the one shown in the given pciture.  [2020]

(a)  (b)  (c)  (d)

**32. Which of the following is mostly used for personal communication?**

(a) 

(b) [2020]

(c)

(d)

**33. Select the odd one out.** [2021]

(a)  (b)  (c)  (d)

**34. Select the option that shows a mode of transport similar to ship.** [2021]

(a)  (b)  (c)  (d)

**35. Vehicles which have engine run on fuel like _________.** [2022]

(a) Petrol  (b) Diesel  (c) CNG  (d) All of these

**36. Which of the following can be used by Rayesha to go from Delhi to Mumbai?**

(a)

(b) [2022]

(c)

(d)

**37. Select the odd one out on the basis of types of means of communication.**

(a) Landline phone  (b) Letter  [2022]

(c) Post card  (d) Television

LEVEL 2

**1. Which of these waterways is the most suitable for:** [2013]

1. Cross continental import and export.
2. Travelling both on the surface of the water and under water.

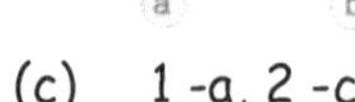
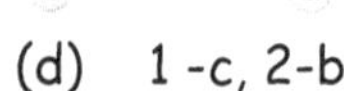

(a)  1 -b, 2 -d  (b)  1 -a, 2 -d  (c)  1 -a, 2 -c  (d)  1 -c, 2 -b

2. **Which of the following statements is wrong?**　　　　　　　　**[2012, Tricky]**

   (a)　Means of travel help us to move people from one place to another.

   (b)　Aeroplane is the fastest means of transportation.

   (c)　Communication means talking or writing to someone.

   (d)　Telephone is the slowest means of communication.

3. **Which of the following means of water transport moves in water?**　　　**[Tricky]**

   (a)　Boat　　　　(b)　Submarine　　　(c)　Steamer　　　(d)　All of these

4. **Match the following.**　　　　　　　　**[2013, Tricky]**

| | Vehicle | | Who use vehicle |
|---|---|---|---|
| (A) | Ambulance | 1 | Police |
| (B) | Police van | 2. | Vegetable seller |
| (C) | Bullock cart | 3. | Fireman |
| (D) | Fire engine | 4. | Hospital |

|  | A | B | C | D | |  | A | B | C | D |
|---|---|---|---|---|---|---|---|---|---|---|
| (a) | 1 | 2 | 3 | 4 | | (b) | 2 | 4 | 1 | 3 |
| (c) | 4 | 1 | 2 | 3 | | (d) | 2 | 3 | 1 | 4 |

5. **Match the column I with the column II and select the correct option.**　　　**[2014]**

   | Column I | Column II |
   |---|---|
   | **(Means of Transport)** | **(Importance)** |

   1.　Rickshaw　　　　　　　　(A)　Fastest means of transport

   2.　Aeroplane　　　　　　　　(B)　Best for the transport of petrol

   3.　Ship　　　　　　　　　　　(C)　Best for door to door service

   (a)　1 -A, 2 - C, 3-B　　　　　　(b)　1 -C, 2 -A, 3 -B

   (c)　1 -C, 2 -B, 3 -A　　　　　　(d)　1 -B, 2 -A, 3 -C

**Directions (Qs. 6 to 8): Read the passage carefully and answer the following questions.**

Amar and his family were going to Mumbai from Delhi by air to attend his cousin's wedding. They reached airport by car. After reaching Mumbai, they took autorickshaw to his cousin's house. After wedding, they came back to Delhi by train.　　　**[Critical Thinking]**

6. **Which of the following means of transport is used by Amar and his family to go to Mumbai from Delhi?**

   (a)　Train　　　　　　　　　　(b)　Car

   (c)　Autorickshaw　　　　　　(d)　Aeroplane

7. **Which of the following means of transport is not used by Amar and his family?**

   (a)　Car　　　　　　　　　　　(b)　Cycle

   (c)　Autorickshaw　　　　　　(d)　Train

8. **What is the total number of vehicles used by Amar and his family in the whole journey?**
   (a)  1          (b)  2          (c)  3          (d)  4

9. **Select the group in which odd one out is wrongly encircled.**       **[2013]**
   (a)  Camel, Elephant, (Rocket), Mule      (b)  Bus, (train), aeroplane, cycle
   (c)  Pilot, (Baker), Driver, Captain      (d)  (Rickshaw), Bus Van, Truck

10. **Which of the following vehicle/s do/does not need petrol to move? [Critical Thinking]**
    (i)  Bullock cart     (ii)  Aeroplane     (iii)  Cycle     (iv)  Car
    (a)  (i) only      (b)  Both (i) and (iii)   (c)  (iii) only      (d)  None

11. **The _______ brings postcards and _______.**       **[2014]**
    (a)  doctor, letter                    (b)  plumber, letter
    (c)  postman, letter                (d)  pilot, car

12. **Your friend Amit is a poor boy. His grandmother lives in a village and is very sick. Amit wants to meet her for the last time. He is sad and does not know what to do. As a friend how will you help him?**
    (a)  Shout at him for being sad.
    (b)  Help him to arrange train tickets to his village.
    (c)  Ask him to come and play with you.
    (d)  Ignore him and play with other friends.

13. **Which of the following statement about communication is not true? [2014, Tricky]**
    (a)  It means talking or writing to someone.
    (b)  It means exchanging ideas.
    (c)  It means moving from one place to another.
    (d)  Telephone is a means of communication.

14. **Why do people travel? Choose from the following reasons.**
    (a)  To meet relatives               (b)  To go for shopping
    (c)  To go to school and work      (d)  All of these

15. **Which of the following help/s us to travel from one city to another city?**
    (a)  Train      (b)  Bus      (c)  Rickshaw      (d)  Both (a) and (b)

16. **Which of the following means of transport follow/s road traffic signal rules?**
    (a)  Aeroplane                (b)  Rocket     **[2015, Tricky]**
    (c)  Boat                    (d)  None of these

17. **Read the sentences and find true/false (T/F).**       **[Critical Thinking]**
    (a)  Radio and television are the means of mass communication
    (b)  Means of communication keep us in touch with our friends and relatives
    (c)  A newspaper is a written way of communication
    (a)  TFT      (b)  TTT      (c)  FFF      (D)  FET

18. **Match the items of list 1 with the items of list 2**       **[Tricky]**

|  | List 1 |  | List 2 |
|---|---|---|---|
| (A) | Radio | 1 | can hear and can see both |
| (B) | Computer | 2. | needs stamp |

| (C) | Television | 3. | can hear only |
|-----|-----------|----|----|
| (D) | Post card | 4. | e-mails |

|     | A | B | C | D |     |     | A | B | C | D |
|-----|---|---|---|---|-----|-----|---|---|---|---|
| (a) | 1 | 4 | 2 | 3 | | (b) | 3 | 4 | 1 | 2 |
| (c) | 2 | 1 | 3 | 4 | | (d) | 4 | 1 | 3 | 2 |

19.  Isha's mother bought 3 kgs of milk daily from a shop near to their house. One day, she found that the milk was not fresh and milkman was adding chemicals in the milk as a result Isha got ill after drinking the milk. She is upset. She wants to share this information to other people also. As a friend, what will you suggest to her mom?

(a)  She can share the news with media.

(b)  She can send post card to each and every person.

(c)  She can call every person.

(d)  All of the above.

20.  If you want to travel with your family from India to America, which of the following transport will be a good choice?

(a)  Aeroplane  (b)  Scooter  (c)  Train  (d)  Both (a) and (c)

**Directions (Qs. 21 to 28): Fill in the blanks in the passage given below:**

Means of transport helps _________ (21) people and goods from one place to another. Vehicles such as cycles, scooters, vans move on _________ (22). Vehicles like boat, steamer are means of _________ (23) transport. _________ (24) transport is the fastest means of transport. In early times, humans did not have vehicles so they used _________ (25) _________ to transport things. Air transport is the _________ (26) _________ means of transport. Aeroplane is the _________ (27) means of transport. It moves in _________ (28).  **[Critical Thinking]**

21.  (a)  move  (b)  stop  (c)  run  (d)  walk

22.  (a)  water  (b)  land  (c)  grass  (d)  air

23.  (a)  land  (b)  air  (c)  water  (d)  none

24.  (a)  Air  (b)  Train  (c)  Water  (d)  Land

25.  (a)  helicopter  (b)  animals  (c)  birds  (d)  air

26.  (a)  costliest  (b)  cheapest  (c)  slowest  (d)  none of these

27.  (a)  longest  (b)  shortest  (c)  slowest  (d)  fastest

28.  (a)  people  (b)  oil  (c)  dust  (d)  air

29.  Govind is a farmer. He wants to carry vegetables to the market. Which of the following means of transport he will use?

(a)  Helicopter  (b)  Car  (c)  Ship  (d)  Bullock cart

30.  Look at the pictures and answer the question.  **[Critical Thinking]**

(a)

(b)

(c)

(d)

Which of the above means of transport can carry more than 20 people at a time.

(a)    (a) and (c) Only

(b)    (c), and (b) Only

(c)    (b), (c) and (d)

(d)    (a), (b) and (c)

31.    Which of the following means of transport has/have no wheels?    [2016, Tricky]

(i)    Aeroplane    (ii)    Boat    (iii)    Ship    (iv)    Cycle

(a)    (i) only

(b)    (ii) and (iii)

(c)    (i), (ii) and (iii)

(d)    (i), (ii), (iii) and (iv)

32.    Which of the following do/does not run on roads?    [Tricky]

(a)    Metro train

(b)    Steamer

(c)    Truck

(d)    Both (a) and (c)

33.    _____________ is a letter sent through internet.

(a)    Post card    (b)    E-mail    (c)    Telegram    (d)    Fox

34.    Which phone is very handy?    [2017, Tricky]

(a)    Telephone    (b)    Mobile    (c)    Cellular    (d)    Pager

## RESPONSE GRID

### LEVEL 1

| | | | | |
|---|---|---|---|---|
| 1. a b c d | 2. a b c d | 3. a b c d | 4. a b c d | 5. a b c d |
| 6. a b c d | 7. a b c d | 8. a b c d | 9. a b c d | 10. a b c d |
| 11. a b c d | 12. a b c d | 13. a b c d | 14. a b c d | 15. a b c d |
| 16. a b c d | 17. a b c d | 18. a b c d | 19. a b c d | 20. a b c d |
| 21. a b c d | 22. a b c d | 23. a b c d | 24. a b c d | 25. a b c d |
| 26. a b c d | 27. a b c d | 28. a b c d | 29. a b c d | 30. a b c d |
| 31. a b c d | 32. a b c d | 33. a b c d | 34. a b c d | 35. a b c d |
| 36. a b c d | 37. a b c d | | | |

### LEVEL 2

| | | | | |
|---|---|---|---|---|
| 1. a b c d | 2. a b c d | 3. a b c d | 4. a b c d | 5. a b c d |
| 6. a b c d | 7. a b c d | 8. a b c d | 9. a b c d | 10. a b c d |
| 11. a b c d | 12. a b c d | 13. a b c d | 14. a b c d | 15. a b c d |
| 16. a b c d | 17. a b c d | 18. a b c d | 19. a b c d | 20. a b c d |
| 21. a b c d | 22. a b c d | 23. a b c d | 24. a b c d | 25. a b c d |
| 26. a b c d | 27. a b c d | 28. a b c d | 29. a b c d | 30. a b c d |
| 31. a b c d | 32. a b c d | 33. a b c d | 34. a b c d | |

# Answers with Explanations

## LEVEL 1

1. **(c)** Autorickshaw moves on land only.

2. **(b)** Boat is not a means of air transport. It moves on water.

3. **(a)** Ship is a means of water transport.

4. **(d)** Telephone is a means of verbal communication by which we can speak to any person we want to, by just dialling a number. We cannot communicate to a large number of people at the same time using a telephone, so it is not a means of mass communication. We cannot see the picture of the person, while using a telephone, so, it is not a visual means of communication.

5. **(c)** Aeroplane is the fastest of all.

6. **(c)** Helicopter and rocket fly in air only.

7. **(b)** Cycle does not produce smoke.

8. **(c)** The symbol @ shown here is related to e-mail. Email is the modern and one of the fastest means of communication.

9. **(d)** Cycle is means of transportation.

10. **(c)** An ambulance carries sick people to the hospital.

11. **(a)** Post card is the slowest means of communication.

12. **(d)** Internet and computer both are necessary to send an e-mail.

13. **(d)** A radio, television and newspaper are means of communication.

14. **(c)** Telephone is the fastest means of two-way communication. Telegram and letter are slow means of two-way communication. Loudspeaker is a means of mass communication.

15. **(a)** Rickshaw

16. **(b)** School bus

17. **(a)** Boat and Ship move on water. However, Aeroplane does not move on water.

18. **(d)** Goods can be transported by means of cargo ships, cargo airplanes and goods trains.

19. **(c)** Telephone is used to make calls.

20. **(d)** Post card is not a means of mass communication.

21. **(c)** Letter is the cheapest means of communication

22. **(b)** Here X is mass communication. Mass communication gives information to many people at a time. Radio is an example of masscommunication. Telegram, telephone and fax are means of personal communication.

23. **(d)** Police van is used by police only not by common people.

24. **(c)** Stamp

25. **(b)** E-mail is the fastest means of sending message.

26. **(d)** Telephone

27. **(d)** The picture shown is of hot balloon that flows in the air. The

Aeroplane is means of transportation.

option (d) that is an aeroplane also flows in the air.

28. **(c)** X could be boat whereas Y could be bicycle. X (boat) moves on water and Y(bicycle) does not move on water.

29. **(c)** We use telescope  to see the stars in the sky at night.

30. **(a)** The full form of e-mail is electronic mail.

31. **(c)**

32. **(c)** Telephone is used for personal communication.

33. **(a)**

34. **(a)**

35. **(d)** All of these

36. **(c)** Train is used to travel from Delhi to Mumbai.

37. **(d)** Television is a means of mass communication.

## LEVEL 2

1. **(b)** Important means bringing goods from a foreign country and export means sending out goods to a foreign country. Continents are separated by large oceans, thus cross continental export and import is possible only via either sea route (large ships ) or airways.

   Submarines (d) can travel both above and under water surface

2. **(d)** Telephone is the fastest means of communication.

3. **(d)** All these means of transport move in water.

4. **(c)** Ambulance is used in hospital; Police van is used by police; Bullock cart is used by vegetable seller; Fire engine is used by fireman.

5. **(b)** Rickshaw - Best for door to door service. Aeroplane – Fastest means of transport. Ship - Best for the transport of petrol.

6. **(d)** Aeroplane

7. **(b)** Cycle is not used by Amar's family.

8. **(d)** 4 (car, aeroplane, autorickshaw, train).

9. **(b)** Aeroplane is an air transport. Whereas, bus, train and cycle are land transport.

10. **(b)** Both bullock cart and cycle do not need petrol to move.

11. **(c)** The postman brings postcards and letters.

12. **(b)** Help him arrange train tickets to his village.

13. **(c)** Means of transport helps in moving from one place to another.

14. **(d)** People travel to meet relatives for shopping or to go to school and work.

15. **(d)** Both train and bus help us to travel from one city to another.

16. **(d)** None of these follow road traffic signal rules.

17. **(b)** All the statements are true.

18. **(b)** We can only hear through radio; we can send e-mails through computer; we can hear and see both on television; There has to be stamps on post card.

19. **(a)** Media is a means of mass communication.

20. **(a)** Aeroplane

21. **(a)** move

22. **(b)** land

23. **(c)** water

24. **(a)** Air

25. **(b)** Animals

26. **(a)** costliest

27. **(d)** fastest

28. **(d)** air

29. **(d)** Bullock cart is used by farmers for transportation.

30. **(c)** Aeroplane, bus and ship can carry more than 20 people at a time.

31. **(b)** Boats and ships do not have wheels. Aeroplane and cycles do have wheels.

32. **(d)** Both metro train and steamers do not run on roads.

33. **(b)** E-mail

34. **(b)** Mobile

Do you wash your hands before eating your dinner? You should wash your hands everytime before having meal because it is a good habit and it also keeps us healthy. Each one of us have either good or bad habits. But, we should learn good habits to become a good and healthy person. Why your mother always stops you when you play with electrical objects? It is because you may get an electric shock. Why your teacher tells you not to run up and down on the stairs because you can get injured by doing these things. So, we should keep ourselves away from the things which can harm us.

**Write a few good habits that you follow in the given space?**

______________________________  ______________________________

______________________________  ______________________________

After reading this chapter, you will learn about good habits, safety rules and first aid which will help you in your daily life.

# 8
## Chapter

# Good Habits, Safety and First Aid



**This lesson will help you to:**

* learn about good habits.
* understand how accidents happen.
* study how accidents can be avoided.
* know about first aid and how to give medical help to the injured person.

## INTRODUCTION

Each one of us has some habits either good or bad. We should learn good habits. We go to school everyday to learn. Our teacher teaches us good habits. Let us study these habits.

## GOOD HABITS

1. Take bath every-day in the morning.

2. Brush your teeth twice a day. After getting up in the morning and before going to the bed at night.

3. Exercise daily as it will keep your bones and muscles strong.

4. Wash your hands before and after eating food.

5. Comb your hair daily.

6. Do not bite your nails, use nail cutter to cut your nails.

7. Always cover your mouth and nose while sneezing and coughing.

**Did you know ?**

* Injured people are carried to the hospitals in an ambulance. Ambulance has all the necessary equipments that a patient might need.

**Do you know ?**

* We should not operate any electrical switches when there is a gas leaking because the electrical switches generate sparks while being switched on and off.

8. Wash your hands after going to toilet.

We heard many news of accidents everyday. Accidents cause harm to life and property. Accidents can be avoided if we follow safety rules at home, at school, in the play-ground and on the road.

## SAFETY AT HOME

Make your home a safe place. A person can slip and fall on a wet floor. To avoid such accidents:

- keep the floor of your home clean and dry.
- bathroom and kitchen floor should not be slippery.
- do not play with sharp things like scissors, blades and knife.
- do not leave your toys and sharp items on the floor.
- turn off the gas stove when you are not using the gas.
- do not touch the electrical fittings with wet hands, you may get an electric shock.
- do not touch table fans and electric heaters.
- while giving medicine to any person, always check the date of expiry.

## SAFETY AT SCHOOL

In school, accidents can happen when children rush and push each other. To avoid accidents in school:

- do not run up and down on the stairs, you may fall and hurt yourself.
- always go in the school bus in line. Never put your hand or neck outside the window of the bus.
- do not climb on desks and chairs, you may fall and hurt yourself.
- do not throw anything on anyone in class.

## SAFETY ON ROAD

Safety on roads is important for your own safety and the safety of others. Carelessness on the road can cause accidents.

- To avoid accidents we should walk on the footpath.
- Cross the road using zebra crossing.
- Do not run or play on the road.
- Always follow traffic rules while walking on the road.

### Misconcept/Concept

- ❖ **Misconcept**: If you have a nose bleed, you should tilt your head back.

  **Concept**: Instead of doing this, tilt your head forward, pinch your nostrils shut and breathe through your mouth.

### Real Life Examples

- ❖ Do not use electric switches with wet hand.

- ❖ A first aid box consists of bandaid, cotton, antiseptic lotion, scissor, thermometer and soap.

### Traffic Signals

- ❖ **Red**      Stop
- ❖ **Yellow**   Ready
- ❖ **Green**    Go

## SAFETY ON THE PLAYGROUND

- Always follow the rules of the game. Never push your friends while playing.
- Use a swimming tube for swimming . Always swim in presence of an adult.

## FIRST AID

Immediate first aid can save a person's life and prevent injury.

First aid is the medical help given to an injured or sick person before doctor arrives.

While giving first aid, be calm and make the injured or sick person comfortable. Make him lie down. Do not panic after an accident. Common emergencies which need first aid are minor cuts, fainting, insect/snake bite and burning.

## 1. FOR MINOR CUTS

First wash the cut with water. Then, apply an antiseptic lotion over it. Tie a bandage on the cut.

## 2. IF A PERSON FAINTS

If a person faints, make him lie down with his head at a level lower than the body. This helps the blood to reach his brain faster. Allow fresh air around the person. Let the person rest quietly.

## 3. FOR BURNS

If a burn is minor, wash the burnt area with cold running water. Put an ice pack on the burnt area. Apply an antiseptic cream on the affected area.

| Type of an accident | Type of first aid given |
|---|---|
| 1. Bites and Stings | **Dogs, monkeys and some other animals can cause rabies** <br> • Wash the wound with soap and water <br> • Apply antiseptic <br> • Get tetanus injection from a doctor |
| | **Snake (poisonous)** <br> • Tie a tight bandage above the wound (between the wound and heart) , it slows down the circulation of venom. <br> • Use ice to sooth the area |
| 2. Broken bones | • Do not move broken part of the body. <br> • If a bone of hand is broken make a sling using a cloth or a bandage. |
| 3. Sprain | • Do not move sprained part of the body <br> • An elastic bandage can be wrapped around the joint to keep it from moving <br> • First day the sprained joint should be soaked in cold water <br> • From the second day onwards soak it in warm water two or three times a day. <br> • Ointment should be lightly rubbed over sprained joint |

# Multiple Choice Questions

## LEVEL 1

1. Which of the following activity/ies we should do every morning?
   (a) Cooking　　　　　　　　　(b) Bathing
   (c) Brushing　　　　　　　　(d) Both (b) and (c)

2. Which of the following activity/ies we should do twice a day?　　　[2012, Tricky]

   (a)

   (b)

   (c)

   (d) All of these

3. Which of the following is a good habit?
   (a) Bite your nails daily
   (b) Take bath daily
   (c) Dance on the road
   (d) Wash your hand before going to toilet

4. _________ is the immediate help given to a person who is hurt, before the doctor comes.　　　[2013]
   (a) Critical aid　　　　　　　(b) First aid
   (c) Medical treatment　　　　(d) Intensive treatment

5. It is not a good habit to _________.　　　[Tricky]
   (a) throw waste in the dustbin.　　　(b) put clean water for birds to drink.
   (c) waste food by taking excess food.　(d) eat healthy food.

6. Green light means to _________.　　　[Tricky])
   (a) come　　　　　　　　　　(b) run
   (c) go　　　　　　　　　　　(d) dance

7. Select the things from the box given below, with which we should not play.　　　[2014, Tricky]



   (a) 1, 2 and 6　　　　　　　(b) 2, 4 and 5
   (c) 4, 5 and 6　　　　　　　(d) 2, 3 and 6

8.  **Which of the following do we use while crossing the road?**                    [Tricky]
    (a)  Footpath                    (b)  Zebra crossing
    (c)  Traffic light               (d)  Both (b) and (c)

9.  **Which of the following activity we should do with the help of an adult?**

                                                                    [2015, Tricky]
    (a)  Eating food                 (b)  Playing with teddy bear
    (c)  Learning swimming           (d)  Bathing

10. **It is NOT necessary to wash your hands ________.**
    (a)  before eating               (b)  after eating
    (c)  both (a) & (b)              (d)  after bathing

11. **Which of the following rule/s we should follow when we are in a swimming pool?**
    (a)  Jump into the swimming pool                          [2016, Tricky]
    (b)  Do not go deep inside the swimming pool
    (c)  Do not enter alone in the swimming pool
    (d)  Both (b) and (c)

12. **At home, we should stay away from which of the following things?**        [Tricky]

    (a)                              (b)

    (c)                              (d)  Both (a) and (b)

13. **Which of the following is a wrong statement?**                            [2016]
    (a)  Walk on the footpath.       (b)  Stand in a queue at the bus stop
    (c)  Do not get into or off a moving bus    (d)  Do not obey the traffic rules

14. **At home, never play with ________.**
    (a)  teddy bear                  (b)  knife
    (c)  ball                        (d)  video game

15. **Which of the following activity/ies you should never do in the playground?**
    (a)  Jump off a see-saw          (b)  Go slow on slides
    (c)  Wait for your turn on slides    (d)  None of these

16. **Which of the following should be followed to prevent accidents at home?** [2017, Tricky]
    (a)  Carelessness at home        (b)  Safety rules at home
    (c)  Neglecting safety rules at home    (d)  All of these

**17.** At homes, stay away from _________.    [Tricky]

(a)   toys                          (b)   knife

(c)   match box                (d)   both (b) and (c)

**18.** Which of the following body postures is correct?    [2012]

(a)          (b)          (c)          (d)

**19.** Which of the following is not a good habit ?

(a)   Not Washing hand after going to toilet.

(b)   Washing hand before and after eating food.

(c)   Brushing teeth once in a week.

(d)   All of the above.

**20.** Which of the following statements are correct?    [2012]

1.   Use your hanky when you sneeze.

2.   Turn off the tap after washing your hands.

3.   Throw wastes in the garden.

4.   Always bite your nails.

(a)   1 and 4                     (b)   1 and 2

(c)   3 and 4                     (d)   1, 2 and 3

**21.** Which of the following is/are correct option/s for traffic signal?    [Tricky]

(a)   Red $\rightarrow$ stop              (b)   Blue $\rightarrow$ go

(c)   Green $\rightarrow$ go            (d)   Both (a) and (c)

**22.** What is  INCORRECT about the given picture?    [2013]

(a)   Drinking water is being used to take bath

(b)   Kitchen utensils are being used for bath

(c)   Child is taking bath in the bathroom

(d)   Both a and c

**23.** Which of the following item should be used if a person gets minor cut?    [Tricky]

(a)   Cold cream                (b)   Ice pack

(c)   Antiseptic lotion         (d)   None of these

**24.** Which of these is correct? [2013]

|     | Do's | Don'ts |
|-----|------|--------|
| (a) | Bite your nails | Lick your fingers after eating |
| (b) | Clean your ears with earbuds | Finger your nose |
| (c) | Cover your mouth while coughing | Comb your hair daily |
| (d) | Cut nails with nail cutter | Rinse mouth with water after eating |

**25.** Which of the following article of your home should not be touched with wet hands?

(a) Toys     (b) Knife     [Tricky]

(c) Gas stove     (d) Electric switch

**26.** Select the INCORRECT option. [2014]

|     | Do's | Don'ts |
|-----|------|--------|
| (a) | Drink clean and pure water | Eat uncovered food |
| (b) | Wash hands before and after meals | Finger your nose |
| (c) | Cover your mouth while coughing | Comb your hair daily |
| (d) | Cut nails with nail cutter | Rinse mouth with water after eating |

**27.** Which of the following activity keeps your bones and muscles strong?

(a) Brushing     (b) Bathing     (c) Exercise     (d) Eating

**28.** Which of the following activity should be done at least thrice a week? [2015]

(a)      (b)      (c)      (d)

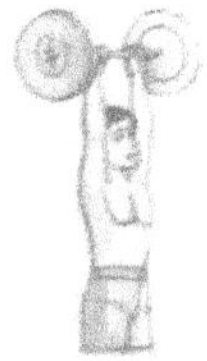

**29.** Manya and Siddi were playing. Suddenly, Siddhi fell down and started crying. Manya should __________. [2015]

(a) Run away from there

(b) Start crying with Siddhi

(c) Wipe the wound carefully with her hands

(d) Call an adult immediately

**30.** Which of following child/ren is/are NOT showing a good habit? [2015]

(a)      (b)      (c)      (d) Both A and B

**31.** Which of these is correct? [2018]

| | Dos | Don'ts |
|---|---|---|
| (a) | Bite nails | Spit on the floor |
| (b) | Put wastes in dustbin | Pluck flowers from parks |
| (c) | Throw wrappers on the road | Cover mouth while sneezing |
| (d) | Talk while eating | Chew the food properly |

**32.** Which of the following statements is correct ? [2019]

(a) We should help people in our neighbourhood.

(b) We should litter our neighbourhood with garbage.

(c) Market can never be in our neighbourhood.

(d) Garden in our neighbourhood is very harmful for us.

**33.** Which road sign is NOT given in the box? [2018]

(a) Overtaking prohibited
(b) School ahead
(c) U-turn prohibited
(d) No parking

**34.** Refer to the given picture. Is the boy following safety rules? [2018]

(a) Yes, because he is not flying kite in the ground.

(b) No, because he is not wearing swimming float.

(c) Yes, because he is wearing a cap.

(d) No, because he is flying kite on terrace without railings.

**35.** If there is a doctor's clinic on the way to market from your house, which sign will you come across ? [2019]

(a)   (b)   (c)   (d) 

**36.** Which portion of the road is shown in the given figure ? [2019]

(a)    Zebra crossing        (b)    Footpath

(c)    Mid of road        (d)    None of these

**37.** Where should one place dolls and toys after playing with them ?  **[2019]**

(a)    In the book shelf        (b)    In the showcase

(c)    On the floor        (d)    In the dustbin

**38.** Which of these children follows good habits?  **[2020]**

(a) Avinash always obeys traffic rules on the road.

(b) Deepa eats uncovered food the vendors.

(c) Suman always runs and plays in the corridors of her school.

(d) Saira eats food that has fallen on the floor.

**39.** Ashish went to the market in a car and parked his car near a shop. When he returned after shopping, he was fined by the traffic police. He realised that he had not noticed the road sign of __________.  **[2020]**

(a)      (b)      (c)      (d)

**40.** Which of the following road signs shows men at work?  **[2021]**

(a)      (b)      (c)      (d)

**41.** You will go to the place shown in the given picture, when you  **[2022]**

(a) Are ill and have to see a doctor

(b) Need to keep your money and jewellery safe

(c) Have to post letters

(d) Want to worship.

**42.** Which of the following activities is unsafe?  **[2022]**

(a)      (b)

(c)      (d)

**43. In case of cuts and wounds you should**      **[2022]**

  (a) Not tie a bandage over it

  (b) Never take any first aid

  (c) Clean the wound with a piece of cotton dipped in an antiseptic liquid.

  (d) Never put a band-aid around it.

**44. When a sick person coughs or sneezes, he/she releases _________ into the air which c make other people sick.**      **[2022]**

  (a) Water vapour    (b) Smoke     (c) Dust     (d) Germs

## LEVEL 2

**Directions (Qs. 1 to 10): Fill in the blanks in the passage given below:**    **[Critical Thinking]**

We should learn good habits from our teachers and elders. We should take _________ (1) _________ daily in the morning before going to school. We should _________ (2) our teeth twice a day. _________ (3) daily to keep your bones and muscles strong. Wash your _________ (4) before and after eating food. Use _________ (5) for cutting your nails. Never play with _________ (6) objects, for example: _________ (7). We should always follow safety rules. While _________ (8) on road, use footpath and always use _________ (9) while crossing the road. Never _________ (10) on the road.

| | | | | | | | |
|---|---|---|---|---|---|---|---|
| 1. | (a) | medicine | (b) | bath | (c) | dance | (d) Both (a) or (b) |
| 2. | (a) | wash | (b) | brush | (c) | cook | (d) comb |
| 3. | (a) | Eat | (b) | Drink | (c) | Cook | (d) Exercise |
| 4. | (a) | legs | (b) | eyes | (c) | hands | (d) ears |
| 5. | (a) | knife | (b) | blade | (c) | nailcutter | (d) teeth |
| 6. | (a) | hard | (b) | soft | (c) | sharp | (d) All of these |
| 7. | (a) | teddy | (b) | balloon | (c) | knife | (d) All of these |
| 8. | (a) | walking | (b) | dancing | (c) | eating | (d) singing |
| 9. | (a) | footpath | (b) | zebra crossing | (c) | swimming pool | (d) None of these |
| 10. | (a) | play | (b) | walk | (c) | sleep | (d) Both (a) and (c) |

**11. Which of these is correct?**      **[2012, Tricky]**

| | Do's | Dont's |
|---|---|---|
| (a) | Bite your nails | Lick your fingers after eating |
| (b) | Clean your ears with earbuds | Talk while eating |
| (c) | Eat junk foods | Eat food at a fixed time everyday |
| (d) | Chew food properly | Eat food from roadside vendor |

**12.**

Safety Rules

At home → A

At school → B

While crossing the road → C

While playing → D

Study the above given flowchart and select the correct option regarding it.

[Critical Thinking]

(a)   B – Do not stand in the queue

(b)   A - Do not touch stoves, heaters, toasters or electric fan when they are switched ON

(c)   D - Do not fly kites in open fields

(d)   C - Do not cross the road when the traffic light is red

13.   **Match the coloumn I and the coloumn II**                    (2013, Tricky)

| Column I | | Column II | |
|---|---|---|---|
| A | Burning | 1. | Zebra crossing |
| B | Cut | 2. | Rub ice on the affected area |
| C | Traffic rules | 3. | Make the person lie down |
| D | Faint | 4. | Apply antiseptic lotion after washing |

|  | A | B | C | D |  |  | A | B | C | D |
|---|---|---|---|---|---|---|---|---|---|---|
| (a) | 3 | 1 | 2 | 4 |  | (b) | 2 | 4 | 1 | 3 |
| (c) | 1 | 2 | 3 | 4 |  | (d) | 2 | 1 | 3 | 4 |

14.   **Which one of the following is least likely to get hurt?**

(a)   

(b)   

(c)   

(d)   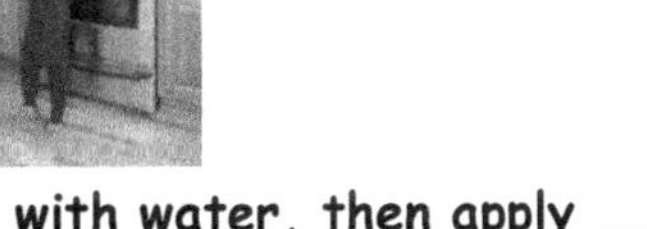

15.   **If a person gets minor cut, first _________ the cut with water, then apply _________ over it.**                    [2014, Tricky]

(a)   wash, cold cream

(b)   remove, band-aid

(c)   wash, antiseptic

(d)   wash, icepack

16.   **Read the following statements and choose the correct option**    [Critical Thinking]

**Statement A:** We should take bath twice

**Statement B:** We should cross the road using footpath.

(a)   Statement A is true, statement B is false

(b)   Statement A is false, statement B is true

(c)   Both the statement are true

(d)   Both the statement are false

**17.** **Which of the following safety rule we should follow while walking on road?**
                                                                        (2015, Tricky)
(a)  Do not play in the play-ground        (b)  Do not run on the play-ground
(c)  Do not run on the road                (d)  Do not eat on the road

**18.** **Which of the following activity can harm us?**                    [Tricky]
(a)  Walking on zebra crossing             (b)  Running on the wet floor
(c)  Playing with knife                    (d)  Both (b) and (c)

**19.** **While handling electric points, we should touch them with ________.**    [Tricky]
(a)  wet hands        (b)  dry hands        (c)  iron rod        (d)  ice

**20.** **What is the main aim of giving first-aid?**                    (2016, Tricky)
(a)  To prevent further injury             (b)  To save life
(c)  To prevent surgery                    (d)  Both (a) and (b)

**21.** **Your friend got hurt while playing football with you in school. He got a cut on his knee, which was bleeding. What should you do first of all?**          [Tricky]
(a)  Send him to the doctor immediately    (b)  Wash the cut with water
(c)  Apply an antiseptic lotion over it    (d)  Both (b) and (c)

**22.** **The given items can be categorised in two groups as**             [2013]
1.  Things that can ____(A)____.           2.  Things that can ____(B)____.

Select the correct option.

|     | A                     | B                     |
|-----|-----------------------|-----------------------|
| (a) | Cut                   | Infect                |
| (b) | Burn                  | Give electrical shock |
| (c) | Give electrical shock | Burn                  |
| (d) | Burn                  | Cut                   |

**23.** **Study the given flowchart and select the correct option regarding it.**        [2013]

Safety Rules

At home | At school | While crossing road | While Playing

d | e | f | g

(a)  e - Do not stand in the queue

(b)  d - Do not touch stoves, heaters, toasters or electric fan when they are switched ON

(c)  g - Do not fly kites in open fields

(d)  f - Do not cross the road when the traffic light is red for vehicles

**24.** **Which of the following safety rule you should follow in school?**
(a)  Do not run on the stairs
(b)  Do not push each other while playing
(c)  Do not climb on the chairs and tables in the classroom
(d)  All of the above

**25.** Which of the following is a good habit?

(a) Walking on zebra crossing

(b) Pushing each other during play

(c) Moving in a line while entering in the school bus

(d) Both (a) and (c)

**26.** [2013]

> Pooja : After playing, I keep my things in their proper place.
>
> Deepika : If you do not, you or someone else might trip on them.

Read the above conversation and select the correct option regarding them.

(a) Pooja is right, while Deepika is wrong.

(b) Both Pooja and Deepika are right.

(c) Deepika made the correct explanation of Pooja's statement.  (d)  Both B and C

**27.** In which of the following emergency, first aid should be given?   (Tricky)

(a) Bone fracture       (b) Minor cut

(c) High fever       (d) Cold and cough

**28.** Which of the following is the most important practice to stay healthy?   [2014]

(a) Exercising outdoors in fresh air

(b) Saying thank you when someone does you a favour

(c) Sharing you things with your friends

(d) Praying before a meal to offer thanks to God

**29.** Which of the following is a good habit?   (Tricky)

(a) Getting into a moving school bus.

(b) Keep your hand outside the moving bus.

(c) Enter into the school bus in a line.

(d) Pushing each other in the moving bus.

**30.** Which of the given actions show the correct way to take care of our pets?   [2014]

(a) 1 and 2       (b) 2 and 3

(c) 3 and 4       (d) 1 and 3

**31.** Read the following sentences carefully and write true/false (T/F)

[Critical Thinking]

(A) We should run on a wet floor

(B) Toys should not be scattered on the floor

(C) Always cross the road using zebra crossing

(a) TTF       (b) FTT       (c) TFT       (d) TTT

**32.** The traffic police officer is signalling to stop vehicles approaching from __________.

[2015]

(a) Behind

(b) Front

(c) Left and right sides

(d) Both A and B

**Directions (Qs. 33 to 35): Read the following passage carefully and answer the following question.** [Critical Thinking]

Accidents can be avoided if we are careful. We should never run on a wet floor and should not scatter our toys on the floor in our house. In the kitchen, we should stay away from the gas stove, knife and scissors. When you are in school, do not run on the stairs and always follow safety rules while playing in the play-ground and in the swimming pool.

**33.** We should follow __________ to avoid accidents at home.

(a) zebra crossing (b) safety rules
(c) traffic rules (d) All of these

**34.** Which of the following rule/s we should follow at our home?

(a) We should not run on the wet floor (b) Do not touch sharp objects like knife
(c) Do not scatter toys on the floor (d) All of these

**35.** Which of the following object/s we should not touch at our home?

(a) Knife (b) Toys (c) Gas stove (d) Both (a) and (c)

**36.** While your mother was frying samosa in the kitchen her hand got burnt.

Which of the following first aid you would give to her? (Tricky)

(a) Apply ice on the burnt area (b) Make her lie down on the bed
(c) Stick a band aid on the burnt area (d) Both (a) and (c)

**37.** Which of the following traffic signal indicates the vehicles that you can cross the road? (2017, Tricky)

(a) Red light (b) Green light (c) Yellow light (d) Orange light

**38.** The object X shown in the given picture is used while [2021]

(a) Driving a car (b) Riding a bike
(c) Swimming in the pool (d) Travelling in the bus.

**39.** Read the given conversation between two sisters Anamika and Siya. [2021]

Select the correct option regarding it.
(a) Both Anamika and Siya are correct.
(b) Both Anamika and Siya are incorrect.
(c) Anamika is correct and Siya is incorrect.
(d) Siya is correct and Anamika is incorrect.

40. **Which of the following is/are unsafe activity/activities?** [2021]
    1. Walking on the footpath.
    2. Running while crossing the road.
    3. Wearing a seat belt while sitting in a moving car.
    4. Taking medicines on your own when you are sick.
    (a) 1 only      (b) 2, 3 and 4 only
    (c) 2 and 4 only      (d) 1.2,3 and 4

41. **Look at the given picture of a room of a house. The good habits to be followed here include __________ .** [2022]

    (a) Flushing toilet after every use
    (b) Turning off tap after use
    (c) Turning off shower after use
    (d) All of these

## RESPONSE GRID

### LEVEL 1

| | | | | |
|---|---|---|---|---|
| 1. a b c d | 2. a b c d | 3. a b c d | 4. a b c d | 5. a b c d |
| 6. a b c d | 7. a b c d | 8. a b c d | 9. a b c d | 10. a b c d |
| 11. a b c d | 12. a b c d | 13. a b c d | 14. a b c d | 15. a b c d |
| 16. a b c d | 17. a b c d | 18. a b c d | 19. a b c d | 20. a b c d |
| 21. a b c d | 22. a b c d | 23. a b c d | 24. a b c d | 25. a b c d |
| 26. a b c d | 27. a b c d | 28. a b c d | 29. a b c d | 30. a b c d |
| 31. a b c d | 32. a b c d | 33. a b c d | 34. a b c d | 35. a b c d |
| 36. a b c d | 37. a b c d | 38. a b c d | 39. a b c d | 40. a b c d |
| 41. a b c d | 42. a b c d | 43. a b c d | 44. a b c d | |

### LEVEL 2

| | | | | |
|---|---|---|---|---|
| 1. a b c d | 2. a b c d | 3. a b c d | 4. a b c d | 5. a b c d |
| 6. a b c d | 7. a b c d | 8. a b c d | 9. a b c d | 10. a b c d |
| 11. a b c d | 12. a b c d | 13. a b c d | 14. a b c d | 15. a b c d |
| 16. a b c d | 17. a b c d | 18. a b c d | 19. a b c d | 20. a b c d |
| 21. a b c d | 22. a b c d | 23. a b c d | 24. a b c d | 25. a b c d |
| 26. a b c d | 27. a b c d | 28. a b c d | 29. a b c d | 30. a b c d |
| 31. a b c d | 32. a b c d | 33. a b c d | 34. a b c d | 35. a b c d |
| 36. a b c d | 37. a b c d | 38. a b c d | 41. a b c d | |

# Answers with Explanations

## LEVEL 1

1. **(d)** We should take bath and brush everyday in the morning.
2. **(a)** We should brush our teeth twice a day.
3. **(b)** Taking bath daily is a good habit.
4. **(b)** First aid
5. **(c)** It is not a good habit to waste food by taking excess food.
6. **(c)** Green light says 'go'
7. **(b)** We should not play with screwdriver, knife and scissors.
8. **(d)** We use zebra crossing and traffic light while crossing the road.
9. **(c)** We should learn swimming with the help of an adult.
10. **(d)** Washing your hands after bathing is NOT necessary.
11. **(d)** Both (b) and (c) rules should be followed when we are in swimming pool.
12. **(d)** At home we should stay away from both electric heater and electric fan.
13. **(d)** We should obey the traffic rules.
14. **(b)** At home we should never play with knife.
15. **(a)** You should never jump off a see-saw in the play-ground.
16. **(b)** We should follow safety rules at home.
17. **(d)** At homes, stay away from both knife and match box.
18. **(b)** We should always sit, walk or stand with straight back.
19. **(c)** We should brush teeth twice a day.
20. **(b)** We should throw wastes in the dustbin and not in the garden. We should not bite our nails, but should cut them regularly with a nail cutter.
21. **(d)** Both Red → Stop and Green → Go are correct options for traffic signal.
22. **(c)** Child is taking bath in the kitchen, not in the bathroom. It is a bad habit. We should always take bath in the bathroom.
23. **(c)** Antiseptic lotion should be used if a person gets minor cut.
24. **(b)** We should always clean ears with ear-buds and we should not put finger into our nose.
25. **(d)** Electric switch should not be touched with wet hands as it may give you electric shock.
26. **(c)** Combing our hair daily is a good habit.
27. **(c)** Exercise keeps your bones and muscles strong.
28. **(d)** Exercise should be done at least thrice a week. All the other activities should be done daily.
29. **(d)** As Siddhi fell down and started crying, she might have got injuries. So, Manya should immediately call an adult who can give her first aid.
30. **(d)** According to option 'a' a small child is teasing a cat, by pulling its tail. It is not a good habit to hurt animals. In option 'b' a girl is wasting water while brushing her teeth. Both option 'a' and 'b' are showing bad habits whereas, option 'c' shows a girl throwing garbage in a dustbin which is a good habit.
31. **(b)** We should put waste in dustbin and we should not pluck flowers in the park.
32. **(a)** We should help people in our neighbourhood.
33. **(d)** The sign for no parking is not shown.
34. **(d)** No, because he is flying kite on terrace without railings. The terrace should have railings.
35. **(a)** The cross sign is red tells us about doctor clinic.
36. **(a)** The picture shown is of zebra crossing. We should cross road on zebra crossing.
37. **(a)** The toys and dolls should be placed properly in the bookshelf. They should not be thrown on the floor and in the dustbin.
38. **(a)** Avinash always obeys traffic rules on the road.

| | | |
|---|---|---|
| 39. | (c) | No parking |
| 40. | (b) | |
| 41. | (a) | |
| 42. | (b) | Running on the stairs is unafe. |
| 43. | (c) | |
| 44. | (d) | Germs |

## LEVEL 2

1. **(b)** bath    2. **(b)** brush
3. **(d)** Exercise    4. **(c)** hands
5. **(c)** nail cutter    6. **(c)** sharp
7. **(c)** knife    8. **(a)** walking
9. **(b)** zebra crossing
10. **(a)** play
11. **(c)** We should not eat junk foods as they are not good for our health. We should eat food at a fixed time everyday as this helps in proper digestion of food and is good for our digestive system.
12. **(b)** At home we should not touch electric appliances when they are switched ON.
13. **(b)** A → 2, B → 4, C → 1, D → 3 when burnt, rub ice on the affected area, when there is a cut, apply antiseptic lotion after washing the wound, traffic - rules are followed when zebra crossing is used, when someone faints, make him lie down.
14. **(a)** Walking on zebra crossing will not hurt you.
15. **(c)** If a person gets minor cut, first wash the cut with water, then apply antiseptic over it.
16. **(d)** Both the statements are false as we should brush our teeth twice a day and we should cross the road using zebra crossing.
17. **(c)** Do not run on the road.
18. **(d)** Running on the wet floor and playing with knife can harm us.
19. **(b)** While handling electric points, we should touch them with dry hands.
20. **(d)** To prevent further injury and to save life.
21. **(d)** Wash the cut with water first of all, then apply an antiseptic lotion on it.
22. **(d)** Among the given items, matchbox and cracker are items which can burn (a) and blade and scissors are items which can cut (b). Never play with these things. These things can hurt you.
23. **(b)** At school (e), we should stand in queue. While playing (g) we should fly kites in open fields. While crossing the road (f) we should cross the road only when traffic light is red for vehicles. At home (d), we should not touch stoves, heaters, toasters or electric fan, when they are switched ON.
24. **(d)** Do not run on the stairs, do not climb on the chairs and tables in the class-room and do not push each other while playing.
25. **(d)** Walking on zebra crossing and entering into the school bus in line is a good habit.
26. **(d)** Both Pooja and Deepika are right Deepika made the correct explanantion of Pooja's statement.
27. **(b)** First aid can be given for minor cut.
28. **(a)** Exercising outdoor in fresh air will keep our body and mind healthy.
29. **(c)** Enter into the school bus in line.
30. **(d)** We should feed our pets timely and properly and give them proper place for resting and playing. We should never tease them.
31. **(b)** We should not run on a wet floor.
32. **(d)** In the given figure, the police officer is using his both hands to stop vehicles. Left hand is used horizontally to stop vehicles coming from his back side and right hand is used vertically to stop vehicles coming from his front side.
33. **(b)** We should follow safety rules to avoid accidents at home.
34. **(d)** All of these rules should be followed at our home.
35. **(d)** We should not touch knife and gas stove at over home.
36. **(a)** Apply ice on the burnt area.
37. **(b)** Green light means to go.
38. **(c)** Swimming in the pool
39. **(a)** Both Anamika and Siya are correct.
40. **(c)** 2 and 4 only
41. **(d)** All of these

# 9 | CHAPTER FOREWORD

We can't live without food, clothes and shelter. Do you know our food comes from plants and animals? You and your family live in a house. In the same  way, people need houses where they can eat, sleep and rest. A shelter protects us from heat, rain, cold and other extreme weather conditions. We  wear clothes to cover our body and to protect ourselves from various weather conditions.

**Fill the blanks with one word.**

1.  Cow gives us ___________________.

2.  Eskimo lives in an___________________.

3.  We get honey from _______________.

4.  King of fruits ___________________.

After reading this chapter, you will know about different types of foods and their functions, different types of houses and clothes.

# 9

## Chapter

# Food, Shelter and Clothes



**This chapter will help you to:**

* learn about different types of food and their function.
* know about the food we get from plants and animals.
* study about different types of houses.
* learn about different types of clothes we wear on different occasions.

## INTRODUCTION

We cannot live without food, clothes and shelter. These are the basic necessities of life. Food gives us energy to work and play. We eat different types of food. Some food comes from plants and some from animals. Let us discuss about different types of food.

## 1. ENERGY GIVING FOOD

Energy giving food gives us energy to work and play. **For example,** rice, wheat butter, ghee, jaggery, bread, sugar, potato etc give us energy. These contain carbohydrates. They have lots of sugar and starch.

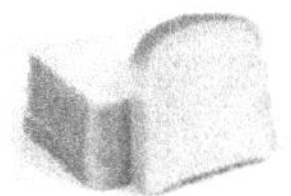

## 2. BODY-BUILDING FOOD

Body building food helps in building our body.
**For example,** meat, milk, fish and cheese.

---

### Historical Preview:

* In early times, the early man used to eat raw food. Later, on they produced fire by rubbing two rocks. After this, they started cooking their food.

### Amazing Facts

* Strawberries and Cashews are the only fruits that have their seeds on the outside unlike all other fruits which have their seeds inside.

## 3. PROTECTIVE FOOD

Protectivefoodarethefoodwhichprotectsusfromdiseases. **For example,** fruits, nuts and vegetables. Food like fruits & vegetable skin are rich in roughage.

All type of food should be eaten in proper amount. Food which contains all the nutrients in right amount is known as **balanced diet**.

### FOOD FROM PLANTS

We get fruits and vegetables from plants. We eat different parts of plants as food. **For example:** we eat the root of **radish, carrot and turnip**. We eat the stem of many plants as vegetables such as **onion, potato and ginger**. We eat the leaves of many plants like **spinach, mint, and coriander**. We eat flower of **cauliflower and broccoli**.

### FOOD FROM ANIMALS

Animals such as cow, buffaloes, camel and goats give us milk. Milk is used to produce cheese, curd and sweets. Animals also give us meat and egg. We get honey from honeybee. Milk is the only food for infants.

### SHELTER (HOUSES)

A house is a place where we live together. It is a place where we eat, sleep and relax. It protects us from heat, rain, cold and other weather conditions.

### DIFFERENT KINDS OF HOUSES

Early man did not live in houses. They lived in caves or on trees. Today people live in many different kinds of houses. Let us discuss them in detail.

1. **Kutcha House:** Houses made up of mud, straw, and bamboo stick are known as **kutcha houses**. These houses are not very strong. People of villages, live in kutcha houses. **For example:** A hut is a kutcha house.

2. **Pukka House:** Strong houses made up of bricks, cement, steel and mortar are called pukka houses. **For example:** Flats, bungalows, apartments are the examples of pukka houses. People of cities, live in pukka houses. These houses are also known as **permanent houses**.

### SPECIAL KINDS OF HOUSES

There are many special kinds of houses that are found in a particular area. The different kinds of houses depend upon the climate of the place and material available to build the house.

> **Do You Know?**
>
> ❖ Dry fruits like Cashew, Almond & Walnuts are nuts where pears, grams, Rajmas are Pulses

Kutcha House

Pukka house

**Igloo:** These are dome shaped houses present in snow. These houses are made up of block of ice. Eskimos live in igloo.

People who do not stay in one place, live in caravans and tents that can move from one place to another. Such type of houses are called **temporary houses**.

**Caravan:** These are the houses on wheels. These houses can be moved from place to place. Nomads like gypsies live in carvans.

**Tent:** A tent is made up of canvas and can be folded easily. These houses are used in forest, desert and camps.

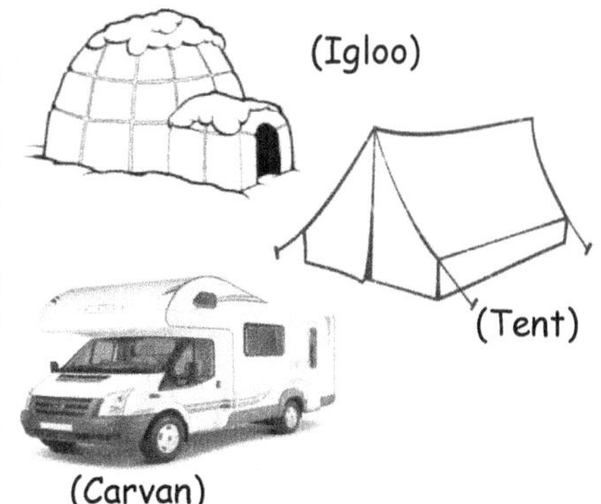


Fact box houses in hills have sloping roof so that rain water flows down easily.

## KEEPING THE HOUSE CLEAN

We should keep our house clean. A clean house is free from diseases.

A clean house needs to dispose off garbage in a proper way.

The houses should have doors and windows with wire netting to allow fresh air in, but keep flies and mosquitos away.

## DECORATION OF HOUSE

Clothes are made from fibres which are obtained either from plants or from animals. People decorate their house to make them look nice. They do so in many ways. They decorate homes by making **rangoli** which is made of colours and flowers. People hang paintings on the wall of their house.

All members of the family should help to keep the house neat and clean. They can also keep wind chimes and flowers in their houses.

## CLOTHES

People wear variety of clothes of different materials, colours, and designs. Main factors that determine what people wear are: the climate of the place; the culture and tradition; the latest fashion and trends. In India, people living in villages generally wear traditional clothes.

In cities men wear shirts and trousers, t-shirts and jeans, where as women wear salwar-kameez, saris, t-shirts and jeans and dresses.

## CLOTHES WE WEAR

Clothes can be worn in different ways, either stitched or unstitched. A fabric or textile can be cut and stitched to make clothes. A cloth that is not stitched is an unstitched cloth.

## UNSTITCHED CLOTHES

1. **Saree:** In India, women mostly wear sarees. A saree is a long unstitched fabric that women wrap around themselves in different styles.

2. **Lungi and dhoti:** Men also wear unstitched clothes in the form of lungis.

3. **Dupatta:** A dupatta is a long unstitched cloth which is worn by women to cover their heads.

4. **Shawl:** A shawl is an unstitched piece of cloth that is usually woollen. It is worn by both men and women, especially in winter.

## DIFFERENT TYPES OF CLOTHES

The clothes that we wear vary due to lots of factors. Some of the factors are climate we live in, the occasion we are attending and the profession we are working in.

## CLOTHES ACCORDING TO CLIMATE

We use to wear clothes according to the climate of a place.

1. In summer, we wear mostly light coloured cotton clothes because they absorb sweat and keep us cool. Cotton is obtained from plants.

2. In winter, we wear dark coloured clothes made of wool. Woollen clothes trap the body heat and keep us warm. Wool is obtained from animals like sheep, other than wool, leather & silk are also obtained from animals. Leather is obtained from skin of animals, whereas silk is obtained from silkworm.

Summer clothes

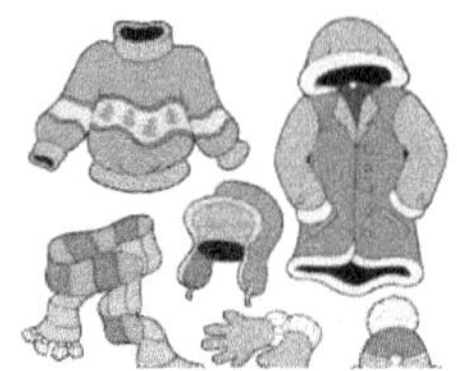

Winter clothes

## CLOTHES ACCORDING TO OCCASION

School uniform   Sports wear   Party dress   Night dress

For different occasions, we wear different kinds of clothes. We wear special clothes on different festivals. The clothes we wear at home and school are not the same.

## CLOTHES ACCORDING TO PROFESSION

People in certain profession wear uniform. A uniform helps us to identify the profession of a person. For example, we can identify a policeman, a doctor and a lawyer by their uniform.

Lawyer         Soldier         Doctor

Pilot         Policeman         Nurse

# Multiple Choice Questions

## LEVEL 1

1. Which of the following is body building food? [Tricky]
   (a) Meat    (b) Potato    (c) Pizza    (d) Fruits

2. Which of the following food item is made up of milk?
   (a) Fish    (b) Potato    (c) Cheese    (d) Egg

3. Which of the following is/are a protective food/s? [Tricky]
   (a) Mango        (b) Apple
   (c) Spinach      (d) All of these

4. Which of the following food comes from animal?
   (a) Egg    (b) Mango    (c) Potato    (d) Rice

5. Types of clothes we wear, depend on which of the following factor? [2012]
   (a) Climate      (b) Family
   (c) Occasion    (d) Both (a) and (c)

6. Which of the following is not a body building food? [Tricky]
   (a) Milk    (b) Fruits    (c) Meat    (d) Soyabean

7. An Eskimo lives in an ________ [2012]
   (a) Tent    (b) Tree    (c) Igloo    (d) Hut

8. Which of the following food we do not get from animals? [2013, Tricky]
   (a) Honey      (b) Nuts
   (c) Milk        (d) Chicken

9. Which of the following type of house is made up of ice? [Tricky]
   (a) Igloo    (b) Tent    (c) Stilt house    (d) None

10. Which of the following you will not find in a house?
    (a) Kitchen    (b) Bathroom    (c) Playground    (d) Bedroom

11. Which of these is a Kutcha house? [2014]

    (a)      (b)      (c)      (d)

12. Which of the following type of cloth is not worn by men?
    (a) Shirts    (b) Saree    (c) Jeans    (d) Trousers

13. Which of the following houses can be easily moved from place to place? [Tricky]
    (a) Caravans    (b) Igloo    (c) Stilt house    (d) Hut

14. **What is the shape of an Igloo?** [2015]
    (a) Square (b) Dome-shaped (c) Round (d) Triangular

15. **Which of the following you will not see in cities?**
    (a) Trees (b) Bungalows (c) Huts (d) Apartments

16. **Which of the following is/are used to decorate houses?**
    (a) Wind chimes (b) Paintings (c) Flowers (d) All of these

17. **People living in plains usually make** [2015, Tricky]

(a)

A house with sloping roof

(b)

A house with flat roof

(c)

A house boat

(d)

A Kutcha house

18. **Choose odd one out** [Tricky]
    (a) Saree (b) Salwar-kameez (c) Skirt (d) Igloo

19. **Which of the following can be eaten without cooking?**
    (a) Cucumber (b) Carrot (c) Radish (d) All of these

20. **Which of the following structures of a house can be flat, sloping or semi-ciruclar?** [2016]
    (a) Floor (b) Mud (c) Roof (d) Door

21. **Which of the following protect/s us from diseases?**
    (a) Fruits (b) Vegetables
    (c) Milk (d) Both (a) and (b)

22. **Which of the following is/are energy giving food/s?**
    (a) Rice (b) Cereals (c) Wheat (d) All of these

23. **Which of the following has many houses in it?** [2017, Tricky]

(a)

(b)

(c)

(d)

24. **Which of the following can be eaten only after cooking?**
    (a) Cucumber (b) Rice (c) Radish (d) All of these

**25.** A house built with stones, bricks and cement is called a      [Tricky]

    (a)  Hut     (b)  Tent     (c)  Caravan     (d)  Pucca house

**26.** The food shown in the given picture falls under which food group?      [2012]

    (a)  Protective foods

    (b)  Body-building foods

    (c)  Energy-giving foods

    (d)  Roughage-giving foods

**27.** Which of the following is a house on wheels?      [Tricky]

    (a)  Igloo     (b)  Hut     (c)  Tent     (d)  Caravan

**28.** What type of cloth is best suited for winter?

    (a)  Cotton     (b)  Linen     (c)  Woolen     (d)  Polyester

**29.** Our house keeps us safe from ________.      [2013]

    (a)  Heat, cold and family     (b)  Rain, winds and food

    (c)  Heat, cold and rain     (d)  Cold, winds and school

**30.** Which of the following house is made of canvas?

    (a)  House boat     (b)  Caravan     (c)  Igloo     (d)  Tent

**31.** Which of the following house has roof made of straw or palm leaves?

    (a)  Igloo     (b)  Caravan     (c)  Mud house     (d)  Tent house

**32.** Foods with lots of sugar and starch are rich in ________ .      [2014]

    (a)  Fats     (b)  Proteins

    (c)  Carbohydrates     (d)  Cold, winds and school

**33.** If you look around, you will find two types of houses: Kutcha and Pucca houses. Select the correct examples for the houses.      [2014]

| | Kutcha | Pucca | | Kutcha | Pucca |
|---|---|---|---|---|---|
| (a) | Igloo | Houseboat | (b) | Caravan | Stilt House |
| (c) | Hut | Bungalow | (d) | Bungalow | Tent |

**34.** The kind of roof depends on      [Tricky]

    (a)  Money and material

    (b)  Weather, climate and the availability of material

    (c)  People and weather     (d)  People and place

**35.** A multistorey building where many families live in different housing units is called ________.      [2014]

    (a)  Mall     (b)  Apartment     (c)  Cottage     (d)  Villa

**36.** Which of the following is/are temporary house/s?

(a) Caravans and house boats    (b) Pucca houses

(c) Apartments    (d) All of these

**37.** Shweta was asked to bring a fruit that is juicy, sweet and sour in taste and is rich in vitamin C. Which of the following fruit should she bring?    **[2015]**

(a)    (b)    (c)    (d)

**38.** Match correctly the following terms in the column I with those in the column II.    **[Tricky]**

| | Column I | | Column II |
|---|---|---|---|
| A | Multi storey | 1. | Caravan |
| B | Mobile house | 2. | Igloo |
| C | Semicircular roofs | 3. | Apartment |
| D | Sloping roofs | 4. | Houses in the hill |

|  | A | B | C | D |  | | A | B | C | D |
|---|---|---|---|---|---|---|---|---|---|---|
| (a) | 3 | 1 | 2 | 4 | | (b) | 3 | 1 | 2 | 4 |
| (c) | 4 | 3 | 2 | 1 | | (d) | 3 | 2 | 4 | 1 |

**39.** Why do people put wire mesh on their doors and windows ?    **[2015]**

(a) It allows sunlight and air to come in

(b) It keeps the house warm and dark.

(c) It stops the entry of mosquitoes and flies

(d) Both (a) and (c)

**40.** Cotton clothes are preferred during the summer because these clothes

(a) Do not absorb sweat    (b) Absorb heat

(c) Absorb sweat easily    (d) Do not allow the body heat to escape

**41.** Which of the following houses are made of wood, bamboo and mud?

(a) Caravans    (b) Huts    (c) Igloos    (d) Tents

**42.** Houses in the plains have    **[Tricky]**

(a) Curved roofs    (b) Flat roofs

(c) Sloping roofs    (d) Semi-circular roofs

**43.** Eskimos live in

(a) Caravan    (b) House boats    (c) Igloos    (d) Huts

**44.** Mountain climbers often carry [Tricky]

(a) Cardboards      (b) Tents

(c) Blocks      (d) Asbestos sheets

**45.** ________ is a house built of snow. Eskimos make these to live in.

(a) Caravan    (b) Igloo    (c) Kutcha House    (d) Houseboat

**46.** Food items can be grouped into energy-giving, body-building and protective foods. Select the food item which does NOT belong to the group, to which the other three belong. [2015]

(a)    (b)    (c)    (d)

**47.** Which of the following is placed INCORRECTLY in the given flow chart? [2018]



(a) Potato    (b) Green beans    (c) Butter    (d) Milk

**48.** The type of temporary house shown in the picture, can be seen in [2018]

(a) Mumbai    (b) Kashmir    (c) Rajasthan    (d) Gujarat

**49.** Which of these do the people build to stop flooding ? [2018]

(a) Streets    (b) Dams    (c) Sidewalks    (d) Bridges

**50.** Which among these is a junk food? [2018]

(a)    (b)    (c)    (d)

**51.** Rohan has come back after playing in the park. He is feeling tired and should have ________ to get instant energy. [2018]

(a) Egg    (b) Banana    (c) Butter    (d) Pulses

**52.** How do you keep your bones and muscles healthy ?                    [2019]

(a)   Eating bad food                    (b)   Sleeping late

(c)   Breathing out more oxygen          (d)   Eating healthy

**53.** In which of the following weather conditions do we wear woollen clothes?                    [2021]

(a)                    (b)                    (c)                    (d)

**54.** Select the INCORRECT option.                    [2022]

|     | Vegetaration food | Non-vegetarian food |
|-----|-------------------|---------------------|
| (a) | Cereals           | Chicken             |
| (b) | Pulses            | Prawns              |
| (c) | Meat              | Chapati             |
| (c) | Bread             | Fish                |

**55.** Which among the following is the same type of house as the one shown in the given picture?                    [2022]

(a)   Bungalow          (b)   Tent          (c)   Caravan          (d)   Houseboat

**56.** Curd is prepared from the:                    [2022]

(a)   fruit juice          (b)   vegetable juice  (c)   honey          (d)   milk

## LEVEL 2

**1.** Find which of the following is under wrong heading?                    [Critical Thinking]

| Body-building food | Protective food | Energy giving food |
|--------------------|-----------------|--------------------|
| Milk               | Fish            | Sugar              |
| Meat               | Fruits          | Cashew nuts        |

(a)   Milk          (b)   Cashew nuts          (c)   Fish          (d)   Fruits

2.  **Read the following statements and find true and false (T/F).**    [2012, Tricky]

    (A)  We should eat only meat to remain healthy.

    (B)  Eating vegetables makes us ill.

    (C)  An infant drinks only milk.

    (a)  TTT          (b)  FFT          (c)  TFT          (D)  FFF

3.  **Read the following sentences and identify the food item.**    [Critical Thinking]

    (A)  I am a complete food.

    (B)  I help you to grow and give you energy.

    (C)  I protect you from diseases.

    (D)  An infant drinks only me.

    Guess who I am?

    (a)  Egg          (b)  Pumpkin          (c)  Milk          (d)  Meat

4.  **Which of the following thing/s a house should not have?**    [2013, Tricky]

    (a)  Windows for sunlight and fresh air.     (b)  Flies and mosquitoes.

    (c)  Dustbin.                                (d)  Clean and tidy rooms.

5.  **Match the following:**    [Critical Thinking]

    (A)  Orange          (1)  River

    (B)  Sugar           (2)  Cow

    (C)  Milk            (3)  Sugarcane

    (D)  Fish            (4)  Plant

|     | A | B | C | D |     |     | A | B | C | D |
|-----|---|---|---|---|-----|-----|---|---|---|---|
| (a) | 1 | 3 | 2 | 4 |     | (b) | 4 | 3 | 2 | 1 |
| (c) | 2 | 3 | 4 | 1 |     | (d) | 1 | 2 | 3 | 4 |

6.  **Which of the following statement is true?**    [2014, Tricky]

    (a)  Food gives us energy and helps us to grow

    (b)  We cannot eat apple without cooking

    (c)  We should live in dirty house only

    (d)  We should not eat fruits and vegetables daily

7.  **Clothes do not protect us from which of the following?**

    (a)  Rain          (b)  Dust          (c)  Cold          (d)  Plants

8.  **Match the following:**    [Tricky]

|   | List I    |    | List II |
|---|-----------|----|---------|
| A | Hut       | 1  | Brick   |
| B | Apartment | 2. | Ice     |
| C | Tent      | 3. | Mud     |
| D | Igloo     | 4. | Cloth   |

|     | A | B | C | D |     |     | A | B | C | D |
|-----|---|---|---|---|-----|-----|---|---|---|---|
| (a) | 3 | 1 | 4 | 2 |     | (b) | 2 | 1 | 3 | 4 |
| (c) | 1 | 2 | 4 | 3 |     | (d) | 3 | 2 | 1 | 4 |

**9.** Which of the following is NOT obtained from animals? **[2015]**

    (a) Wool      (b) Cotton      (c) Leather      (d) Silk

**Directions (Qs. 10 to 17):** Fill in the blanks in the passage given below: **[Tricky]**

People wear a variety of clothes of different materials, colours and ________ (10) ________. We wear clothes according to climate, ________ (11) ________ and profession. We wear ________ (12) ________ clothes in summers. In winters we wear clothes made of ________ (13) ________. We wear ________ (14) ________ when we go to school and in some profession. We wear ________ (15) ________ when we go to play in a park. A uniform helps us to ________ (16) ________ the profession of a person. We wear________ (17) ________ when we go to the bed.

**10.** (a) designs      (b) animals      (c) thread      (d) wool

**11.** (a) day      (b) occasion      (c) mood      (d) colour

**12.** (a) plants      (b) woollen      (c) cotton      (d) rubber

**13.** (a) cotton      (b) wool      (c) hands      (d) plants

**14.** (a) uniform      (b) dress      (c) night dress      (d) sports wear

**15.** (a) sports wear      (b) night      (c) uniform      (d) all

**16.** (a) make      (b) clean      (c) identify      (d) none

**17.** (a) night dress      (b) uniform      (c) sweater      (d) socks

**18.** Who among the following live in caravans? **[2014, Tricky]**

    (a) Eskimos      (b) Kashmiris      (c) Gypsies      (d) All of these

**Directions (Qs. 19 to 23):** Read the passage carefully and answer the question.

**[Critical Thinking]**

Food is the necessity of life. It provides support and growth to human body. Food consists of many substances called nutrients. Cereals, potato, rice and sugar have carbohydrates. Milk, egg, meat, fish are rich in proteins. Fruits and vegetables consist of minerals and vitamins.

**19.** Food that we eat consists of many substances which are called ________

    (a) Nutrients      (b) Proteins      (a) Vitamin      (b) Carbohydrate

**20.** Which of the following food item consist/s of carbohydrate?

    (a) Rice      (b) Potato      (c) Sugar      (d) All

**21.** Which of the following is/are provided to the human body from food?

    (a) Support, protection against disease      (b) Growth

    (c) Energy      (d) All of these

**22.** Which of the following give/s us minerals and vitamins?

    (a) Fruits      (b) Vegetables

    (c) Butter      (d) Both (a) and (b)

**23.** Which of the following food item is rich in protein?

    (a) Egg      (b) Sugar      (c) Butter      (d) Orange

**24.** People who do special jobs and pupils in schools wear **[2016]**

    (a) Party wears      (b) Uniforms

    (c) Night dress      (d) T-shirts and jeans

**25.** Your friend Ram has fallen from the stairs in school and his left hand has got injured. Ram is suffering from pain. As a friend what will you suggest him so that he can recover soon.

(a) He should eat body building food like sprouts, egg and fish.

(b) He should drink milk, it helps in growth and repair of injured parts.

(c) He should stop going to school.

(d) Both (a) and (b)

**26.** What type of clothes do you prefer to wear when it is cold? [2017]

(a) Cotton  (b) Silk  (c) Woollen  (d) Flax

**27.** Find the incorrect match: [Tricky]

(a) Rice : Cereal  (b) Eskimo : Igloo  (c) Hut : Cities  (d) Mango : Fruits

**28.** Match the column (I) with the column (II). [Critical Thinking]

| | Column I | | Column II |
|---|---|---|---|
| A | Lehenga | 1 | Summer |
| B | Cotton clothes | 2. | Party wear |
| C | Coat and tie | 3. | Winter |
| D | Sweater | 4. | Professional clothes |

|  | A | B | C | D | | | A | B | C | D |
|---|---|---|---|---|---|---|---|---|---|---|
| (a) | 2 | 1 | 4 | 3 | | (b) | 1 | 2 | 3 | 4 |
| (c) | 4 | 3 | 1 | 2 | | (d) | 2 | 1 | 3 | 4 |

**29.** Match the column-I with the column-II and select the correct option. [2012]

| | Column-I | | Column-II |
|---|---|---|---|
| A. | Kutccha house | 1. | Made on wheels |
| B. | Pucca house | 2. | Made of bamboo, mud, straw, leaves |
| C. | Igloo | 3. | Made of wood, bricks, cement, steel |
| D. | Caravan | 4. | Made of snow |

(a) A-2, B-4, C-1, D-3  (b) A-2, B-3, C-4, D-1

(c) A-1, B-3, C-2, D-4  (d) A-4, B-3, C-2, D-1

**30.** Which of the following is/are necessary for keeping our house fresh and germ free?

(a) Fresh air  (b) Cleanliness  [Tricky]

(c) Sunlight  (d) All of the above

**31.** Three groups of food are shown below. Which of these groups: [2013]

A. help us to grow and prevent us from falling sick, respectively

B. give us the most energy and is roughage-rich food, respectively

|     | A      | B      |
| --- | ------ | ------ |
| (a) | M, L   | N, M   |
| (b) | M, L   | N, L   |
| (c) | L, N   | M, N   |
| (d) | M, L   | M, N   |

**32.** Which of the following house/s can be moved from one place to another?

(a) Caravan     (b) Tent     (c) Hut     (d) Both (a) and (b)

**33.** Food, clothes and shelter are the _________ necessities of our life.

(a) basic     (b) good     (c) bad     (d) only

**34.** Select the odd one out.                                                                     [2014]

(a)          (b)          (c)          (d)

**35.** Shweta's mother washed some clothes and hung them out to dry. A strong wind blew away the clothes.

Find out their names by filling in the missing letters and select the correct set of alphabets from the given options.

|     | 1     | 2     | 3     | 4     | 5     |
| --- | ----- | ----- | ----- | ----- | ----- |
| (a) | E, T  | R, A  | I, T  | L, O  | U, E  |
| (b) | O, L  | M, P  | M, O  | G, E  | U, E  |
| (c) | I, T  | E, T  | R, A  | H, T  | A, E  |
| (d) | I, T  | E, T  | G, L  | H, T  | L, A  |



**36.** Study the given flowchart and select the option which can fill the empty spaces: d, e and f correctly.                                                                     [2014]

(a) d-Egg, e-Fish, f-Soyabean

(b) d-Rice, e-Egg, f-Nuts

(c) d-Bread, e-Fruits, f-Cheese

(d) d-Jaggery, e-Butter, f-Fruits



**37.** Ram, noticed his younger brother that daily after playing with his friends, when he comes back home, he eats his dinner first and then goes to the bedroom to sleep. What should Ram tell him to do when he comes home after playing?

(a) Change dirty clothes as they cause skin diseases

(b) Wash hands before eating dinner

(c) Change night clothes before sleeping

(d) All of these

38. **Which of the following type of food gives us strength to fight diseases?**
    - (a) Body building food
    - (b) Protective food
    - (c) Energy giving food
    - (d) All of these

39. **Read the following sentences and find the incorrect one?**                    [Tricky]
    - (a) Caravan are the houses on wheel.
    - (b) Rangoli is made of clothes.
    - (c) Curd is made of milk.
    - (d) In winter, we wear woollen clothes.

40. **Which of following protect/s us from heat, cold, dust and rain?**          [Tricky]
    - (a) A house without roof
    - (b) Park
    - (c) Clothes
    - (d) Playground

41. **The picture given below shows children wearing clothes that are suitable to wear in winter season.**

    [Tricky]

    **Which of these gives fibre that is used to make a sweater?**

    - (a)
    - (b)
    - (c)
    - (d)

42. **During the rainy season, we need to**
    - (a) Wear a raincoat
    - (b) Carry an umbrella
    - (c) Keep our body dry
    - (d) All of these

43. **Which of the following gives us silk fibre?**
    - (a) Plant
    - (b) Sheep
    - (c) Silkworm
    - (d) Polar bear

44. **Which of the following statement is NOT correct?**                    [Tricky]
    - (a) The houses in the hills have sloping roofs
    - (b) The houses in the plains have flat roofs
    - (c) Caravans are houses on wheels
    - (d) All houses are built of mud only

45. **Which of the following cloth absorbs sweat easily?**
    - (a) Silk
    - (b) Cotton
    - (c) Woollen
    - (d) Nylon

46. **Woollen clothes protect us from**
    - (a) Cold
    - (b) Rain
    - (c) Heat
    - (d) All of these

**47.** The picture given below shows a boy getting wet in the rain.    [Critical Thinking]

Which of the following is/are to be worn to keep dry in this season?

(a)   Woollen clothes  (b)   Raincoat        (c)   Cotton clothes (d)   Silk clothes

**48.** The picture given below is that of a silk saree.    [Tricky]

**Silk saree**

Identify the living organism from which the fibre was obtained to make the saree?

(a)   Sheep            (b)   Goat            (c)   Silkworm        (d)   Plant

**49.** Cotton clothes are preferred during the ___________ season.

(a)   Rainy            (b)   Summer          (c)   Winter          (d)   Spring

**50.** Clothes are made from    [Tricky]

(a)   Fibres           (b)   Barks           (c)   Microbes        (d)   Webs

**51.** Which of the following sentence is correct?

(a)   Wheat  and rice are pulses.        (b)   Pea and gram are pulses.

(c)   Pea and tomato are cereals.        (d)   Mango has many seeds.

**52.** Ayush's elder brother regularly goes to gym and wants to build muscles. Ayush, on the other hand is weak and easily falls ill. Which of the following foods should be taken more by (a) Ayush and (b) his elder brother?    [2015]

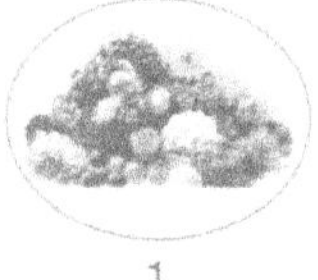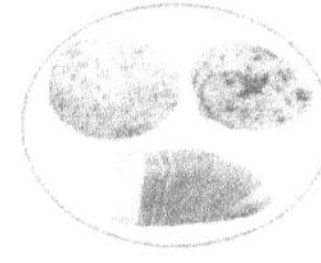

|     | a    | b |
|-----|------|---|
| (a) | 1, 2 | 2 |
| (b) | 2    | 4 |
| (c) | 3, 4 | 3 |
| (d) | 2    | 1 |

53. **Read carefully what Amol is saying. What should Amol include in his diet to develop strong muscles that are required for becoming a sports person?** **[2015]**

    (a)  Fish, sweets and butter

    (b)  Yoghurt, eggs and pulses

    (c)  Fruits and vegetables

    (d)  Rice, jaggery and milk

54. **Mira made the following pairs of food items, one each from plant and animal. Unknowingly she made a mistake while pairing them. Find the WRONG pair.**

    (a)  Soybean and honey

    (b)  Egg and salt          **[2020]**

    (c)  Curd and rice

    (d)  Chapati and chicken

55. **Amrita is spending her holidays in Assam. She noticed that many houses there are raised on wooden poles. What can be the reason for this?**

    **[2020]**

    (a)  Such houses are temporary and can be moved from one place to another.

    (b)  Such houses are fire proof.

    (c)  Such houses are built to collect water in drought prone areas.

    (d)  Such houses are safe in areas where it rains a lot and which are flood prone.

56. **Refer to the given word chop table. Select the boxes that will give answer to the following questions.** **[2021]**

    (a) Name of a temporary house.

    (b) Name of a fabric made from fibres obtained from stem of a plant.

| 1 BUN | 2 CO | 3 LI |
|---|---|---|
| 4 FL | 5 NEN | 6 TE |
| 7 TT | 8 GAL | 9 ON |
| 10 AT | 11 NT | 12 OW |

|     | (a)        | (b)     |
|-----|------------|---------|
| (a) | 1, 8, 12   | 3. 5    |
| (b) | 6, 11      | 3, 5    |
| (c) | 4, 10      | 2, 7, 9 |
| (d) | 6. 11      | 2, 7, 9 |

## RESPONSE GRID

### LEVEL 1

| | | | | |
|---|---|---|---|---|
| 1. a b c d | 2. a b c d | 3. a b c d | 4. a b c d | 5. a b c d |
| 6. a b c d | 7. a b c d | 8. a b c d | 9. a b c d | 10. a b c d |
| 11. a b c d | 12. a b c d | 13. a b c d | 14. a b c d | 15. a b c d |
| 16. a b c d | 17. a b c d | 18. a b c d | 19. a b c d | 20. a b c d |
| 21. a b c d | 22. a b c d | 23. a b c d | 24. a b c d | 25. a b c d |
| 26. a b c d | 27. a b c d | 28. a b c d | 29. a b c d | 30. a b c d |
| 31. a b c d | 32. a b c d | 33. a b c d | 34. a b c d | 35. a b c d |
| 36. a b c d | 37. a b c d | 38. a b c d | 39. a b c d | 40. a b c d |

41. a b c d   42. a b c d   43. a b c d   44. a b c d   45. a b c d
46. a b c d   47. a b c d   48. a b c d   49. a b c d   50. a b c d
51. a b c d   52. a b c d   53. a b c d   54. a b c d   55. a b c d
56. a b c d

## LEVEL 2

1. a b c d   2. a b c d   3. a b c d   4. a b c d   5. a b c d
6. a b c d   7. a b c d   8. a b c d   9. a b c d   10. a b c d
11. a b c d   12. a b c d   13. a b c d   14. a b c d   15. a b c d
16. a b c d   17. a b c d   18. a b c d   19. a b c d   20. a b c d
21. a b c d   22. a b c d   23. a b c d   24. a b c d   25. a b c d
26. a b c d   27. a b c d   28. a b c d   29. a b c d   30. a b c d
31. a b c d   32. a b c d   33. a b c d   34. a b c d   35. a b c d
36. a b c d   37. a b c d   38. a b c d   39. a b c d   40. a b c d
41. a b c d   42. a b c d   43. a b c d   44. a b c d   45. a b c d
46. a b c d   47. a b c d   48. a b c d   49. a b c d   50. a b c d
51. a b c d   52. a b c d   53. a b c d   54. a b c d   55. a b c d
56. a b c d

# Answers with Explanations

## LEVEL 1

1. **(a)** Meat is a body building food.
2. **(c)** Cheese is made up of milk.
3. **(d)** All these are protective food.
4. **(a)** Egg comes from hen.
5. **(d)** Types of cloth we wear depends on both climate and occasion
6. **(b)** Fruits are protective food.
7. **(c)** An Eskimo lives in an Igloo.
8. **(b)** We get nuts from plants.
9. **(a)** Igloo is made up of ice.
10. **(c)** You will not find playground in a house.
11. **(b)** A hut is a kutcha house.
12. **(b)** Men do not wear Saree.
13. **(a)** Caravans can be easily moved from place to place.

14. **(b)** An igloo is a dome shaped house.
15. **(c)** Hut is not present in cities.
16. **(d)** All these materials are used to decorate houses.
17. **(b)** People living in plains usually make a house with flat roof.
18. **(d)** Women wear saree, salwar-kameez and skirt. Igloo is a place to live in.
19. **(d)** All these can be eaten without cooking.
20. **(c)** Roof of a house can be flat, sloping and semi circular.
21. **(d)** Fruits and vegetables are protective food that protects us from disease.
22. **(d)** All of these are energy giving food.

23. (c) An apartment has many houses in it.

24. (b) Rice can be eaten only after cooking.

25. (d) Houses built with stones, bricks and cement are called a pucca house.

26. (c) Butter, paranthas and jaggery are rich in carbohydrates and fats and thus, are energy-giving foods.

27. (d) Caravan is a house on wheels.

28. (c) Woollen clothes are best suited during winter season.

29. (c) Our house keeps us safe from heat, cold and rain.

30. (d) Tent houses are made of canvas.

31. (c) Mud house roofs are made of straw or palm leaves.

32. (c) Foods with lots of sugar and starch are rich in carbohydrates. For example wheat, rice and potatoes.

33. (c) Kutccha house and pucca house are two types of permanent houses. Bungalow is a pucca house while hut is a kutccha house. Stilt house can be a kutccha or pucca house. Igloo caravan and tent are temporary houses.

34. (b) Kind of roof depends on weather, climate and availability of material.

35. (b) A multistory building with many housing units is called apartment.

36. (a) Caravans and house boats are temporary houses.

37. (b) Fruits in option A, C and D are apple, lemon and muskmelon, respectively. Option B is an orange, which is juicy, sweet and sour in taste and rich in vitamin C. Option 'C' is lemon, although it is juicy and sour and is rich in vitamin C, but it is not sweet. Hence, Shweta should bring orange.

38. (b) The correct option is multistorey-apartment, mobile house-caravan, semicircular roofs-igloo, sloping roofs-houses in the hills.

39. (d) Doors and window should be fitted with wire-mesh to keep flies and mosquitoes away. It also allows fresh air and sunlight to enter in the house. Sunlight kills germ and we get fresh and clean air to breathe.

40. (c) Cotton clothes absorb sweat easily.

41. (b) Huts are made of wood, bamboo and mud.

42. (b) Houses in the plains have flat roofs.

43. (c) Eskimos live in igloos.

44. (b) Mountain climbers move from one place to another and so, they often carry tents to have shelter and take rest.

45. (b) Eskimos, who live in very cold places like polar regions make houses of snow, which are called igloos. An igloo keeps them warm because snow is a bad conductor of heat.

46. (d) Egg, option (d) is rich source of protein and is referred to as body-building food. It helps to build our muscles and bones. Butter, french-fries and biscuits can be grouped into energy giving foods.

47. (c) Butter is an body building food. Protective foods are fruits and vegetables.

48. (b) The type of temporary house shown in the picture can be seen in Kashmir. It is known as house boat.

49. (b) People build dams to stop flooding.

50. (a) The picture (a) is of burger. It is a junk food.

51. (b) Banana is an energy giving food. Rohan should eat bananas for instant energy.

**52.** **(d)** We should eat healthy to keep our bones and muscles healthy. Eating healthy means eating fruits and vegetables more and no junk food.

**53.** **(d)**

**54.** **(c)** Chapati is a vegetarian food.

**55.** **(a)** Bungalow

**56.** **(d)**

## LEVEL 2

**1.** **(c)** Fish is body building food.

**2.** **(b)** We should eat proteins, minerals, vitamins and carbohydrates also. Eating vegetable is good for our health.

**3.** **(c)** Milk is a complete food. Milk helps us to grow. Milk gives us energy. Milk protect us from diseases. A small baby drinks only milk.

**4.** **(b)** A house should not have flies and mosquitoes.

**5.** **(b)** We get orange from plant, sugar from sugarcane, milk from cow, fish from river.

**6.** **(a)** Food gives us energy and helps us to grow. Apple can be eaten row ; we should live in clean house; we should eat fruits and vegetables daily.

**7.** **(d)** Clothes protect us from rain, dust and cold.

**8.** **(a)** Hut is made up of mud. Apartment is made up of bricks. Tent is made up of cloth. Igloo is made up of ice.

**9.** **(b)** Cotton is obtained from cotton plant.

**10.** **(a)** Designs

**11.** **(b)** Occasion

**12.** **(c)** Cotton

**13.** **(b)** Wool

**14.** **(a)** Uniform

**15.** **(a)** Sports wear

**16.** **(c)** Identify

**17.** **(a)** Night dress

**18.** **(c)** Gypsies are nomads. Nomads move from one place to another. They live in caravans.

**19.** **(a)** Nutrients

**20.** **(d)** All of these contain carbohydrates

**21.** **(d)** All of these are provided to the human body from food.

**22.** **(d)** We get minerals and vitamins from fruits and vegetables.

**23.** **(a)** Eggs are rich in protein.

**24.** **(b)** People who do special jobs and school students wear uniforms.

**25.** **(d)** Both (a) and (b).

**26.** **(c)** Woollen clothes provide warmth to the body.

**27.** **(c)** Huts are present in villages.

**28.** **(a)** Lehenga is a party wear dress, we wear cotton clothes in summer, coat and tie are professional clothes, we wear sweater in winters.

**29.** **(b)** Kutccha house – Made of bamboo, mud, straw, leaves.

Pucca house – Made of wood, bricks, cement, steel.

Igloo – Made of snow

Caravan – Made on wheels

**30.** **(d)** All of these are necessary to keep our house clean and free from germs.

**31.** **(c)** Carbohydrates and fats are the energy giving food. Proteins are the body building food. Vitamins and minerals protect us from diseases. From the food shown in the figures, food L (dal, egg, milk and meat) is food of proteins and, thus helps us to grow. Food N (fruits and vegetables) is full of vitamins, minerals and roughage.

Vitamins and minerals prevent us from falling sick and roughage helps in digestion. Food M (butter, bread, rice, chapati) is rich in carbohydrates and fats and, thus gives us the most energy.

**32. (d)** Caravan and tent can be moved from one place to another.

**33. (a)** Food, clothes and shelter are the basic necessities of our life.

**34. (b)** Rajma seeds are pulses while cashew, almond and walnut are nuts.

**35. (c)** 1. SKIRT    2. VEST    3. KURTA
4. SHIRT    5. SAREE

**36. (b)** Rice is a carbohydrate rich, thus energy giving food. Egg is a protein rich, thus body building food. Nuts are rich in vitamins and minerals and thus are grouped under protective foods.

**37. (d)** To change dirty clothes, wash hands before eating food and change into night dress before sleeping.

**38. (b)** Protective foods gives us strength to fight disease.

**39. (b)** Rangoli is made of flowers and colours.

**40. (c)** Clothes protect us from heat, cold, dust and rain.

**41. (c)** We get wool fibre from the fleece of sheep.

**42. (d)** During the rainy season, we need to keep our body dry, we should wear a rain-coat and carry an umbrella.

**43. (c)** We get silk fibres from silkworms.

**44. (d)** Only kutccha houses like the hut are made of mud.

**45. (b)** Cotton clothes absorb sweat easily.

**46. (a)** Woollen clothes protect us from cold.

**47. (b)** A rain-coat is made of a water proof material. A raincoat should be worn during rains to keep us dry.

**48. (c)** Silk fibre is obtained from the cocoons of silkworms.

**49. (b)** Cotton clothes absorb sweat easily and keep the body cool. Cotton clothes are preferred during summer season.

**50. (a)** Clothes are made from fibres.

**51. (b)** Pea and gram are both pulses. Wheat and rice are grains; tomato is a fruit and mango has one seed.

**52. (a)** Ayush is a weak boy and easily falls ill, so he needs protective foods (which protect us from falling ill) and body building foods (which help to grow and make bones and muscles strong). He should eat food 1 and food 2, as food 1 contains fruits and vegetables (protective food) and food 2 contains milk, eggs, cheese and pulses, a source of body building food. His brother should take food 2, in order to build strong muscles.

**53. (b)** As Amol wants to become a sports person, he must eat protein rich, body-building food items that would help him to build his bones and muscles. So, he must include body-building foods like yoghurt, eggs and pulses in his diet.

**54. (b)** Soyabean, rice, chapati are plant products while honey, curd, chicken are animal products. Salt is neither obtained from plants nor from animals.

**55. (d)** In Assam, houses are raised on wooden poles to prevent water from entering the houses during floods.

**56. (b)** (a) – 6, 11 (TENT); (b) – 3, 5 (LINEN)

# 10 CHAPTER FOREWORD

Can you see air? No, you can't see, you can only feel it. It is all around us. We can't even breathe without air. So, air is very important for us. Do you know the taste of water? It is tasteless. Water is essential for life. Water helps us in cooking food, cleaning the house and washing clothes. In which season we wear woollen clothes? We wear woollen clothes in winter to protect ourselves from chilly breeze.

**Now, answer the following questions.**

1. We get water from

    (a) Rain        (b) Oceans        (c) Rivers        (d) All of these

2. Match the clothes to their related seasons.

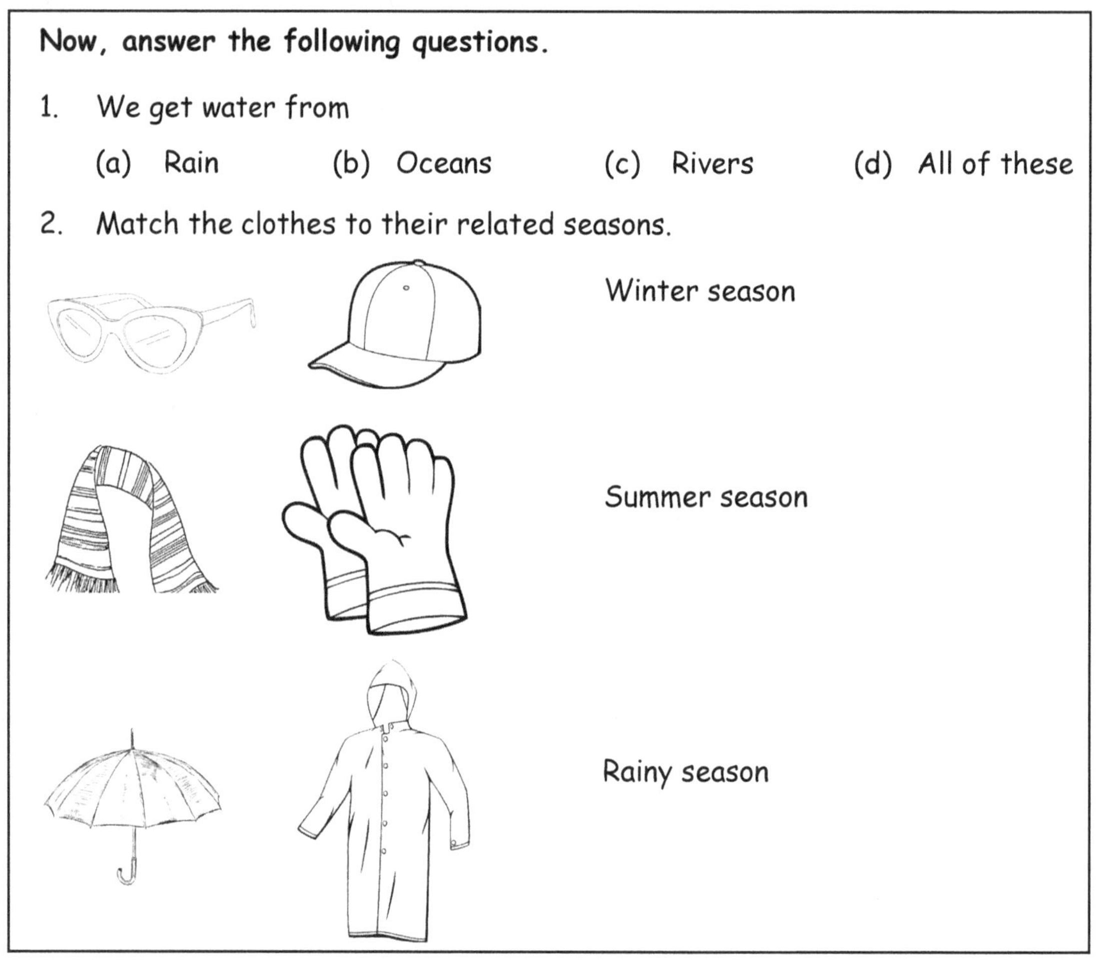


After reading this chapter, you will learn about the sources and forms of water, air and its constituents and different seasons.

# 10
## Chapter

# Air, Water and Weather



## LEARNING OBJECTIVES

**This lesson will help you to:**

- ❖ study about air and its constituents.
- ❖ know the importance of air.
- ❖ learn about the sources and forms of water.

## INTRODUCTION

In the previous class, we have studied that air is necessary for our life. Air is present all around us. Air occupies space, it has weight and it cannot be seen, only we can feel it. It gives shape to things. Let us study the components of air.

> **Do you know?**
>
> ❖ Air contains 78% nitrogen, 21% oxygen and 1% other gases which contain carbon dioxide and water vapour.

## AIR AS A MIXTURE OF GASES

Air is not man-made. It is a natural resource, and it is present everywhere. It cannot be seen, and it is not exhaustible. Air is very important for the living things because without air a living organism will die. This is the reason why air is called invisible friend of living organisms. Air is necessary for burning. Air is not a single component. In-fact, it is a mixture of different gases like nitrogen, oxygen, carbon dioxide, hydrogen, argon, neon, helium, krypton, xenon and radon.

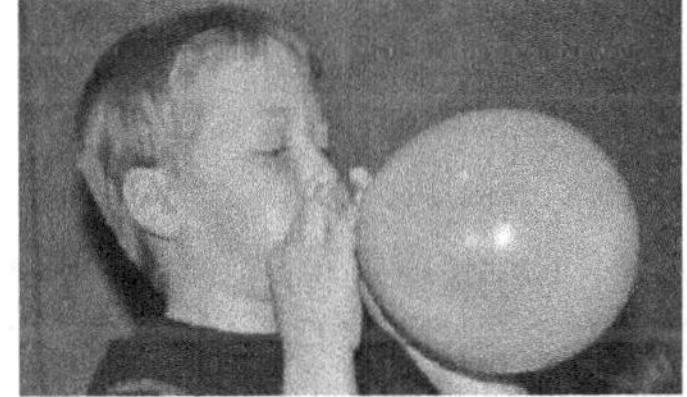

## TYPES OF WIND

Fast movement of air is called wind. There are mainly two types of wind depending on its motion.

1. Global Wind
2. Local Wind

**1. Global Wind**

Global winds are the large movements of air that happen all over the world because of the following reasons :

- The rotation of the earth.
- The movement of the earth around the sun.
- Because of the round shape of the earth.

2. **Local Wind**

   Every region has their own type of winds. These winds are limited to that particular area and caused by temperature difference. They can move up, down and horizontal. Mountain areas are good example of such kind of winds. In these areas, wind blows against the mountain and is forced to go up. Because wind is usually going into one direction, the other side of the mountain almost does not have any wind.

## OTHER GENERAL CLASSIFICATION OF WIND

### Breeze

It is a light, pleasant air, and not very fast moving air. Motion of air from sea to land is called **sea breeze** and land to sea is called **land breeze.**

Sea Breeze

Land Breeze

### Storm

Storm is a strong wind and it contains, dust particles, snow and rain. Therefore, a storm may be categorized as dust storm, snowstorm and rainstorm. This type of wind can have a circular motion also. Cyclone is the perfect example of circular storm. This kind of wind may cause damages to trees, houses and other things.

### Cold Wave

Movement of cold air in winter is called **cold wave.** This is not a pleasant wind and harmful for living organisms. It may cause cold related diseases.

### Heat Wave

Movement of hot air in summer is called **heat wave.** This is not a pleasant wind and may cause summer related diseases.

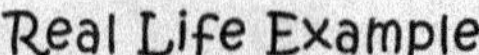

### Uses of Wind

The following are the uses of wind :

- It is very important for living things as they inhale air to be alive. The living things inhale oxygen and exhale carbon dioxide. While plants inhale carbon dioxide and exhale oxygen.
- It is very important for the growth of plants.
- Fresh and cool air is needed for living things to be energetic and active.
- Fresh and natural air makes a good environment.
- It is used for electricity generation.
- In the gas form, it is used for cooking.
- In the gas form, it is used as a fuel for mode of transportations like buses and cars.
- Wind is used to fill in balloons, football, wheels of buses, cars, cycle and motorcycles.

## GERMS IN AIR

Germs are very small or tiny organisms that can cause disease. They are so small that they creep into our bodies without being noticed and cause troubles. Germs in the air take birth because of the air pollution.

**The following are the reasons for germs or airborne germs in air:**

- Various kinds of smokes from industries and vehicles.
- Garbage and filthy materials at improper places.
- Excretions of living organisms at open spaces.
- Any kind of unpleasant smells.
- Living organisms carry various germs through sneeze and breath.

**Pollution** means contamination that causes harm to humans and other living organisms. Various kind of pollutions are given below :

### Air Pollution :

Air get contaminated in such type of pollution because of the following :

- Various kind of smokes from industry, vehicles and other things.
- Excretion of living organisms at improper places.
- Filthy and garbage materials lying at improper places.
- Sneeze and breath living organisms carry diseases.

## WATER

We all need water. Water is required for drinking, bathing, cooking and washing. Plants and animals need water. But do you know, where water comes from?

We get water from rain. Rainwater gets collected in oceans, river, ponds, lake and ground water. Water has no fixed shape. It can take the shape of a vessel in which it is kept.

## FORMS OF WATER

Have you noticed when water is heated in a kettle, steam comes out of it? Steam is a water vapour.

Water is found in three forms. Solid (ice), liquid (water) and gas (water vapour).

The process of changing the water into water vapour is known as **evaporation**.

When water vapour gets cooled, it becomes liquid (water). This process is called **condensation**.

When water is cooled, it becomes ice. This process is known as **freezing**.

## WATER CYCLE

In this cycle, water from oceans, lakes and rivers is converted into water vapour. Water vapour condenses into tiny droplets to form clouds. Clouds lose their water as rain or snow.

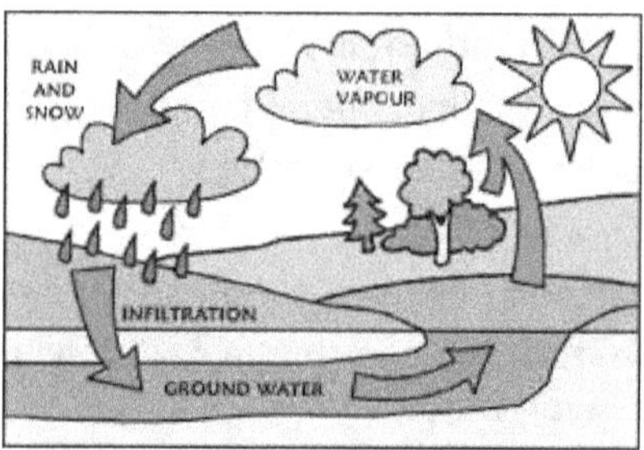


## WATER POLLUTION

Water bodies (seas, oceans, rivers, lakes ponds and ground water) get contaminated when:
- Garbage and dirty materials are thrown into the rivers, ponds and lakes.
- Industrial wastes and chemicals get mixed into the water of rivers, ponds, seas and lakes.
- Detergents are used while washing clothes and taking bath into rivers, lakes and ponds.
- Dead bodies of water animals cause water pollution.

## WEATHER

Has it happened with you that you were out on a sunny day and suddenly it started raining? Who caused this change in weather?

Weather of a place is influenced by the condition of air and the quantity of water available in the atmosphere.

Weather is the condition of atmosphere at a particular time in terms of temperature, pressure, wind and moisture. The weather can be hot, cold, windy, dry or humid. Depending on the weather, there are 5 seasons in India.

## 1. SUMMER SEASON

This is a hot season. Summer stays from April to June. Heat waves are common in this season. Therefore, light and cotton clothes are the most favourable clothes in the summer season.

Summer Season

## 2. RAINY SEASON (MONSOON)

Monsoon season comes after summer and it stays from July to August. This season is necessary for agriculture because plants and crops need water to grow.

Rainy Season

## 3. AUTUMN SEASON

Autumn comes after monsoon. In this season, trees shed their leaves. Temperature is neither too hot nor too cold.

Autumn Season

## 4. WINTER SEASON

The months of November, December and January is the time of winter when the temperature is very low and the atmosphere is cold. This is the season when people wear woollen and warm clothes.

Winter Season

## 5. SPRING SEASON

This is the most pleasant season of the year. Because this is the season of moderate temperature when atmosphere is neither extreme cold nor extreme hot. This season stays from February to March.

Spring Season

# Multiple Choice Questions
## LEVEL 1

1.  Which of the following is present all around us and cannot be seen?
    (a)  Food          (b)  Paper          (c)  Air          (d)  Ice

2.  Which of the following activity/activities need/s water?          [2012]
    (a)  Drinking      (b)  Bathing        (c)  Cooking       (d)  All of these

3.  Choose odd one out.          [Tricky]
    (a)  Kite          (b)  Airplane       (c)  Bird          (d)  Boat

4.  Which of the following is not a form of water?
    (a)  Ice           (b)  Oil            (c)  Water vapour  (d)  Steam

5.  Which of the following is present in liquid form?          [2013, Tricky]
    (a)  Milk          (b)  Pulses         (c)  Egg           (d)  Plant

6.  Which of the following process changes water into water vapour?          [Tricky]
    (a)  Melting       (b)  Cooling        (c)  Heating       (d)  None

7.  Which of the following is not a source of water?          [2014]
    (a)  Pond          (b)  Lake           (c)  Rain          (d)  Desert

8.  Wet clothes dry under the sun. This is an example of _________ .
    (a)  Melting       (b)  Evaporation    (c)  Boiling       (d)  Condensation

9.  A windmill needs which of the following to rotate?          [2014]
    (a)  Air           (b)  Gas            (c)  Water         (d)  Rain

10. Which of the following name is given for gentle wind?
    (a)  Rain          (b)  Storm          (c)  Breeze        (d)  Air

11. Windmills are used to          [2015]
    (a)  Pump water                        (b)  Produce electricity
    (c)  Grind gains                       (d)  All of the above

12. Air occupies space and has _________ .
    (a)  Weight                            (b)  Force
    (c)  Temperature                       (d)  Both (a) and (b)

13. Which of these activity/activities needs wind?          [2016, Tricky]

    (a)                                    (b)

    (c)                                    (d)  All of the above

14. **Which of the following does not have definite shape?** [Tricky]
    (a) Book  (b) Ice  (c) Smoke  (d) Water bottle

15. **Fast and strong winds are called** [2016]
    (a) Breeze  (b) Storm  (c) Wind  (d) Earthquake

16. **Which of the following process changes water vapour into water by cooling?** [Tricky]
    (a) Melting  (b) Condensation  (c) Boiling  (d) Freezing

17. **Which of the following is NOT a property of air?** [2017, Tricky]
    (a) Air fills space  (b) Air has weight
    (c) Air gives shapes to things  (d) Air can be seen

18. **Which of the following activity makes air unclean?** [Tricky]
    (a) Smoke from automobiles  (b) Washing clothes
    (c) Watering plants  (d) Boiling milk

19. **Which of the following is the main source of heat and light on earth?**
    (a) Earth  (b) Moon  (c) Sun  (d) None

20. **Weather depends on which of the following factor/s?**
    (a) Sun  (b) Wind  (c) Rain  (d) All of these

21. **Choose odd one out:** [Tricky]
    (a) Summers  (b) Monsoons  (c) Winters  (d) Evaporation

22. **Which of the following thing we do not use in summers?**
    (a) Cooler  (b) Ice-cream  (c) Blanket  (d) Fan

23. **The given pictures show ____________.** [2012]

    (a) Summer season  (b) Winter season
    (c) Autumn season  (c) Both (a) and (b)

24. **Which of the following is not present in the air?**
    (a) Germs  (b) Smoke  (c) Dust  (d) Ice

25. **Cloud : Rain :: Water : ________** [Tricky]
    (a) Ice  (b) Chocolate  (c) Wood  (d) Oil

26. **The picture given below shows a girl blowing air into a balloon. Air has**
    [Critical Thinking]

    (a) Weight and occupies space

    (b) Water and water vapour

    (c) Water and germs

    (d) Water vapour and dust

27. A student carried out an experiment as shown in the figure given below.

[Critical Thinking]

Which is the best conclusion drawn from the above experiment?

(a) Air moves things
(b) Air is needed for burning
(c) Air occupies space
(d) Air has weight

28. The diagram below illustrates the water cycle.

[Tricky]

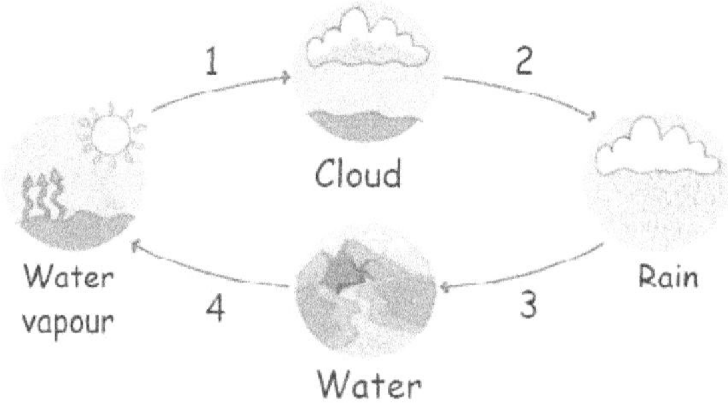


Which arrow represents the gaseous form of water?

(a) 1 and 3
(b) 2 and 4
(c) 2 and 1
(d) 4 and 1

29. In the given figure, which of the following is provided to the plants?

(a) Air
(b) Water
(c) Food
(d) Sunlight

30. In which of the following season, weather is neither hot nor cold?  [2013]

(a) Spring
(b) Winter
(c) Summer
(d) Monsoon

31. Which of the following processes in the given figure of water cycle is responsible for drying of wet clothes?  [2018]

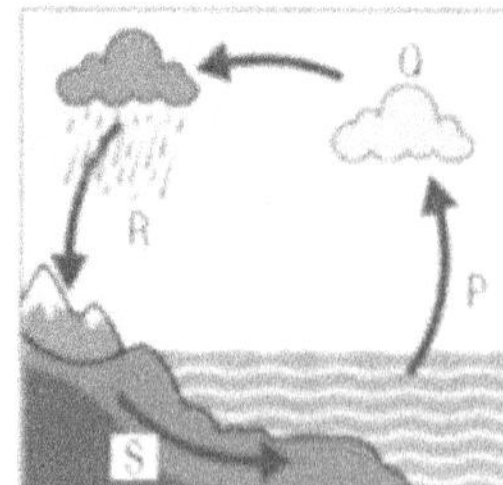


(a) Q
(b) R
(c) P
(d) S

**32.** What will happen to the water in the pot if left over the campfire ?  [2018]

(a)   The water will turn into a liquid  (b)   The water will turn into ashes

(c)   The water will turn into a gas  (d)   The water will turn into a solid

**33.** Which of these weather conditions caused the corn field to look as shown in the picture ?  [2018]

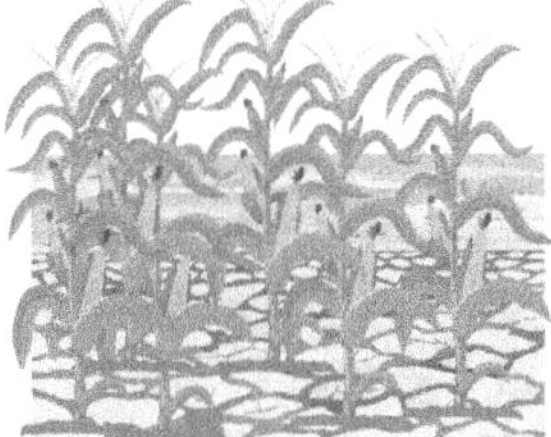

(a)   A tornado  (b)   A flood  (c)   A drought  (d)   A snowstorm

**34.** Shreya filled some water in a glass tumbler as shown. Her friends Swati, Sumit and Rati saw this and made following statements.  [2018]

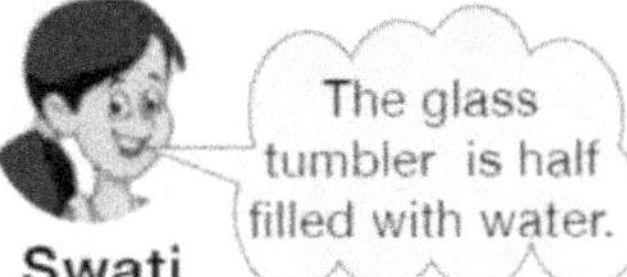

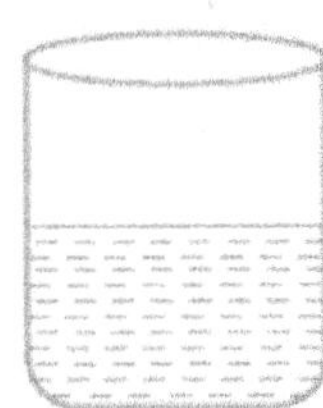

Who among them made the correct statement?

(a)   Rati only  (b)   Sumit only

(c)   Swati and Rati only  (d)   Swati and Sumit only

**35.** Which of the following ways of travelling pollutes the air the least ?  [2019]

(a)   Riding the bus  (b)   Riding a car

(c)   Riding an airplane  (d)   Riding a bike

**36.** Refer to the given weather forecast report for 30ᵗʰ November. Which of the following is most suitable to be worn on this day?    [2020]
    (a) Cotton shirt         (b) Woollen sweater
    (c) Silk saree         (d) Shorts

**37.** _______ causes day and night on Earth.    [2020]
    (a) Earth's tilt on its axis
    (b) Rotation of Earth on its axis
    (c) Revolution of Earth in its orbit
    (d) Revolution of Moon around the Earth

**38.** The given picture represents water cycle. Which of the labelled parts represents processes : (A) condensation and (B) evaporation?    [2020]
    (a) (A) - 1; (B) - 4
    (b) (A) - 1; (B) - 3
    (c) (A) - 2; (B) - 4
    (d) (A) - 2; (B) - 1

**39.** Select the correct match from the following.
    (a) Valley      –     Small low mountain    [2020]
    (b) Pond      –     Still water
    (c) Plateau      –     Piece of land surrounded by water on all sides
    (d) Ocean      –     Freshwater

**40.** The given figure proves that __________.    [2020]
    (a) Air gives shape to things

    (b) Air helps to move things

    (c) Air has weight

    (d) Air helps in burning

**41.** From which of the following sources of water, underground water is obtained?
    (a) Ocean     (b) Sea     (c) Tubewell     (d) River   [2021]

**42.** Which of the following is also known as a blue planet?    [2021]
    (a) Mercury     (b) Venus     (c) Jupiter     (d) Earth

**43.** What does the given activity show?    [2022]
    (a) Air fills up space.
    (b) Air is present all around us.
    (c) Air has weight.
    (d) Air is needed for burning.

**44.** Which of the given statements is NOT correct for water?    [2022]
    (a) Water helps to digest our food.
    (b) Water helps to keep our body cool.
    (c) Water helps to flush out wastes from our body.
    (d) None of these

**45.** Select the correct match from the following.  [2022]

(a) Valley       –    Small low mountain

(b) Pond      –    Still water

(c) Plateau      –    Land surrounded by water on all sides

(d) Ocean      –    Feshwater

**46.** When the wind blows gently, it is called __________.  [2022]

(a) storm     (b) air     (c) breeze     (d) water

**47.** How many planets are there in our solar system?  [2022]

(a) 1     (b) 5     (c) 8     (d) 12

**48.** In the picture shown below, there is/are:  [2022]

(a) two stars

(b) two planets

(c) two moons

(d) a planet and a star

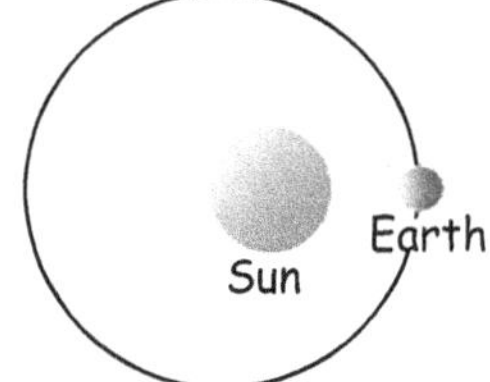


## LEVEL 2

**1.** Which of the following picture represents water cycle?  [Critical Thinking]

(a) Clouds → Water Vapour → Sea → Rain → Clouds

(b) Sea → Water Vapour → Rain → Clouds → Sea

(c) Clouds → Rain → Sea → Water Vapour → Clouds

(d) Rain → Clouds → Sea → Water Vapour → Rain

**2.** Match the list I with the list II.  [2012, Tricky]

| | List I | | List II |
|---|---|---|---|
| A | 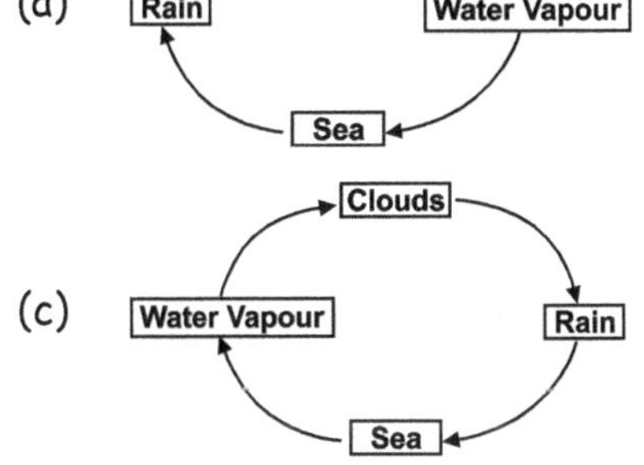 | 1 | Summer |
| B | 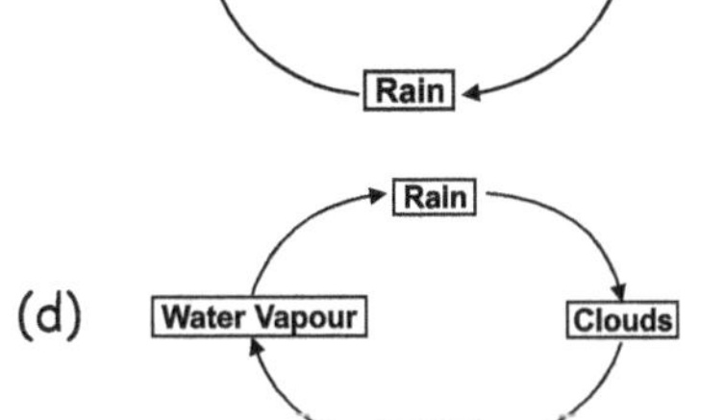 | 2. | Winter |

| | | | |
|---|---|---|---|
| C | | 3. | Monsoon |
| D | | 4. | Autumn |

|  | A | B | C | D |  |  | A | B | C | D |
|---|---|---|---|---|---|---|---|---|---|---|
| (a) | 3 | 1 | 2 | 4 | | (b) | 1 | 2 | 3 | 4 |
| (c) | 4 | 3 | 2 | 1 | | (d) | 1 | 4 | 2 | 3 |

**Directions (Qs. 3 to 12): Read the passage carefully and fill the blanks in the passage given below.** **[Tricky]**

Air is necessary for all _________ (3) _________ things. It is present _________ (4) _________. It occupies _________ (5) _________ and has _________ (6) _________. It gives _________ (7) _________ to things. We must breathe _________ (8) _________ air. We should keep our doors and _________ (9) _________ open for fresh air. Dirty air is bad for health and make us _________ (10) _________. Moving air is called _________ (11) _________. A gentle wind is known as _________ (12) _________.

| | | | | | | | | |
|---|---|---|---|---|---|---|---|---|
| **3.** | (a) | living | (b) | non-living | (c) | liquid | (d) | solid |
| **4.** | (a) | nowhere | (b) | everywhere | (c) | in kitchen | (d) | in garden |
| **5.** | (a) | earth | (b) | sun | (c) | space | (d) | light |
| **6.** | (a) | direction | (b) | shape | (c) | height | (d) | weight |
| **7.** | (a) | shape | (b) | colour | (c) | smell | (d) | taste |
| **8.** | (a) | dirty | (b) | fast | (c) | slow | (d) | fresh |
| **9.** | (a) | windows | (b) | mouth | (c) | lungs | (d) | none |
| **10.** | (a) | fit | (b) | ill | (c) | healthy | (d) | strong |
| **11.** | (a) | wind | (b) | breeze | (c) | storm | (d) | none |
| **12.** | (a) | storm | (b) | breeze | (c) | windmill | (d) | speed |

**Directions (Qs. 13 to 14): Read the passage carefully and answer the following questions.**
**[Critical Thinking]**

What we eat, drink, and types of clothes we wear depend on weather. In summers, we like to drink something cold and in winters, we like to drink something hot. Fruits like mango, litchi and watermelon are there in summer. In winter we get fruit like oranges, grapes, apples and guavas. Carrot, cabbage, peas and radish are winter vegetables. Cucumber, pumpkin and bottle gourd are summer vegetables.

**13.** **Read the following statements and answer the question?** **[2013, Tricky]**

**Statement 1:** Wind is the movement of air.

**Statement 2:** Monsoon comes after summer and it stays from July to August.

(a)   Both Statement 1 and Statement 2 are false.

(b)   Both Statement 1 and Statement 2 are true.

(c)   Statement 1 is true and Statement 2 is false.

(d)   Statement 1 is false and Statement 2 is true

14.   **Weather depends upon ________.**                                    **[Critical Thinking]**

(a)   Food we eat                          (b)   Clothes we wear

(c)   Milk we drink                        (d)   None of these

15.   **Read the following sentences carefully and find true and false. (T/F)**        **[2014]**

(a)   In autumn season trees shed their leaves.

(b)   Condensation changes water vapour into water.

(c)   Rain-water is drinking water.

(a)   FFT              (b)   TTF              (c)   FTF              (D)   TTT

16.   **Which of the following is not a winter fruit?**

(a)   Grapes          (b)   Guava          (c)   Apple          (d)   Watermelon

17.   **After reading the weather forecast in the newspaper today, Sunidhi and her mother went out with an umbrella and gumboots. What may be the weather forecast symbol in the newspaper?**        **[2015]**

(a)                  (b)                  (c)                  (d)

18.   **Look at the pictures given below:**                              **[2014, Tricky]**

(A)                  (B)                  (C)

(Kite is flying)        (Birds flying)        (Windmill rotating)

Which is the common thing they all need?

(a)   Rain            (b)   Air            (c)   Water            (d)   Wings

19.   **Which of the following cause/s water pollution?**                      **[Tricky]**

(i)    Garbage thrown in rivers and lakes.

(ii)   Dead bodies of water animals.

(iii)  Movement of air.

(iv)   Factory wastes released into water.

(a)   Both (i) and (ii)                    (b)   (ii) and (iv)

(c)   (i), (ii) and (iv)                    (d)   All of the above

**20.** What does the following figure represents? [2015]

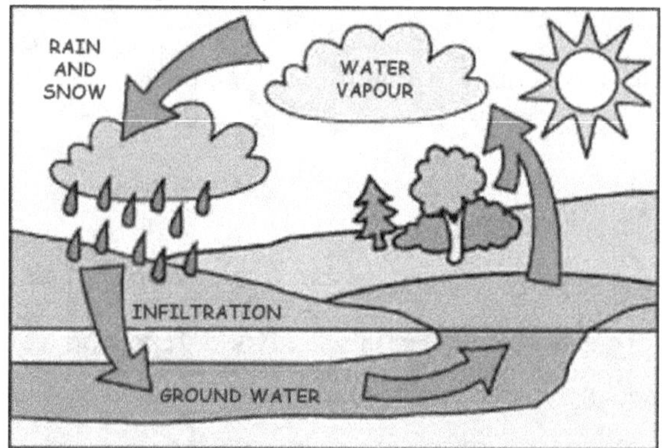


(a) Path of germs in air  (b) Water cycle

(c) Storm  (d) Formation of clouds

**21.** Akhil is a farmer's son, he gives water to the crops everyday with his father. But, his crops are not healthy. They use water from the nearby river. His mother washes clothes in the same river and throws all the waste of her house into it. What will you suggest to Akhil's family for the good growth of their crops?

(a) They should stop throwing garbage into the river.

(b) His mother should not wash clothes in the river as detergent pollutes water.

(c) His father should use good fertilizers and clean water for crops.

(d) All of the above.

**22.** Which of the following is a feature of summer season? [2016, Tricky]

(a) In summer season we go to hill stations.

(b) It stays from April to June.

(c) We wear cotton clothes in this season.

(d) All of the above.

**23.** Which of the following statement is false. [Tricky]

(a) Wind has speed and exerts pressure.

(b) Air contains dust, smoke and germs.

(c) We must breathe in fresh air.

(d) Dirty air is good for health.

**24.** The heat of the sun changes water into _____________? [2016]

(a) Smoke  (b) Air  (c) Gas  (d) Water vapour

**25.** What happens when you keep a bowl of water on the gas stove? [Tricky]

(a) Water turns into steam  (b) Water turns into ice

(c) No change in water  (d) None of the above

**26.** Which of the following give/s out smoke on burning? [2017, Tricky]

(a) Wood  (b) Plastic  (c) Garbage  (d) All of these

**27.** Which of the following statement is wrong about evaporation?    [Tricky]

    (a)    Evaporation turns water into water vapour.

    (b)    Evaporation takes place on heating.

    (c)    It transfers water from land to the air.

    (d)    Evaporation is the cooling of air.

**28.** Water drops fall from the clouds as rain. Where does rain-water go?    [2015]

    1.    It is absorbed into the soil

    2.    It collects in the oceans and rivers.

    3.    It collects in the ponds and reservoirs.

    (a)   1 only     (b)   2 only     (c)   1 and 3 only     (d)   1, 2 and 3

**29.** What does the given picture show?    [2012]

    (a)    The car is getting dirty.

    (b)    The air is getting dirty.

    (c)    The water is getting dirty.

    (d)    All of the above.

**30.** During which of the following season we eat ice cream?

    (a)    Rainy           (b)    Spring

    (c)    Summer        (d)    Autumn

**31.** Rajat read the weather forecast of the coming week as shown below.    [2013]
Which of these items will be used best by him in such weather?

| Monday | Tuesday | Wednesday | Thursday | Friday |
|---|---|---|---|---|
| | | | | |

    (a)    Umbrella, raincoat and woollen socks
    (b)    Sunglasses, gumboots and woollen gloves
    (c)    Raincoat, umbrella, gumboots
    (d)    Heaters, quilts, sunglasses

**32.** Which of the following is an/the effect/s of a storm?    [Tricky]

    (a)    Storm uproots trees        (b)    Weak and old building collapse
    (c)    There will be less rain      (d)    Both (a) and (b)

**33.** Solve the crossword given on names of different sources of getting water. Which
of the following words is NOT hidden in the crossword?    [2013]

    (a)    HANDPUMP     (b)    TUBEWELL

    (c)    SNOW           (d)    RIVER

**34.** **What role does sun play in a water cycle?** [Tricky]
 (a) It helps in formation of cloud   (b) It helps in evaporation
 (c) It helps in condensation   (d) Both (a) and (c)

**35.** **A teacher asked her students to write a heading for the given poster.**
 **Amongst these students, which student gave the most appropriate heading for the poster?** [2014]
 (a) Leena  - Save water
 (b) Rohit  - Save Trees
 (c) Meena - Save the Earth
 (d) Rahul  - Save Wild Life

**36.** **Which of the following is the gaseous form of water?**
 (a) Ice   (b) Water vapour   (c) Rock   (d) Evaporation

**37.** **Amayra lives in a place where temperature in December is below 0°C. Water vapours in the air in such places in December fall to the ground as ___________.** [2015]
 (a) Rain drops   (b) Snow flakes   (c) Hailstones   (d) All of these

**38.** **Which of the following is a summer vegetable?**
 (a) Peas   (b) Raddish   (c) Carrot   (d) Bottle gourd

**39.** **Amar is a brilliant student and he loves studies. But during winters he was absent for many days as he was suffering from high fever and cold. As a teacher of Amar what will you suggest his mother?**
 (a) Make him wear proper woollen clothes in winters.
 (b) Take Amar to the doctor.
 (c) Amar should take proper rest and healthy food like soup, fruits and milk.
 (d) All of these.

**40.** **Select the INCORRECT statement regarding water.** [2015]
 (a) Water can exist in three forms, which can be changed into one another.
 (b) River water is salty water.
 (c) Hand pumps can be used to draw underground water.
 (d) None of these

**41.** **Some events are shown in the box.** [2015]
 **Select the correct option regarding them.**
 (a) Events 1 and 2 show that air moves things.
 (b) Events 1 and 3 show that air fills space.
 (c) Events 2 shows that moving air has direction.
 (d) Events 3 shows that air is present all around us.

**42.** **Which of the following is the shape of a screscent Moon?** (2020-21)
 (a)    (b)
 (c)    (d)

43. Read the given table carefully about processes X and Y involved in water cycle.

(2020-21)

|   | Features | Process X | Process Y |
|---|---|---|---|
| 1. | It converts one form of water to another. | ✓ | ✓ |
| 2. | It needs heating. | ✗ | ✓ |
| 3. | It needs cooling. | ✓ | ✗ |

**Select the INCORRECT option regarding processes X and Y.**

(a) In process X, water may change from a gas to a liquid state.

(b) In process Y, water changes from a liquid to a gas state.

(c) Process Y will be slower on a warm day than on a cold day.

(d) An example of process X is may be the formation of drops of water on the outer surface of a glass of ice water.

## RESPONSE GRID

### LEVEL 1

| | | | | |
|---|---|---|---|---|
| 1. a b c d | 2. a b c d | 3. a b c d | 4. a b c d | 5. a b c d |
| 6. a b c d | 7. a b c d | 8. a b c d | 9. a b c d | 10. a b c d |
| 11. a b c d | 12. a b c d | 13. a b c d | 14. a b c d | 15. a b c d |
| 16. a b c d | 17. a b c d | 18. a b c d | 19. a b c d | 20. a b c d |
| 21. a b c d | 22. a b c d | 23. a b c d | 24. a b c d | 25. a b c d |
| 26. a b c d | 27. a b c d | 28. a b c d | 29. a b c d | 30. a b c d |
| 31. a b c d | 32. a b c d | 33. a b c d | 34. a b c d | 35. a b c d |
| 36. a b c d | 37. a b c d | 38. a b c d | 39. a b c d | 40. a b c d |
| 41. a b c d | 42. a b c d | 43. a b c d | 44. a b c d | 45. a b c d |
| 46. a b c d | 47. a b c d | 48. a b c d | | |

### LEVEL 2

| | | | | |
|---|---|---|---|---|
| 1. a b c d | 2. a b c d | 3. a b c d | 4. a b c d | 5. a b c d |
| 6. a b c d | 7. a b c d | 8. a b c d | 9. a b c d | 10. a b c d |
| 11. a b c d | 12. a b c d | 13. a b c d | 14. a b c d | 15. a b c d |
| 16. a b c d | 17. a b c d | 18. a b c d | 19. a b c d | 20. a b c d |
| 21. a b c d | 22. a b c d | 23. a b c d | 24. a b c d | 25. a b c d |
| 26. a b c d | 27. a b c d | 28. a b c d | 29. a b c d | 30. a b c d |
| 31. a b c d | 32. a b c d | 33. a b c d | 34. a b c d | 35. a b c d |
| 36. a b c d | 37. a b c d | 38. a b c d | 39. a b c d | 40. a b c d |
| 41. a b c d | 42. a b c d | 43. a b c d | | |

# Answers with Explanations

## LEVEL 1

1. **(c)** Air is present all around us.
2. **(d)** We need water for drinking, bathing and cooking.
3. **(d)** Kite, airplane and bird fly in the air. Boat floats on water.
4. **(b)** Oil is not a form of water.
5. **(a)** Milk is in liquid form. Pulses, egg and plant are in solid forms.
6. **(c)** Heating changes water into water vapour.
7. **(d)** Desert is not a source of water.
8. **(b)** Evaporation
9. **(a)** Windmill needs air to rotate.
10. **(c)** A gentle wind is called a breeze.
11. **(d)** Windmills generate electricity. They are used to pump water, produce electricity and grind grains.
12. **(a)** Air occupies space and has weight.
13. **(d)** A windmill, a boat and a parachute need air to move.
14. **(c)** Smoke does not have definite shape.
15. **(b)** Fast and strong winds are called storm.
16. **(b)** The condensation changes water vapour into water by cooling.
17. **(d)** Air cannot be seen, but felt.
18. **(a)** Smoke from automobiles makes air unclean.
19. **(c)** Sun is the main source of heat and light on earth.
20. **(d)** The weather depends on the sun, the wind, and the rains.
21. **(d)** Summers, monsoon and winters are seasons. Evaporation is a process.
22. **(c)** We do not use blanket in summers.
23. **(d)** The given pictures show winter season as girl is wearing sweater and snow is falling. It is also showing summer season as people are wearing cotton clothes and eating ice cream.
24. **(d)** Ice is not present in air.
25. **(a)** Cloud gives rain. Water gives ice.
26. **(a)** Air occupies space and has weight.
27. **(b)** The given experiment proves that air is needed for burning.
28. **(d)** Arrows 4 and 1 represent evaporation show gaseous form of water.
29. **(b)** The given figure shows that water is provided to the plants.
30. **(a)** Spring season has a pleasant weather which is neither cold nor heat.
31. **(c)** The clothes are dried due to the process of evaporation. It is a process of water changing water into water vapour.
32. **(c)** The water will turn into a gas due to heating.
33. **(c)** The drought caused the corn field to look as shown. It happens due to shortage of rainfall.
34. **(d)** The glass tumbler is half filled with both water and air. So, Swati and Sumit are correct.
35. **(d)** All the vehicles pollute the environment. Riding bicycle does not pollute environment.
36. **(b)** Woollen sweater is wear in winter season.
37. **(b)** Rotation on Earth on its axis causes day and night on Earth.
38. **(d)**

39. (b) Pond – Still water
40. (b) Air helps to move things.
41. (c) Tubewell
42. (d) Earth
43. (a) Air fills up space.
44. (d) None of these
45. (b) Pond. It is a small body of still water surrounded by land.
46. (c)
47. (c)
48. (d)

## LEVEL 2

1. (c) Picture (c) represents water cycle.
2. (a) Rain comes in monsoon season, days are sunny in summers, we wear cotton clothes as it is sunny in summers, we wear woollen clothes in winter, trees shed their leaves in autumn.
3. (a) Living
4. (b) Every where
5. (c) Space
6. (d) Weight
7. (a) Shape
8. (d) Fresh
9. (a) Windows
10. (b) Ill
11. (a) Wind
12. (b) Breeze
13. (b) Both Statement 1 and Statement 2 are true.
14. (d) Weather depends on none of these.
15. (b) Ground-water is drinking water.
16. (d) Water-melon is a summer fruit.
17. (c) Raincoats, umbrella and gumboots are required on a rainy day to protect ourselves from rain.

Option (C) displaying rain may be the weather forecast symbol in the newspaper for that day.

18. (b) All these activities need air.
19. (c) All these cause water pollution.
20. (b) The given figure represents water cycle.
21. (d) All the statements are correct.
22. (d) All of the above.
23. (d) Dirty air is bad for health.
24. (d) The heat of the sun changes water into water vapours.
25. (a) Water turns into steam due to heat.
26. (d) All of these give out smoke on burning.
27 (d) In water cycle, water from ocean and rivers is converted into water vapour which is evaporation.
28. (d) Rainwater goes deep (absorbed) into the soil. It fills up oceans, rivers, ponds, lakes, streams and reservoirs.
29. (b) The figure shows that air is getting dirty or polluted by burning crackers and tyres and also by the smoke coming out of car.
30. (c) In summer season, we eat icecream.
31. (c) The weather forecast predicts heavy rains on Monday, moderate rains on Tuesday, partly cloudy on Wednesday, cloudy on Thursday and partly cloudy again on Friday.

    It indicates that the rain is the prevalent weather and it is monsoon season. Rajat will use raincoat, umbrella and gumboots to protect himself from rain.
32. (d) Both (a) and (b) are correct.
33. (b) The names of different sources of getting water hidden in the crossword are : River, Snow, Rain,

Pond and Handpump. Tubewell is not hidden in the crossword.

34. **(b)** In a water cycle, sun helps in evaporation.

35. **(c)** As the poster says to conserve the trees, animals (wildlife), air and water, thus it is concerned with protection of entire Earth, not just any one factor.

    Hence the title given by Meena 'Save the Earth' is the most appropriate one.

36. **(b)** Water vapour is the gaseous form of water.

37. **(b)** Snow flakes fall on the ground in the month of December when the temperature is below 0°C. Rain drops and hailstones cannot occur at 0°C.

38. **(d)** Bottle gourd is a summer vegetable.

39. **(d)** All of the above

40. **(b)** River water is not salty. Water present in sea and oceans is salty.

41. **(c)** Event '2' shows a wind sock flying in the direction of blowing wind, indicating that moving air has direction. Event '1' shows that air occupies space.

42. **(b)** Crescent moon is defined as the Small portion of Moon visible in the sky on the day before or after new moon day.

43. **(c)** Process X is condensation while process Y is evaporation. Evaporation will be faster on a warm day as compared to cold day.

# 11 CHAPTER FOREWORD

Who teaches you in your class? Do you know? Yes, you know him / her as your teacher. Who brings milk to your house early in the  morning? You know him as a milkman. Occupation is the job that a person does to earn money. Different people  have different occupations and they helps us in many ways. For example, when you fall ill, you go to the doctor for treatment. Police helps us and protects our lives.-

**Match the following occupations with their description.**

| A. | Teacher | 1. | Stiches our clothes |
| B. | Milkman | 2. | Treat us when we fall ill |
| C. | Policeman | 3. | Catches thieves |
| D. | Doctor | 4. | Brings milk to our house |
| E. | Tailor | 5. | Teach us many things |

After reading this chapter, you will identify different helpers of a society and famous personalities of the world.

# 11
## Chapter

# Occupation





## LEARNING OBJECTIVES

**This chapter will help you to :**
- ❖ identify different helpers of the society.
- ❖ understand their role in community service.
- ❖ study about famous personalities of the world.

## QUICK CONCEPT REVIEW

Every person has to do some work to earn money that becomes his/her job. Occupation is the job that a person does. Different people have different occupation. Some people work at our home and some at our neighborhood. These are many people who help us. In the last class, we have studied that a farmer grows food grains, cobbler mends our shoes, plumber repairs pipes in our kitchen and bathroom.

## TYPES OF HELPERS AROUND US

There are a number of helpers around us, whom we need most necessarily to complete our daily life routine. Our helpers can be classified in two categories:

**1) Direct Helpers      2) Indirect Helpers**

**1) Direct Helpers:** Helpers who come to our contact regularly and we usually talk to them for our needs are called direct helpers. For example, parents and neighbors are the direct helpers for a kid. But for a grown person a number of direct helpers like a security guard, doctor, a lawyer, a barber and a carpenter are available to provide their support when needed.

**2) Indirect Helpers:** Helpers who do not come directly in our contact, but serve us indirectly are called indirect helpers. For example, a soldier standing at the border for our nation never comes to our contact, but he is providing us security from international threats. The police administration provides us security from evil elements and criminals in our society.

## WHY DO WE NEED DIFFERENT TYPES OF HELPERS?

As we can't bring all of our required goods from their source like news-papers from press, vegetables from farms, packed food from factories and can't do all works ourselves like securing our society, school and offices, prescribing medicine while illness and building our house. So we need persons who can do these jobs for us. So our different types of needs and inability to do our every work ourselves, force us to take help of others.

For example:

**Milkman:** A milkman gives milk to our houses early in the morning.

**Teacher:** We learn to read and write from our teachers in school. We learn good habits and good manners from them. A teacher is the future maker of a nation. A good teacher serves his country and society by giving better education to the students. A teacher makes doctors, engineers and officers for the future. A teacher must be respected in the society for doing such an important work.

**Dentist:** Dentist is a doctor who takes care of our teeth and cavities.

**Police officer:** We can see a police officer in every area. A police officer helps to keep law and order and protects our lives and property.

**Fisherman:** Fishing is the common occupation of people who live by the sea coast, ocean and river. Fish is an important source of food and oil.

**Shopkeeper:** A large number of people use to sell goods to the customers and are called shopkeepers.

**Firefighters:** A firefighter is a trained person who can put off fires using water pumps and fire extinguishers. We can dial 101 to call a firefighter.

**A Newspaper Hawker:** In morning, most of us like to sip a cup of tea while reading a newspaper. A news-paper hawker delivers news-papers door to door before we get up in the morning without thinking about good or bad weather.

**Doctor and Nurse:** A doctor is the life saver in a hospital. Not only he prescribes medicines to a patient but also gives moral support to them. They can be both male & female. A nurse serve the patients like a mother and sister in hospital. She also helps a doctor by taking care of patient. A doctor treats us when we fall ill. A doctor tells ways to stay healthy and strong.

**Engineers, Architects and Labours:** These persons develop infrastructure of the nation. They contribute to work on different fronts like constructing our homes to live in as well as all buildings like offices to work, school and colleges to read, malls for shopping and mega structures like bridges to travel, stadiums to play and dams to generate electricity. These components of infrastructure are necessary to make not only a good society, a city, but also a nation. Architects design the structures and do interior designing of such monuments. Whereas, an engineer with the support of labours and many more helpers works on their projects to complete them.

**Security Guard:** The security guards guard a house, a society, an office, a school and a colony. They protect us from thieves and stray animals on road.

**Soldier:** Soldiers from Air Force, Army and Naval forces secure our nation from external enemies of our country. Forces help us to remain citizen of an independent country. Forces keep us safe from terrorists also. Their services for our nation have remained admirable forever. The soldiers are always ready to die for their nation. We must feel proud of them and their spirit for patriotism should be saluted by every countryman.

**Other helpers are barber, tailor, plumber, carpenter, cobbler and porter.**

There are many more helpers we have in our society such as a barber to get our haircut, a tailor stitches our clothes, a carpenter makes or repairs our furniture and a cobbler mends our shoes while a porter helps us to carry heavy loads. Likewise, there are many other helpers as well that we require in our daily life routine.

## FAMOUS PERSONALITIES

1. **APJ Abdul Kalam** was an Indian scientist and who was also the 11th President of India.
2. **Narendra Modi** is the 15th and current Prime Minister of India.
3. **Bill Gates** is the founder of the largest software company 'Microsoft'.
4. **Kiran Bedi** is an indian politician, social activist, and a retired police officer. She is the first female IPS officer.
5. **Sunita Williams:** Sunita Williams is an American astronaut. She holds the records for the longest single space flight by a woman.

# Multiple Choice Questions

## LEVEL 1

1. Who treats the patients?

   (a) Policeman     (b) Doctor     (c) Farmer     (d) Tailor

2. I stitch your school uniform. Guess who I am?     **[2012]**

   (a) Doctor     (b) Tailor     (c) Cobbler     (d) Painter

3. What does a carpenter make?     **[Tricky]**

   (a) Furniture     (b) Pot     (c) Shoes     (d) Cloth

4. Choose odd one out

   (a) Nurse     (b) Patient     (c) Medicine     (d) Tailor

5. The kind of work a person does to earn money is called ________.

   (a) Job     (b) Skill     (c) Walking work     (d) Occupation

6. Which of the following things is used by potter to make pots?     **[2013, Tricky]**

   (a) Scissors            (b) Potter's wheel

   (c) Brush             (d) Comb

7. Which of the following thing people do when they want to relax?

   (a) Mend shoe     (b) Watch T.V     (c) Stitch cloth     (d) Repair tap

8. Who among the following comes to your house everyday?

   (a) Policeman     (b) Plumber     (c) Milkman     (d) Tailor

9. Who devoted her life in serving poor and old people?     **[2014]**

   (a) Kiran Bedi          (b) Mother Teresa

   (c) Kalpana Chawla       (d) None of these

10. Who among the following is not a helper at school?     **[Tricky]**

    (a) Watchman     (b) Teacher     (c) Gardener     (d) Policeman

11. Who among the following helps your mother in washing and cleaning?

    (a) Tailor             (b) Housekeeper

    (c) Teacher           (d) Doctor

12. Nandu washes and irons our clothes. Who is he?     **[2015, Tricky]**

    (a) Fisher man     (b) Tailor     (c) Fireman     (d) Washerman

13. Shalu wants to have a haircut. Which of the following person will help her?

    (a) Barber     (b) Baker     (c) Tailor     (d) Cobbler

**14.** Which of the following thing a barber will not need to do his work? **[Tricky]**

  (a) Comb    (b) Scissors    (c) Chair    (d) Potter's wheel

**15.** The duty of a doctor is to _______________ **[2016, Tricky]**

  (a) Take care of the patient    (b) Earn lot of Money

  (c) Treat the patient    (d) Both (a) and (c)

**16.** Who was the Prime Minister of India after Independence? **[Tricky]**

  (a) Jawaharlal Nehru    (b) APJ Abdul Kalam

  (c) Mahatma Gandhi    (d) Narendra Modi

**17.** Which of the following famous person worked in the field of writing?

  (a) Rabindranath Tagore    (b) Bill Gates

  (c) Narendra Modi    (d) Kiran Bedi

**18.** The activity done by us to earn money is called________ **[2017]**

  (a) Learning    (b) Occupation    (c) Teaching    (d) Practicing

**19.** Who among the following is known to be a famous scientist?

  (a) Sachin Tendulkar    (b) Narendra Modi

  (c) Albert Einstein    (d) Bill Gates

**20.** The shown tools are used by a ________. **[2012]**

  (a) Potter

  (b) Grocer

  (c) Tailor

  (d) Carpenter

**21.** Who is known as the 'Father of the Nation'? **[Tricky]**

  (a) Jawaharlal Nehru    (b) Bill Gates

  (c) Narendra Modi    (d) Mahatma Gandhi

**22.** Jagan is a ________ . He mends **[2013]**

  (a) Potter    (b) Blacksmith    (c) Cobbler    (d) Mason

**23.** Who among the following is not required to build a house ?

  (a) Plumber    (b) Barber    (c) Electrician    (d) Carpenter

24. Identify the professional who makes drawing of the house before it is built.
[2013]

(a)  (b)  (c)  (d)

25. Who is the 15th Prime Minister of India?                [Tricky]
    (a)  Narendra Modi                    (b)  Bill Gates
    (c)  Rabindranath Tagore              (d)  APJ Abdul Kalam
26. Reena has to buy a band-aid for her brother. She should go to a ______ .[2015]
    (a)  Greengrocer    (b)  Chemist     (c)  Florist      (d)  Baker
27. Unscramble the given letter groups and select the option that gives the name of a professional who fits and repairs water pipes.                [2018]

    (a)  TOLIAR        (b)  MNICEHAC     (c)  PBEMULR      (d)  CTAEPERNR

28. Three of the following tools are used by the same professional. Select the odd one.
[2018]

(a)  (b)  (c)  (d)

29. The weather is part of the daily news. Tracking the weather is most important for people who–                [2018]

    (a)  Work in banks   (b)  Sell televisions  (c)  Grow crops  (d)  Use computers

30. Four different professionals are hidden in the given puzzle. Solve the puzzle and select the professional who is NOT hidden in the puzzle.                [2018]

|   | O |   | T |   | R |   |
|   |   | A |   | L |   | R |
|   | T |   |   |   |   |   |
|   |   |   |   |   |   |   |
|   | R |   |   | E | R |   |

    (a)  A person who makes clay pots          (b)  A person who treats the patients

    (c)  A person who stitches clothes          (d)  A person who sells medicines

31. Who builds our house with bricks and cement?                [2019]

    (a)  A Mason       (b)  A Plumber      (c)  A Carpenter   (d)  An Electrician
32. We get __________ fibre from the animal shown here.                [2022]
    (a) Woollen
    (b) Cotton
    (c) Silk
    (d) Nylon

**33.** Who of the following treats the sick people? [2022]

 (a)  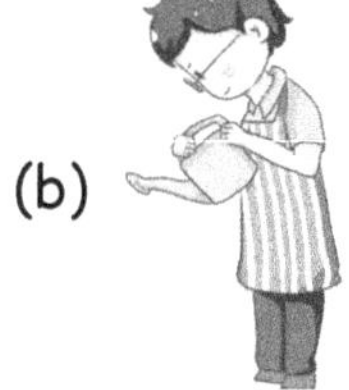 (b)   (c)   (d)

**34.** A house caught fire in your neighbourhood. Whom should you call to blow out the fire? [2022]

(a) Ambulance  (b) Fire Brigade  (c) School  (d) Police Station

## LEVEL 2

**1.** Match the following. [Tricky]

| | List I | | List II |
|---|---|---|---|
| (A) | Nurse | (1) | Post office |
| (B) | Farmer | (2) | Bank |
| (C) | Postman | (3) | Hospital |
| (D) | Banker | (4) | Field |

|  | A | B | C | D |  | | | | |
|---|---|---|---|---|---|---|---|---|---|
| (a) | 1 | 2 | 3 | 4 | (b) | 4 | 2 | 1 | 3 |
| (c) | 3 | 4 | 1 | 2 | (d) | 4 | 3 | 2 | 1 |

**2.** Look at the pictures given below and find who uses the things given below.

[2012, Tricky]

(A)      1. Barber

(B)      2. Farmer

(C)      3. Doctor

(D) 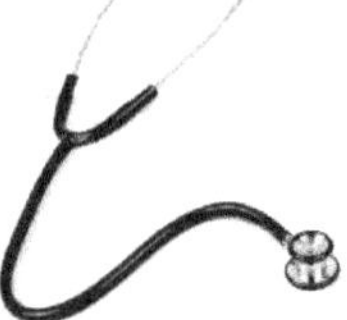     4. Driver

|     | A | B | C | D |
|-----|---|---|---|---|
| (a) | 1 | 2 | 3 | 4 |
| (b) | 2 | 4 | 1 | 3 |
| (c) | 4 | 2 | 1 | 3 |
| (d) | 1 | 4 | 2 | 3 |

**Directions (Qs. 3 to 6): Read the passage carefully and answer the questions.**

The work people do to earn money is their occupation. There are teachers who teach students in school, lawyers who help people to get their rights, writers who write interesting stories, plumbers who mend and fix water pipes and sweepers who clean streets. We should respect all jobs. No job is big or small.                    **[Critical Thinking]**

3. **Who among the following writes  interesting stories?**
   (a)  Writers          (b)  Plumbers          (c)  Sweeper          (d)  Teachers

4. **Who among the following help to clean streets?**
   (a)  Lawyers         (b)  Sweepers         (c)  Plumbers         (d)  Writers

5. **Which of the following statement/s is/are correct?**                    **[Tricky]**

   **Statement 1:** No job is big or small.

   **Statement 2:** We should respect all jobs.

   (a)  Both the statements are correct.

   (b)  Both the statements are incorrect.

   (c)  Statement 1 is correct statement 2 is incorrect.

   (d)  Statement 1 is incorrect statement 2 is correct.

6. **Who helps people to get their rights?**
   (a)  Plumber         (b)  Police         (c)  Lawyer         (d)  Teacher

7. **A child should do which of the following job/s?**                    **[2013]**
   (a)  Working in a tea stall              (b)  Cleaning dishes in people's home
   (c)  Going to school to study           (d)  Both (a) and (b)

**Directions (Qs. 8 to 18) Fill in the blanks in the passage given below:**

Every person of our society has to do some work to earn ________ (8) ________ that becomes her/his job. There are ________ (9) ________ who drive buses, cobbler who repairs ________ (10) ________ , (11) ________ who grow crops, tailors make ________ (12) ________ for us. An ________ (13) ________ checks electrical wires at home. A ________ (14) ________ takes care of the safety of our house. A carpenter makes ________ (15) ________ . A ________ (16) ________ works in a salon and cut ________ (17) ________ . When we fall ill, a ________ (18) ________ treats us.

8.  (a)  respect       (b)  money        (c)  gesture       (d)  all
9.  (a)  drivers       (b)  doctors      (c)  dentist       (d)  teachers
10. (a)  wall          (b)  house        (c)  shoes         (d)  fan
11. (a)  farmers       (b)  watchman     (c)  milkman       (d)  plumbers
12. (a)  shoes         (b)  furniture    (c)  clothes       (d)  wires

13. (a)  plumber      (b)  barber      (c)  cobbler      (d)  electrician
14. (a)  Housekeeper  (b)  fireman     (c)  watchman     (d)  doctor
15. (a)  furniture    (b)  house       (c)  cloth        (d)  shoes
16. (a)  policeman    (b)  barber      (c)  carpenter    (d)  milkman
17. (a)  nail         (b)  trees       (c)  hair         (d)  tooth
18. (a)  nurse        (b)  doctor      (c)  dentist      (d)  patient

19. **Mrs. Geeta teaches English to you and her husband Mr. Kamal treats you when you are ill. What are Mrs. Geeta and Mr. Kamal occupations?**    [2013, Tricky]
    (a)  Mrs. Geeta – Teacher, Mr. Kamal – Doctor
    (b)  Mrs. Geeta – Doctor,  Mr. Kamal – Teacher
    (c)  Mrs. Geeta – Writer,  Mr. Kamal – Plumber
    (d)  Mrs. Geeta – Nurse,   Mr. Kamal – Carpenter

20. **Your friend Amit teases his maid, Madhu, everytime because he thinks Madhu does a small work of cleaning and washing at other people's houses. You find this wrong. As a friend what will you tell Amit ?**
    (a)  No work is small or big
    (b)  We should respect all jobs
    (c)  You will ask Madhu not to go to Amit's house
    (d)  Both (a) and (b)

21. **Read the following sentences and find true/false (T/F).**    [2014, Tricky]
    (1)  Bill Gates is the founder of Microsoft.
    (2)  Kalpana Chawla was the first Indian woman to go in space.
    (3)  Sachin Tendulkar is a famous scientist.
    (a)  TTT        (b)  FFF        (c)  TTF        (d)  FFT

22. **Match the following.**    [Tricky]
    (A)  Kalpana Chawla           (1)  Cricketer
    (B)  Sachin Tendulkar         (2)  Prime Minister
    (C)  Narendra Modi            (3)  Scientist
    (D)  Albert Einstein          (4)  Astronaut

|      | A | B | C | D |      |      | A | B | C | D |
|------|---|---|---|---|------|------|---|---|---|---|
| (a)  | 4 | 1 | 2 | 3 |      | (b)  | 1 | 2 | 3 | 4 |
| (c)  | 3 | 4 | 2 | 1 |      | (d)  | 1 | 2 | 4 | 3 |

23. **Who was the former captain of Indian cricket team?**    [2015]
    (a)  Narendra Modi           (b)  Bill Gates
    (c)  Sachin Tendulkar        (d)  Albert Einstein

24. **When your school is on fire, whom you will call to put off the fire?**
    (a)  Policeman    (b)  Milkman    (c)  Firefighter    (d)  Carpenter

**25.** See the image below. It shows a ______________?  [2016]

(a)  Postman  (b)  Policeman  (c)  Doctor  Pilot

**26.** Your mother received a letter from your grandmother. Who among the following has delivered that letter to your mother?  [Tricky]

(i)  Fireman  (ii)  Post-man  (iii)  Barber  (iv)  Cobbler

(a)  (i) only  (b)  (ii) only  (c)  (iii) and (iv)  (d)  (i) and (iv)

**27.** Read the given conversation between a teacher and her students. Select the correct option regarding this.  [2014]

(a)  Varun's father is a grocer.

(b)  Ram's father is a doctor.

(c)  Shweta's father is a banker.

(d)  Varun's father is a baker.



**28.** Who among the following was an Indian scientist as well as was the President of India?  [Tricky]

(a)  Rabindra Nath  (b)  Jawaharlal Nehru

(c)  Narendra Modi  (d)  APJ Abdul Kalam

**29.** Refer the given box to find out the occupations of Hari and Jagan.  [2014]

|     | Hari | Jagan |
|-----|------|-------|
| (a) | Blacksmith | Cobbler |
| (b) | Greengrocer | Plumber |
| (c) | Chemist | Potter |
| (d) | Tailor | Carpenter |

**30.** Who is the first woman police officer?

(a)  Kiran Bedi  (b)  Mother Teresa

(c)  Kalpana Chawla  (d)  Both (b) and (c)

31. Names of some occupations are hidden in the given word grid.  [2014]

    A. How many names are hidden?

    B. How many of them require hands-on-skills for the work and not classroom education?

    |   |   |   |   |   |   |   |
    |---|---|---|---|---|---|---|
    | N | T | A | F | T | S | S | N |
    | O | A | B | A | R | B | E | R |
    | A | I | S | R | C | H | E | H |
    | P | L | U | M | B | E | R | N |
    | P | O | R | E | H | G | I | A |
    | Q | R | V | R | I | K | B | A |

    |       | a     | b     |
    |-------|-------|-------|
    | (a)   | Four  | Two   |
    | (b)   | Five  | Three |
    | (c)   | Four  | Four  |
    | (d)   | Three | Two   |

32. You are going to Shimla with your family for summer vacation. Who will take care of the safety of your house in your absence?

    (a) Watchman    (b) Milkman    (c) Policeman    (d) Housekeeper

33. Read the conversation between two friends. Which of the following persons should they visit?  [2015]

    |       | Rahul       | Advika    |
    |-------|-------------|-----------|
    | (a)   | Greengrocer | Plumber   |
    | (b)   | Plumber     | Stationer |
    | (c)   | Doctor      | Stationer |
    | (d)   | Greengrocer | Doctor    |



34. Who among the following is a businessman?

    (a) Mother Teresa

    (b) Bill Gates

    (c) Mahatma Gandhi

    (d) All of these

35. If your neighbour is beating his/her housekeeper, whom do you inform to?

    (a) Fireman    (b) Barber

    (c) Milkman    (d) Police

36. _____________ is the occupation of a large number of people living in a village.  [2017, Tricky]

    (a) Mining    (b) Fishing

    (c) Producing    (d) Farming

37. Who designs the structure of a house or a building?

    (a) Carpenter    (b) Architect

    (c) Builder    (d) Engineers

38. Who among the following did things to help poor and old people and children?

    (a) Kiran Bedi

    (b) Mary Kom

    (c) Mother Teresa

    (d) Lata Mangeshkar

39. Match the following: [2022]

    I.   Post office.    A. Nurse
    II.  Police          B. Police station
    III. School          C. Post man
    IV.  Hospital        D. Teacher

    (a) I → c, II → a, III → b, IV → d
    (b) I → c, II → d, III → a, IV → b
    (c) I → a, II → b, III → c, IV → d
    (d) I → c, II → b, III → d, IV → a

## RESPONSE GRID

### LEVEL 1

1. a b c d    2. a b c d    3. a b c d    4. a b c d    5. a b c d
6. a b c d    7. a b c d    8. a b c d    9. a b c d    10. a b c d
11. a b c d   12. a b c d   13. a b c d   14. a b c d   15. a b c d
16. a b c d   17. a b c d   18. a b c d   19. a b c d   20. a b c d
21. a b c d   22. a b c d   23. a b c d   24. a b c d   25. a b c d
26. a b c d   27. a b c d   28. a b c d   29. a b c d   30. a b c d
31. a b c d   32. a b c d   33. a b c d   34. a b c d

### LEVEL 2

1. a b c d    2. a b c d    3. a b c d    4. a b c d    5. a b c d
6. a b c d    7. a b c d    8. a b c d    9. a b c d    10. a b c d
11. a b c d   12. a b c d   13. a b c d   14. a b c d   15. a b c d
16. a b c d   17. a b c d   18. a b c d   19. a b c d   20. a b c d
21. a b c d   22. a b c d   23. a b c d   24. a b c d   25. a b c d
26. a b c d   27. a b c d   28. a b c d   29. a b c d   30. a b c d
31. a b c d   32. a b c d   33. a b c d   34. a b c d   35. a b c d
36. a b c d   37. a b c d   38. a b c d   39. a b c d

# Answers with Explanations

## LEVEL 1

1.  **(b)**  A doctor treats the patients.
2.  **(b)**  A tailor stiches your school uniform.
3.  **(a)**  A carpenter makes furniture.
4.  **(d)**  Tailor. All the other options are found in a hospital.
5.  **(d)**  The work a person does to earn money is called occupation.
6.  **(b)**  A potter uses potter's wheel to make pots.
7.  **(b)**  People watch T.V. when they want to relax.
8.  **(c)**  A milkman comes to our house everyday.
9.  **(b)**  Mother Teresa devoted her life in serving poor and old people.
10. **(d)**  Police does not work in a school.
11. **(b)**  A housekeeper helps your mother with washing and cleaning.
12. **(d)**  Nandu is a washerman.
13. **(a)**  Barber will help her to get a hair-cut.
14. **(d)**  A barber needs comb, scissors and chair to do a haircut.
15. **(d)**  Both (a) and (c)
16. **(a)**  Jawaharlal Nehru was the first Prime Minister of India after independence.
17. **(a)**  Rabindranath Tagore worked in the field of writing.
18. **(b)**  Occupation is the activity done by us to earn money.
19. **(c)**  Albert Einstein is known to be a famous scientist.
20. **(d)**  The tools shown are used by a carpenter who uses wood to make furniture.
21. **(d)**  Mahatma Gandhi is known as 'Father of the Nation'.
22. **(c)**  Cobbler is a person who mends foot-wears like sandals and shoes. A potter makes clay pots for us, a blacksmith makes objects using iron. A mason is a person who constructs buildings and houses.
23. **(b)**  Barber is not required to build a house.
24. **(d)**  A painter (option A) colours the walls and windows. of the house. A carpenter (option B) makes articles of wood like furniture and doors. A plumber (option C) fits and repairs water pipes, taps and wash basins. An architect (option D) makes design plan of a house before it is built, depending upon the area available and the needs of the owner. The house is built according to this plan.
25. **(a)**  Narendra Modi is the 15th Prime Minister of India.
26. **(b)**  Reena should go to a chemist to buy a band-aid for her brother. A greengrocer sells vegetables, a florist sells flowers and a baker sells cakes and cookies.
27. **(c)**  A plumber fits the pipes and taps. The other options are tailor, mechanic and carpenter.
28. **(d)**  The tool shown in picture (d) is used by a cobbler whereas all the other tools are used by a farmer.
29. **(c)**  Tracking the weather is most important for people who grow

crops. Every crop needs different weather condition and a farmer tracks it through weather conditions.

**30.** **(d)** A person who sells medicines is a chemist. The other occupations are potter, doctor and tailor.

**31.** **(a)** A mason builds houses using bricks and cement.

**32.** **(a)** We get woollen fibre from yak.

**33.** **(a)**

**34.** **(b)**

## LEVEL- 2

**1.** **(c)** A nurse works in a hospital, a farmer works in a field, a postman works in a post office and a banker works in a bank.

**2.** **(b)** A farmer uses a sickle, a driver drives a bus, a barber uses a scissor and a doctor uses a stethoscope.

**3.** **(a)** Writers write interesting stories.

**4.** **(b)** Sweepers help in cleaning streets.

**5.** **(a)** Both the statements are correct.

**6.** **(c)** A lawyer helps people to get their rights.

**7.** **(c)** A child should go to school to study.

**8.** **(b)** Money

**9.** **(a)** Drivers

**10.** **(c)** Shoes

**11.** **(a)** Farmers

**12.** **(c)** Clothes

**13.** **(d)** Electrician

**14.** **(c)** Watchman

**15.** **(a)** Furniture

**16.** **(b)** Barber

**17.** **(c)** Hair

**18.** **(b)** Doctor

**19.** **(a)** Mrs. Geeta is a teacher and Mr. Kamal is a doctor.

**20.** **(d)** Both (a) and (b) options are correct.

**21.** **(c)** The third sentence is false. Sachin Tendulkar is a famous circketer.

**22.** **(a)** Kalpana Chawla was an astronaut, Sachin Tendulkar is a cricketer, Narendra Modi is the Prime Minister of India and Albert Einstein was a scientist.

**23.** **(c)** Sachin Tendulkar was the former captain of India cricket team.

**24.** **(c)** When a school is on fire, you will call firefighters or firemen to put off the fire.

**25.** **(a)** Postman

**26.** **(b)** A postman has delivered the letter to your mother.

**27.** **(d)** Ram's father is a banker, Shweta's father is a postman and Varun's father is a baker.

**28.** **(d)** APJ Abdul Kalam was an Indian Scientist as well as the President of India.

**29.** **(b)** A green-grocer sells fruits and vegetables. A plumber mends broken taps, pipelines. and fits new ones.

**30.** **(a)** Kiran Bedi is the first woman police officer.

**31.** **(c)** The names of occupations hidden in the word grid are tailor, farmer, barber and plumber. All these occupations required skills for the work and not high education.

**32.** **(a)** Watchman will take care of the safety of your house in your absence.

**33. (c)** According to Rahul's statement, his knee was hurt badly, thus, he should visit a doctor. Advika needs to buy a new notebook so, she should visit a stationer. A plumber fits and repairs water fittings and a greengrocer sells fruits and vegetables.

**34. (b)** Bill Gates is a businessman. He is the founder of the largest software company Microsoft.

**35. (d)** If someone is beating his/her housekeeper, you should inform to police.

**36. (d)** Farming

**37. (b)** An architect designs structure of buildings and houses.

**38. (c)** Mother Teresa helped poor and old people and children.

**39. (d)**

**12** # CHAPTER FOREWORD

Do you know an early man used leaves and animal skins as clothes? But nowadays, clothes are made up of  cotton, silk, wool, nylon, jute, wool and polyesters. The materials  used for making clothes are called fabrics.

---

**Answer the following questions.**

1.  Name any two knitted clothes we wear.

    _______________________________________________

2.  Name any two clothes we wear in summer season.

    _______________________________________________

3.  We get silk from_________________________________ .

---

After reading this chapter, you will know about different fabrics and fibres. You will also understand how to take care of the clothes and their importance.

# 12 Chapter

# Fibres and Fabrics



- ❖ Silk is obtained from an insect, silkworm. Silkworm lays eggs on a specially prepared cloth.



- ❖ A cloth can be dyed with various colours. Certain patterns and designs are made on them to make them look beautiful.

## LEARNING OBJECTIVES

**This lesson will help you to:**
- ❖ know about the fibres.
- ❖ learn about different types of fibres.
- ❖ study the fibres used for making clothes.
- ❖ learn how to take care of the fibres.

## QUICK CONCEPT REVIEW

Long time ago, people use to wear clothes made from leaves and animal skins. But now-a-days we wear clothes made up of a cotton, silk, wool and nylon. These materials are known as fabrics which are made up of fibres.

## FIBRES

Let us study the fibres and their types.

Clothes are usually made from threads. To make threads, we use very thin thread like material called **fibres**. Fibres are mainly of two types:

1. **Natural fibres:** Fibres that we get from plants and animals are called natural fibres. **For example,** Cotton, jute, wool and silk are natural fibres.

2. **Synthetic fibres:** These fibres are not obtained from plants. They are prepared artificially. **For example,** nylon, polyesters and rayon. These fabrics are stretchable, waterproof and wrinkle free.

## NATURAL FIBRES

### 1. Cotton

Cotton is the most widely used fibre. Cotton is obtained from cotton plant. Cotton is used to make shirts, trousers, frocks, skirt and saree. Fruits of cotton plant are called **cotton balls.**

## 2. Jute

Jute is obtained from jute plant. It is used for making mats, rope and gunny bags.

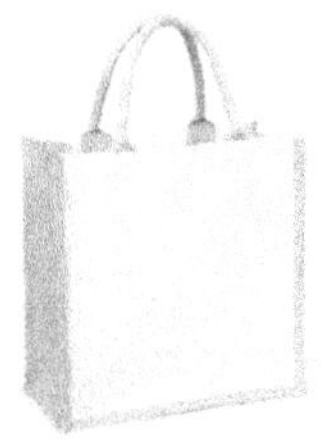



- ❖ We obtain cotton from cotton plant and wool from sheep.
- ❖ Rain coat, gumboots and umbrella are made up of waterproof material.

## 3. Wool

Wool is a fibre obtained from the hair and fur of different animals like sheep, camel and goat. Wool is used in making sweaters, shawls and caps.

## 4. Silk

Silk cotton of is the oldest fabric known to man. Silk is obtained from cocoon of silkmoth. Silk is used to prepare sarees, shirts and tie.

## SYNTHETIC FIBRES

Synthetic fibres are obtained from the raw materials such as chemicals.

### Nylon

Nylon is a synthetic fibre. It is used to make clothes like saree. It is also used to make carpets and ropes.

### Rayon

Rayon is a synthetic fibre obtained from wood pulp. It is used to produce carpets, threads and surgical dressing.

## CARE OF CLOTHES

A good soap or detergent should be used to wash clothes. Washed clothes should be rinsed properly to remove the soap. After the clothes are washed, they should be dried in the sun. Also clothes should be ironed after drying. Ironed clothes not only look good, but also help to kill germs. Woollen, silk and other delicate clothes should be dry cleaned or hand washed. We should use mothballs or dried leaves to store woollen and silk clothes. Insects like moths and silver fish make holes in clothes.

# Multiple Choice Questions

## LEVEL 1

1. Which of the following is not used by humans to make clothes in present days?
 **[Tricky]**
 (a) Wool     (b) Silk     (c) Cotton     (d) Leaves

2. Which of the following fibre is used to make door mats?    **[Tricky]**
 (a) Nylon     (b) Jute     (c) Cotton     (d) Wool

3. Which of the following fibre is obtained from 'silkmoth'?    **[2012, Tricky]**
 (a) Jute     (b) Wool     (c) Cotton     (d) Silk

4. Natural fibres are obtained from which of the following?
 (a) Plants                    (b) Petrol
 (c) Animals             (d) Both (a) and (c)

5. Which of the following is required to make a shirt?    **[2012]**
 (a) Fabric     (b) Scissor     (c) Shawl     (d) Both (a) and (b)

6. Rope is made up of __________ .
 (a) Jute     (b) Nylon     (c) Cotton     (d) Rayon

7. Which of the following is a man-made fibre?    **[2013, Tricky]**
 (a) Cotton               (b) Jute
 (c) Polyester          (d) None of these

8. Which of the following animals gives wool?
 (a) Sheep     (b) Elephant     (c) Lion     (d) All of these

9. Synthetic fibres are __________ .    **[2014, Tricky]**
 (a) Waterproof        (b) Stretchable
 (c) Black in colour     (d) Both (a) and (b)

10. Which of the following is a source of natural fibres?
 (a) Fish     (b) Sunlight     (c) Insect     (d) Air

11. Which of the following can be made from cotton?    **[Tricky]**
 (a) Jacket     (b) Shirt     (c) Sweater     (d) All of these

12. Which of the following is not made up of jute?    **[2015]**
 (a) Gunny bag     (b) Door mat     (c) Rope     (d) Rain-coat

13. Which of the following is made of synthetic fibre?    **[Tricky]**
 (a) Shirt     (b) Hat     (c) Sweater     (d) Carpet

14. Which of the following is/are harmful for clothes?    **[2016, Tricky]**
 (a) Moths     (b) Rats     (c) Silver fish     (d) All of these

15. Delicate clothes should be __________
 (a) Hand washed        (b) Dry cleaned
 (c) Machine washed     (d) Either (a) or (b)

16. __________ protects us from rain.    **[2016]**
 (a) Cotton clothes        (b) Synthetic clothes
 (c) Woollen clothes     (d) Raincoat

17. Which of the following should be used to store woollen and silk clothes?    [Tricky]
    (a)   Dried neem leaves              (b)   Cotton
    (c)   Dried mango leaves             (d)   Flowers
18. Which of the following is not required to keep our clothes clean and safe?
                                                                    [2017, Tricky]
    (a)   Moth balls      (b)   Detergent      (c)   Iron      (d)   Rain
19. Which of the following is/are made up of wool?
    (a)   Gloves      (b)   Raincoat      (c)   Sweaters      (d)   Both (a) and (c)
20. The fibres of some fabrics such as cotton, jute, silk and wool are obtained from plants and animals. These are called ?                    [2017]
    (a)   Artificial fibres   (b)   Natural fibres   (c)   Rayon fibre   (d)   Nylon fibre
21. Jute fibre is obtained from the __________ of the jute plant.
    (a)   Roots      (b)   Leaves      (c)   Stem      (d)   Flower
22. Which of the following clothes keep us warm in winters?
    (a)   Woollen      (b)   Cotton      (c)   Rain-coat      (d)   Synthetic
23. __________ CAN be obtained from source from which object X CAN be obtained.
                                                                    [2018]

Object X

(a)        (b)        (c)        (d)

24. If you could examine a piece of cloth with a hand lens, you would see that the cloth is made of –                                        [2018]
    (a)   Energy      (b)   Threads      (c)   Glue      (d)   Minerals
25. Select the INCORRECT match from the following.              [2019]

    (a)   Feet –                        (b)   Hands –

    (c) Head –                          (d)   Neck –

26. Which of the following weather conditions would make you put on a heavy, warm coat and gloves ?                                       [2019]

    (a)        (b)        (c)        (d)

27. Sheena's mother is making sweater from wool yarn as shown in the picture.
    **What is this method called?**                                    [2020]
    (a) Weaving
    (b) Spinning
    (c) Knitting
    (d) Threading

28. Unscramble the given letters to find out the name of the fibre obtained from an insect.                                    [2022]
    (a) NLIEN         (b) OTCTON         (c) OWLO         (d) ILSK

## LEVEL 2

1. Which of the following is under the wrong heading?          [Critical Thinking]

| Natural fibre | Synthetic fibres |
|---|---|
| Cotton | Rayon |
| Silk | Jute |

   (a) Cotton         (b) Rayon         (c) Silk         (d) Jute

2. Which of the following things we should keep in mind while washing our clothes?
   (a) Good soap or detergent should be used.          [2012, Tricky]
   (b) Rinse them properly to remove soap.
   (c) They should be dried open in the sun.
   (d) All of these

3. Match the following:                                    [Tricky]
   (A) Cotton                    (1) Shirt
   (B) Silk                      (2) Carry bag
   (C) Jute                      (3) Sweater
   (D) Wool                      (4) Saree

|     | A | B | C | D |     |     | A | B | C | D |
|-----|---|---|---|---|-----|-----|---|---|---|---|
| (a) | 2 | 3 | 1 | 4 |     | (b) | 3 | 3 | 3 | 2 |
| (c) | 4 | 1 | 4 | 4 |     | (d) | 1 | 4 | 2 | 3 |

4. Which of the following fibre/s we do not get from plants?          [2013]
   (a) Rayon         (b) Jute         (c) Nylon         (d) Both (a) and (c)

5. Which of the following fibre is prepared artificially?          [Tricky]
   (a) Cotton         (b) Jute         (b) Silk         (d) Nylon

6. In early times, people used to wear clothes made from ________ and ________.
   (a) leaves, animal skin              (b) cotton, animal skin
   (c) flowers, fruits                  (d) papers, leaves

7. Which of the following is/are incorrectly matched?          [2014, Tricky]
   (i) Monsoon : Sweater               (ii) Winter : Woollen clothes
   (iii) Summer : Cotton clothes
   (a) (i) only                         (b) (ii) and (iii)
   (c) (i) and (ii)                     (d) (i), (ii) and (iii)

8. Which of the following is not true about cotton?          [Tricky]
   (a) Cotton is used mostly in summers      (b) It is a synthetic fibre
   (c) It is light and absorbs sweat          (d) It is used to make shirts and trousers

**Directions (Qs. 9 to 13):** Read the passage carefully and answer the following questions.
**[2015, Tricky]**

Silk is a natural fibre. It is obtained from silkworms. Silk is also known as queen of all fabrics. Silkworms eat mulberry leaves. The process of making silk from silkworm is called sericulture. Silk fabric was first developed in China.

9. Silk is a natural _______
   (a) Carbohydrate  (b) Vitamin  (c) Protein  (d) Fibre

10. What do silkworms eat?
    (a) Mulberry leaves (b) Neem leaves  (c) Mango leaves  (d) None of these

11. Which of the following fabric is considered to be the 'queen of all fabrics'?
    (a) Cotton  (b) Silk  (c) Jute  (d) Nylon

12. The process of making silk from silkworm is called ____________.
    (a) Sericulture  (b) Evaporation  (c) Horticulture  (d) All of these

13. Where was silk developed first?
    (a) India  (b) China  (c) Sri Lanka  (d) Thailand

14. Which of the following can be used to make saree?
    (a) Silk  (b) Wool  (c) Cotton  (d) Both (a) and (c)

15. Why do we need to iron clothes? **[Tricky]**
    (a) Ironed clothes look good  (b) Ironing removes wrinkles from clothes
    (c) Cupboard looks neat with ironed clothes (d) All of these

16. Silk fibre is drawn from cocoon of a _______ **[2016]**
    (a) Sheep  (b) Goat  (c) Silkworm  (d) Cow

17. Which of the following correctly define/s the meaning of fibre? **[Tricky]**
    (a) Thin thread like material is known as fibre
    (b) Fibre are natural only
    (c) A cloth is made from fibres
    (d) (a) and (c)

18. You wear washed clothes everyday. Still, they look dirty and cause itching on your skin. What will you do to get rid of this problem?
    (a) You will buy a good detergent.
    (b) Rinse the washed clothes properly.
    (c) Use 2 drops of dettol while washing clothes.
    (d) (b) and (c)

19. Fruits of cotton plants are called _______ **[2017]**
    (a) Cotton fleece  (d) Cotton flower  (c) Cotton balls  (d) Cotton ropes

20. Match the column (I) with the column (II) **[Tricky]**

| | Column I | | Column II |
|---|---|---|---|
| A | Cotton | 1 | Silk moth |
| B | Silk | 2. | Sheep |
| C | Wool | 3. | Cotton plant |
| D | Nylon | 4. | Artificial |

|     | A | B | C | D |     | A | B | C | D |
|-----|---|---|---|---|-----|---|---|---|---|
| (a) | 3 | 1 | 2 | 4 | (b) | 2 | 3 | 4 | 1 |
| (c) | 1 | 3 | 4 | 2 | (d) | 2 | 3 | 1 | 4 |

21. Which of these is made of the material obtained from the animal shown? **[2012]**
    (a) Jute bags
    (b) Woollen socks
    (c) Cotton shirt
    (d) Silk saree

**Directions (Qs. 22 to 31): Fill in the blanks in the passage given below   [Critical Thinking]**

We should take good ________ (22) ________ of our clothes. They should be ________ (23) ________ well with good quality ________ (24) ________ to remove dust and sweat. After the clothes are washed, they should be ________ (25) ________ in the sun. Clothes should be ________ (26) ________ after drying. Ironed clothes look ________ (27) ________ and also help to ________ (28) ________ germs. ________ (29) ________ clothes should be dry-cleaned. Woollen and silk clothes should be stored with ________ (30) ________. This protects the clothes from ________ (31) ________.

| | | | | | | | |
|---|---|---|---|---|---|---|---|
| **22.** | (a) | health | (b) | care | (c) | diet | (d) | sleep |
| **23.** | (a) | washed | (b) | dried | (c) | ironed | (d) | stored |
| **24.** | (a) | water | (b) | machine | (c) | soap | (d) | bucket |
| **25.** | (a) | dried | (b) | kept | (c) | ironed | (d) | washed |
| **26.** | (a) | cleaned | (b) | soaked | (c) | rinsed | (d) | ironed |
| **27.** | (a) | colourful | (b) | small | (c) | good | (d) | healthy |
| **28.** | (a) | grow | (b) | kill | (c) | store | (d) | retain |
| **29.** | (a) | White | (b) | Cotton | (c) | Normal | (d) | Delicate |
| **30.** | (a) | cotton balls | (b) | moth balls | (c) | thermacol | (d) | mango leaves |
| **31.** | (a) | insects | (b) | animals | (c) | rain | (d) | smell |

**32. Match the column (I) with the column (II)**                    [Critical Thinking]

| Column I | | Column II | |
|---|---|---|---|
| A | Jacket | 1. | Cotton |
| B | Gloves | 2. | Polyester |
| C | Saree | 3. | Wool |
| D | Rope | 4. | Jute |

|  | A | B | C | D |  | A | B | C | D |
|---|---|---|---|---|---|---|---|---|---|
| (a) | 1 | 4 | 2 | 3 | (b) | 3 | 2 | 4 | 1 |
| (c) | 4 | 2 | 3 | 1 | (d) | 2 | 3 | 1 | 4 |

**33.** Study the given word grid. How many names of the materials that are used to make clothes are hidden in the word grid?                    [2014]

(a)  2

(d)  3

(c)  4

(d)  5

| L | E | A | T | H | E | R |
|---|---|---|---|---|---|---|
| B | Z | P | C | M | O | A |
| N | Y | L | O | N | F | H |
| A | W | S | T | G | D | K |
| X | O | R | T | I | E | M |
| Z | O | L | O | V | N | X |
| E | L | W | N | Z | P | T |

34. Amit is going to visit his uncle's village next week. You have just come from the same place. The weather is very hot there. Amit has to pack his bag. As his friend what will you suggest Amit?
    (a)  He should carry mostly cotton clothes.
    (b)  He should carry light coloured clothes.
    (c)  Do not go out in afternoon, its very hot there.
    (d)  All of these

## RESPONSE GRID

### LEVEL 1

| | | | | |
|---|---|---|---|---|
| 1. a b c d | 2. a b c d | 3. a b c d | 4. a b c d | 5. a b c d |
| 6. a b c d | 7. a b c d | 8. a b c d | 9. a b c d | 10. a b c d |
| 11. a b c d | 12. a b c d | 13. a b c d | 14. a b c d | 15. a b c d |
| 16. a b c d | 17. a b c d | 18. a b c d | 19. a b c d | 20. a b c d |
| 21. a b c d | 22. a b c d | 23. a b c d | 24. a b c d | 25. a b c d |
| 26. a b c d | 27. a b c d | 28. a b c d | | |

### LEVEL 2

| | | | | |
|---|---|---|---|---|
| 1. a b c d | 2. a b c d | 3. a b c d | 4. a b c d | 5. a b c d |
| 6. a b c d | 7. a b c d | 8. a b c d | 9. a b c d | 10. a b c d |
| 11. a b c d | 12. a b c d | 13. a b c d | 14. a b c d | 15. a b c d |
| 16. a b c d | 17. a b c d | 18. a b c d | 19. a b c d | 20. a b c d |
| 21. a b c d | 22. a b c d | 23. a b c d | 24. a b c d | 25. a b c d |
| 26. a b c d | 27. a b c d | 28. a b c d | 29. a b c d | 30. a b c d |
| 31. a b c d | 32. a b c d | 33. a b c d | 34. a b c d | |

# Answers with Explanations

## LEVEL 1

1.  (d)  Wool, silk and cotton are used by humans to make clothes in present days.
        Leaves are not used by humans to make clothes in present days.
2.  (b)  Jute is used to make door mats.
3.  (d)  Silk is obtained from silkmoth.
4.  (d)  Natural fibres are obtained from plants and animals.
5.  (d)  A fabric and a scissor is required to make a shirt.
6.  (a)  Rope is made up of jute.
7.  (c)  Polyester is a manmade fibre.
8.  (a)  Sheep gives us wool.
9.  (d)  Synthetic fibres are waterproof and stretchable.
10. (c)  An insect is a source of natural fibre that is silk.
11. (b)  Shirt can be made from cotton.
12. (d)  Raincoat is not made up of jute.
13. (d)  Carpet is made of synthetic fibre.
14. (d)  Rats, moths and silver fish are harmful for clothes.
15. (d)  Delicate clothes should be either handwashed or dry cleaned.
16. (d)  Rain coat protects us from rain.

| | | |
|---|---|---|
| 17. | (a) | Dried neem leaves should be used to store woollen and silk clothes. |
| 18. | (d) | Rain is not required to keep our clothes clean and safe. |
| 19. | (d) | Both gloves and sweaters are made up of wool. |
| 20. | (b) | Natural fibres |
| 21. | (c) | Stem |
| 22. | (a) | Woollen clothes keep us warm in winters. |
| 23. | (b) | Tires are made up of rubber. Gloves shown are also made up of rubber. |
| 24. | (b) | Cloth is made up of fine threads so if we see a piece of cloth with a hand lens we observe threads. |
| 25. | (d) | The incorrect match is neck and shirt. We wear shirt on the upper body. |
| 26. | (c) | The picture (c) shows snow. We wear warm clothes in cold. |
| 27. | (c) | Knitting method of converting a single yarn into fabric with hands by using two needles. |
| 28. | (d) | Silk is obtained from the insect silkworm. |

## LEVEL 2

| | | |
|---|---|---|
| 1. | (d) | Jute is under the wrong heading. Jute is a natural fibre. |
| 2. | (d) | All of these things we should keep in mind while washing our clothes. |
| 3. | (d) | A Shirt is made from cotton, a saree from silk carry bag from jute, and a sweater from wool. |
| 4. | (d) | Rayon and Nylon are not obtained from plants. |
| 5. | (d) | Nylon is prepared artificially. |
| 6. | (a) | In early times, people used to wear clothes made from leaves and animals skins. |
| 7. | (a) | (i) only. We do not wear sweaters in monsoon. |
| 8. | (b) | Cotton is a natural fibre. |
| 9. | (d) | Silk is a natural fibre. |
| 10. | (a) | Silkworms eat mulberry leaves. |
| 11. | (b) | Silk is considered to be the 'queen of all fabrics'. |

| | | |
|---|---|---|
| 12. | (a) | The process of making silk from silkworm is called 'sericulture'. |
| 13. | (b) | Silk was 1st developed in China. |
| 14. | (d) | Saree can be made up of cotton and silk. |
| 15. | (d) | All of these are happened when we iron clothes. |
| 16. | (c) | Silkworm |
| 17. | (a) | Fibre is a very thin thread like material. A cloth is made from fibres. |
| 18. | (d) | Rinse the clothes properly and use 2 drops of dettol while washing. |
| 19. | (c) | Cotton balls |
| 20. | (a) | Cotton is obtained from cotton plant. Silk is obtained from silk moth. Wool is obtained from sheep. Nylon is an artificial fibre. |
| 21. | (b) | Woollen socks are made from wool which is obtained from sheep. |
| 22. | (b) | care |
| 23. | (a) | washed |
| 24. | (c) | soap |
| 25. | (a) | dried |
| 26. | (d) | ironed |
| 27. | (c) | good |
| 28. | (b) | kill |
| 29. | (d) | delicate |
| 30. | (b) | moth balls |
| 31. | (a) | insects |
| 32. | (d) | Jacket is made up of polyester. Gloves is made up of wool. Saree is made up of cotton and rope is made up of jute. |
| 33. | (c) | In the given word grid, four names of the materials that are used to make clothes are hidden. These are: LEATHER, NYLON, COTTON AND WOOL. |

| L | E | A | T | H | E | R |
|---|---|---|---|---|---|---|
| B | Z | P | C | M | O | A |
| N | Y | L | O | N | F | H |
| A | W | S | T | G | D | K |
| X | O | R | T | I | E | M |
| Z | O | L | O | V | N | X |
| E | L | W | N | Z | P | T |

| | |
|---|---|
| 34. | (d) |

# 13 CHAPTER FOREWORD

Did you know – Everything is made up of some or the other material. The sunglasses and hats that you wear, the books you read, clothes you wear, or the furniture that you have in your house are all made up of different materials.

**Now, answer the following questions.**

1. Write the three states of matter?

________________, ________________, ________________

2. Match the objects with their types of materials:

A. Furniture               1. Metal

B. Bicycle                2. Glass

C. Mirror                 3. Plastic

D. Toys                   4. Wood

After reading this chapter, you will be able to know about different types of material, states and properties of matter.

<table>
<tr><td>

# 13
## Chapter

</td><td>

# *Materials Around us*

</td></tr>
</table>

## LEARNING OBJECTIVES

**This lesson will help you to:**

❖ know about the different types of materials around us.

❖ study about matter : solid, liquid and gas.

❖ learn about the properties of matter.

## QUICK CONCEPT REVIEW

Everything in this world is made up of some materials. All these materials occupy space and have some weight.

The food you eat, the air you breathe in, the water you drink, your books and notebooks, all these are made up of materials that occupy space, have weight and these are known as matter.

## MATTER

Anything which occupies space and has mass is known as matter. **For example:** Glass, bottle, bag, air, book, chair, and tables.

## STATES OF MATTER

Matter is found in three states: Solid, liquid and gas.

1. **Solid:** Solids have fixed shape and size. **For example,** Wood, cloth, plastic and paper.

2. **Liquid:** Liquids do not have fixed shape. They take up the shape of a container. **For example,** water, milk, juices and oil.

3. **Gas:** Gases spread out. Gases also have no fixed shape. Gases cannot be seen. **For example,** oxygen, carbon dioxide and water vapour.

# TYPES OF MATERIALS

We see different types of objects around us. Each and every object is made up of different materials.

**For example:** A cricket bat is made up of wood, a bicycle is made up of metal, furniture is made up of wood, candle is made up of wax and shoes are made up of leather.

Let us discuss more about these materials:

1. **Paper:** We obtained paper from trees. Paper is used to make many things such as: notebooks, books, newspaper and magazines. We should not waste paper.

2. **Wood:** Wood is obtained from trees. Wood is used to prepare furniture. Wood is very hard and cannot break easily.

3. **Metal:** Metal is very hard and cannot break easily. Metal is used to prepare many things such as trucks, buses, bicycles and artificial jewellery.

4. **Glass:** Glass can break easily. Glass is used to make sunglasses, wall-clocks and mirror.

5. **Plastic:** Plastic is unbreakable. It cannot break easily. Plastic is used to make lunch boxes, water bottles, toys and buckets.

Some of these materials can be recycled and used again and again. These materials are known as recyclable material. **For example,** wood, plastic, paper and glass.

Some materials cannot be recycled again and again and can be used only once. **For example,** coal and petrol.

## TRANSPARENT, TRANSLUCENT AND OPAQUE OBJECT

**Transparent object:** These objects can pass light through their body. **For example,** glass and hand lens.

**Translucent object:** These objects allow only some amount of light through them. **For example,** plastic bag, coloured bottle and butter paper.

**Opaque object:** Opaque object cannot pass light through them. **For example,** Wood and aluminium foil.

> ❖ **Misconcept:** Every matter can be touched and seen.
>
> **Concept:** All three states of matter cannot be touched. We can touch only solid and liquid. Gases cannot be touched.

# Multiple Choice Questions

## LEVEL 1

1. Anything which occupies space and has weight is called?                    **[2012]**
   (a) Salt          (b) Matter          (c) Gas          (d) None of these

2. Which of the following is not a solid matter ?                    **[Tricky]**
   (a) Book          (b) Chair          (c) Juice          (d) Spoon

3. Books are made from ________.
   (a) Paper          (b) Glass          (c) Fabric          (d) Wax

4. Which of the following material is used to make a lunch box?          **[2013, Tricky]**
   (a) Glass          (b) Plastic          (c) Paper          (d) Wax

5. Which of the following is in liquid state?
   (a) Ice          (b) Ice cream          (c) Milk          (d) Rubber

6. Which of the following has fixed shape and size?                    **[Tricky]**
   (a) Solid          (b) Liquid          (c) Gas          (d) All of these

7. Candles are made from ________ .
   (a) Wood          (b) Water          (c) Glass          (d) Wax

8. Which of the following object is made up of leather?
   (a) Shoe          (b) Book          (c) Pot          (d) Spoon

9. Which of the following object is/are not an example of opaque objects? **[2014, Tricky]**
   (a) Wall          (b) Paper          (c) Towel          (d) Glass

10. Which of the following is/are transparent?                    **[Tricky]**
    (a) Water          (b) Air          (c) Orange          (d) Both (a) and (b)

11. Which of the following does/do not have a fixed shape?                    **[Tricky]**
    (a) Air          (b) Water          (c) Candle          (d) Both (a) and (b)

12. Which of the following takes the shape of the container they are put in? **[Tricky]**
    (a) Solid          (b) Liquid          (c) Gases          (d) None of these

13. Which of the following is invisible?                    **[2015]**
    (a) Oxygen          (b) Orange          (c) Book          (d) Wax

14. Which of the following you can't hold in your hand easily?
    (a) Pencil          (b) Bottle          (c) Milk          (d) Bag

15. Which of the following is/are solid?
    (a) Sugar          (b) Salt          (c) Ice cubes          (d) All of these

16. Air is a mixture of many ________ such as oxygen, carbon dioxide and water vapour.                    **[Tricky]**
    (a) Water          (b) Matter          (c) Gases          (d) Wood

17. **Matter can be changed from one form to another by ________.**     [2016]

    (a)  Heating      (b)  Cooling      (c)  Both (a) or (b)  (d)  None of these

18. **Ice cream is a solid form of ________.**

    (a)  Sugar      (b)  Milk      (c)  Juice      (d)  Wax

19. **Which of the following do not have fixed shape?**

    (a)  Juices (liquid)    (b)  Oxygen (gas)    (c)  Pencils (solid)  (d)  Both (a) and (b)

20. **________ takes the shape of its container and has a definite volume.**

    (a)  Solid      (b)  Gas      (c)  Liquid      (d)  None of these

21. **Which of the following we breathe out?**     (2017, Tricky)

    (a)  Carbon dioxide  (b)  Nitrogen      (c)  Oxygen      (d)  All of these

22. **The water is in ________ state in the form of ice.**

    (a)  Liquid      (b)  Water vapour  (c)  Solid      (d)  Gas

23. **Which of these is an example of liquid water ?**     [2018]

    (a)  Ice      (b)  Rain      (c)  Frost      (d)  Steam

24. **The magnet will pick up the nail but not the penny because the nail –**     [2018]

    (a)  Contains iron             (b)  Is lighter than the penny

    (c)  Has rust on it            (d)  Has a sharp point

25. **Ice cubes are an example of which form of water ?**     [2019]

    (a)  Gas      (b)  Liquid      (c)  Solid      (d)  Water vapour

## LEVEL 2

**Directions (Qs. 1 to 14): Fill in the blanks in the passage given below. (Critical Thinking)**

Everything around us is made of ________ (1) ________. Matter is anything that occupies space and has ________ (2) ________ . The food we eat, the air we ________ (3) ________ , the water we drink, are all examples of matter. It is found in ________ (4) ________ states- solid, liquid and gas. ________ (5) ________ have fixed shape and ________ (6) ________ change their shape. They take the ________ (7) ________ of the container they are kept in. Gases ________ (8) ________ out and they do not have a ________ (9) ________ shape ________ . Air is a mixture of ________ (10) ________. Depending on whether ________ (11) ________ can pass through them, materials are of ________ (12) ________ types. Glass is an example of ________ (13) ________ material and ________ (14) ________ is an example of opaque material.

1.   (a)  Air      (b)  Matter      (c)  Water      (d)  Light
2.   (a)  Length      (b)  Area      (c)  Distance      (d)  Weight

3.  (a)  Eat                (b)  Drink         (c)  Breathe        (d)  All of these
4.  (a)  2                  (b)  3             (c)  4              (d)  None of these
5.  (a)  Liquid             (b)  Gas           (c)  Solids         (d)  All of these
6.  (a)  Liquids            (b)  Gas           (c)  Solid          (d)  All of these
7.  (a)  Shape              (b)  Color         (c)  Taste          (d)  Size
8.  (a)  Sink               (b)  Control       (c)  Spread         (d)  Pollute
9.  (a)  Loose              (b)  Tight         (c)  Fixed          (d)  Large
10. (a)  Gases              (b)  Solids        (c)  Liquids        (d)  Matters
11. (a)  Air                (b)  Light         (c)  Water          (d)  Gas
12. (a)  1                  (b)  2             (c)  3              (d)  4
13. (a)  Transparent        (b)  Opaque        (c)  Translucent    (d)  Gaseous
14. (a)  Water              (b)  Air           (c)  Wood           (d)  Glass

**Directions (Qs. 15 to 19): Read the given passage and answer the following questions.**
**[Critical Thinking]**

Matters are made up of very tiny particles called molecules. Molecules in a solid state are very tightly packed. Molecules in liquid and gas states are loosely packed. The state of matter can change on heating or cooling. When solids are heated, they turn into liquid and heating liquid can turn it into a gas.

15. **Matter is made of small particles called __________ .**
    (a)  Cells          (b)  Molecules      (c)  Dust          (d)  None
16. **In which of the following molecules are loosely packed?**
    (a)  Solid                              (b)  Liquid
    (c)  Gases                              (d)  Both liquid and gases
17. **Molecules in solid are packed __________.**
    (a)  Loosely       (b)  Very loosely    (c)  Tightly       (d)  None
18. **Which of the following changes solid into liquid and liquid into gases?**
    (a)  Cooling       (b)  Freezing        (c)  Melting       (d)  Heating
19. **Which of the following states of matter can't be seen or touched?**
    (a)  Solid         (b)  Liquid          (c)  Gas           (d)  All of these
20. **Your mother gave you a glass full of mango milkshake. Your sister poured that into your lunch box and kept the box in freezer. After 2 hours what change/s did you notice?**                     **[Critical Thinking]**
    (a)  Mango milkshake took the shape of lunch box
    (b)  Mango milkshake becomes an ice cream
    (c)  Now mango milkshake evaporates away
    (d)  Both (a) and (b)
21. **Read the following statements and choose the correct answer.**        **[2012, Tricky]**
    **Statement 1:** Gases spread out and they do not have a fixed shape.
    **Statement 2:** A book is made from paper.
    (a)  Statement 1 is true and statement 2 is false
    (b)  Statement 1 is false and statement 2 is true
    (c)  Both the statements are true
    (d)  Both the statements are false

**22.** **Match the following.**    [Tricky]

| | | | |
|---|---|---|---|
| A. | Window panes | (1) | Paper |
| B. | Candle | (2) | Glass |
| C. | Envelope | (3) | Rubber |
| D. | Tyres | (4) | Wax |

|  | A | B | C | D |  |  | A | B | C | D |
|---|---|---|---|---|---|---|---|---|---|---|
| (a) | 2 | 4 | 1 | 3 |  | (b) | 1 | 1 | 2 | 1 |
| (c) | 4 | 2 | 4 | 2 |  | (d) | 3 | 3 | 3 | 4 |

**23.** **Calculate the total number of solid things.**    [2013, Tricky]

| spoon | pot | bottle | ball | mango milkshake |
|---|---|---|---|---|
| tyre | milk | watch | juice | mineral water |

(a)   10        (b)   7        (c)   6        (d)   5

**24.** **Which of the following solid/s can change into liquid if they are kept in sunlight?**    [2014, Tricky]

(a)   Icecream        (b)   Chapati        (c)   Butter        (d)   Both (a) and (c)

**25.** **Which of the following can be seen clearly in the air?**    [Critical Thinking]

(a)   Oxygen gas        (b)   Smoke of a lighted agarbatti

(c)   Nitrogen gas        (d)   Both (a) and (c)

**26.** **Which of the following is not filled with air?**

(a)   Football        (b)   Lemon        (c)   Balloon        (d)   Tyre

**27.** **Identify X and Y.**    [Tricky]

| | X | Milk |
|---|---|---|
| | Solid | Y |

(a)   X = Gas        Y = Fabric
(b)   X = Solid        Y = Spoon
(c)   X = Air        Y = Box
(d)   X = Liquid        Y = Tyre

**28.** **Which of the following is not true about matter?**    [Tricky]

(a)   Matter has weight.
(b)   Matter has 3 states-solid, liquid and gas.
(c)   Matter does not occupy space.
(d)   Everything around us is made of matter.

**29.** Ramu, a little boy was asked to lift a bucket full of water. He tried, but cannot lift it and started crying. Ramu wants to know why he could not lift it. As a friend what will you tell him?

(a) Bucket and water both have weights     (b) It was a difficult task

(c) Two people are required for this     (d) All of these

**30.** Read the given sentences and choose True or False (T/F).     **[Tricky]**

1. Chalk, rice and biscuits are solid matters

2. Oil, honey and tea are liquid matters

3. Ice cream melts in refrigerator

(a) TTT     (b) FFF     (c) TFT     (d) TTF

**31.** What is the process of change of liquid into solid?     **[2016, Tricky]**

(a) Boiling     (b) Melting     (c) Freezing     (d) Evaporation

**32.** Three states of matter are ________     **[2017, Tricky]**

(a) Gas, liquid and mixture

(b) Density, mass and weight

(c) Solid, liquid and gas

(d) None of the above

**33.** P is a rock, yet you can snap it with your hands. P is ________.     **[2015]**

(a) Pumice     (b) Talc     (c) Chalk     (d) Marble

**34.** Refer to the given classification chart and identify d, e and f.     **[2020]**

Rocks/Minerals

Hard rock/Mineral     Soft rock/Mineral

d     Marble     e     Chalk     f

(a) d could be talc while f could be quartz.

(b) e could be granite while f could be sandstone.

(c) d could be sandstone while e could be granite.

(d) e could be graphite while f could be diamond.

**35.** Which of the following rocks was used for making the Taj Mahal?     **[2021]**

(a) Gneiss     (b) Marble     (c) Quartz     (d) Pumice

**36.** Match column I with column II and select the correct option.     **[2022]**

| Column I | Column II |
| --- | --- |
| A Talcum Powder | 1. Granite |
| B. Kitchen counter | 2. Marble |

C. Lotus Temple
D. Red Fort
(a) (a)-4, (b)-1, (c)-2, (d)-3
(c) (a)-1, (b)-3, (c)-4, (d)-2

3. Sandstone
4. Talc
(b) (a)-2, (b)-4, (c)-1, (d)-3
(b) (a)-1, (b)-2, (c)-3, (d)-4

## RESPONSE GRID

### LEVEL 1

| | | | | |
|---|---|---|---|---|
| 1. a b c d | 2. a b c d | 3. a b c d | 4. a b c d | 5. a b c d |
| 6. a b c d | 7. a b c d | 8. a b c d | 9. a b c d | 10. a b c d |
| 11. a b c d | 12. a b c d | 13. a b c d | 14. a b c d | 15. a b c d |
| 16. a b c d | 17. a b c d | 18. a b c d | 19. a b c d | 20. a b c d |
| 21. a b c d | 22. a b c d | 23. a b c d | 24. a b c d | 25. a b c d |

### LEVEL 2

| | | | | |
|---|---|---|---|---|
| 1. a b c d | 2. a b c d | 3. a b c d | 4. a b c d | 5. a b c d |
| 6. a b c d | 7. a b c d | 8. a b c d | 9. a b c d | 10. a b c d |
| 11. a b c d | 12. a b c d | 13. a b c d | 14. a b c d | 15. a b c d |
| 16. a b c d | 17. a b c d | 18. a b c d | 19. a b c d | 20. a b c d |
| 21. a b c d | 22. a b c d | 23. a b c d | 24. a b c d | 25. a b c d |
| 26. a b c d | 27. a b c d | 28. a b c d | 29. a b c d | 30. a b c d |
| 31. a b c d | 32. a b c d | 33. a b c d | 34. a b c d | 35. a b c d |
| 36. a b c d | | | | |

# Answers with Explanations

## LEVEL 1

1. **(b)** Anything which occupies space and has weight is called matter.
2. **(c)** Juice is not a solid matter.
3. **(a)** Books are made from paper.
4. **(b)** Plastic is used to make a lunch box.
5. **(c)** Milk is in liquid state.
6. **(a)** Solids have fixed shape and size.
7. **(d)** Candles are made from wax.
8. **(a)** Shoe is made up of leather.
9. **(d)** Glass is not an example of opaque objects.
10. **(d)** Both water and air are transparent.
11. **(d)** Both air and water do not have fixed shape.
12. **(b)** Liquids take the shape of the container they are put in.
13. **(a)** Oxygen is a gas and it is invisible.
14. **(c)** Milk cannot be held in hand easily.
15. **(d)** All of these are solid as they have fixed shape.
16. **(c)** Air is a mixture of many gases such as oxygen, carbon dioxide and water vapour.
17. **(c)** Matter can be changed from one form to another by heating or cooling.
18. **(b)** Icecream is a solid form of milk.

| | | |
|---|---|---|
| 19. | (d) | Juice is a liquid and oxygen is a gas. Both juice and oxygen do not have fixed shape. |
| 20. | (c) | Liquid |
| 21. | (a) | We breathe out carbon dioxide. |
| 22. | (c) | Solid |
| 23. | (b) | Rain is the source of liquid water. Ice is the solid form of water, frost is frozen dew and snow are forms of ice. |
| 24. | (a) | The magnet will pick up the nail but not the penny because the nail contains iron. Magnet attracts iron. |
| 25. | (c) | Ice is the solid form of water. |

## LEVEL 2

| | | |
|---|---|---|
| 1. | (b) | Matter |
| 2. | (d) | Weight |
| 3. | (c) | Breathe |
| 4. | (b) | 3 |
| 5. | (c) | Solid |
| 6. | (a) | Liquid |
| 7. | (a) | Shape |
| 8. | (c) | Spread |
| 9. | (c) | Fixed |
| 10. | (a) | Gases |
| 11. | (b) | Light |
| 12. | (c) | 3 |
| 13. | (a) | Transparent |
| 14. | (c) | Wood |
| 15. | (b) | Molecules |
| 16. | (d) | Both liquid and gases. |
| 17. | (c) | Molecules in solid are tightly packed. |
| 18. | (d) | Heating changes solid into liquid and liquid into gases. |
| 19. | (c) | Gases cannot be seen or touched. |
| 20. | (d) | Mango milkshake took the shape of the lunch box and became an ice cream. |
| 21. | (c) | Both the statements are true. |
| 22. | (a) | The window panes are made up of glass, a candle is made up of wax, an envelope is made up of paper, the tyres are made up of leather. |
| 23. | (c) | 6 solids are present (spoon, pot, bottle, ball, tyre, watch). |
| 24. | (d) | Both the solids ice-cream and butter will melt and change into liquid when kept in sunlight. |
| 25. | (b) | Smoke of a lighted agarbatti can be seen clearly in the air. |
| 26. | (b) | Lemon is not filled with air. |
| 27. | (d) | 'X' is liquid, 'Y' is tyre which is a solid. |
| 28. | (c) | Matter occupies space. |
| 29. | (a) | Bucket and water both are matters and have weight. |
| 30. | (d) | Ice-cream freezes in the refrigerator. |
| 31. | (c) | Freezing |
| 32. | (c) | Solid, liquid and gas |
| 33. | (c) | Chalk |
| 34. | (c) | Quartz, granite, sandstone and diamond are hard while talc and graphite are soft. |
| 35. | (b) | Marble |
| 36. | (a) | |